CAT
CRIMES II

CAT CRIMES II

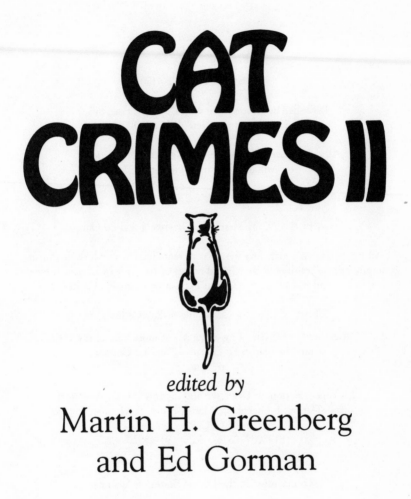

edited by
Martin H. Greenberg
and Ed Gorman

CASTLE BOOKS

This edition published in 1994 by
CASTLE BOOKS
P.O. Box 7100
Edison, NJ 08818-7100

Published by arrangement with Donald I. Fine, Inc.,
19 West 21st Street, New York, NY 10010.

ISBN 0-7858-0203-7

Library of Congress Cataloging-in-Publication Data

Cat crimes II : masters of mystery present more tales of the cat /
edited by Martin H. Greenberg and Ed Gorman.
p.   cm.

1. Crime—Fiction. 2. Detective and mystery stories, American.
3. Cats—Fiction. I. Greenberg, Martin Harry. II. Gorman, Edward.
PS648.C7C39   1992
813'.08720836—dc20   91-45520
CIP

Manufactured in the United States of America

Designed by Irving Perkins Associates

CONTENTS

INTRODUCTION

THE OTHER DAY I was looking through some of the mystery novels in my library and I found three very prominent authors posing with their cats—Raymond Chandler, Ross MacDonald and John D. MacDonald. In fact, John D. looked so delighted about being photographed with his feline that I just stared at the photograph for a long minute or so. Happy vibes at first but then a certain melancholy. I wish John D. and his cat were still around.

Cats and mystery writers seem to have an undue affection for each other. For all the dogs in mystery fiction—and I like dogs just fine—few have earned the enduring stature of the various mystery cats.

Why is that?

I know cats are supposed to be mysterious but actually they aren't mysterious at all. They like food, water, affection and exercise—pretty much the same things we like. As for their alleged inscrutability, I don't find them inscrutable at all, despite Johnny Carson's lame jokes about cats never coming when you call. Who would want to live out his life as a toy for humans, to come trotting across the room every time he was summoned?

Not to put too fine a point on it but I think cats will be around a lot longer than Carson . . .

So here you have it, another collection of stories about some of the best friends most of us will ever have. Cats, and nary a cutesy-poo kitty among them.

—Ed Gorman
April, 1992

AUTHOR NOTES

JOHN SUTER is a celebrated short story writer who has practiced his craft for several decades and is currently active in the affairs of Mystery Writers of America.

EDWARD D. HOCH makes his living as a short story writer, perhaps the only person in the United States to do so. And what stories they are, too, virtually every style and form represented somewhere in his repertoire. He is a modern day master of the traditional mystery tale.

BILL PRONZINI's "Nameless" Detective novels represent one of the most important bodies of work in private eye fiction. Taken together, the "Nameless" books form a spiritual saga of a contemporary middle-aged American male, a saga rife with pleasures and disappointments familiar to all of us. And Pronzini and "Nameless" are just as good at shorter length.

CAROLE NELSON DOUGLAS has worked in a number of genres for a number of years but lately her fine Sherlockian novels about Ms. Adler and her "Midnight Louie" books have turned her into a genuine mystery star. Pick one up and you'll see why.

JUNE HAYDON is new to the mystery field, but not new to the writing market; she has authored six novels, including *Reluctant Ward* and *Winds of Fury*. June has always had cats and currently lives with three.

CHRISTOPHER FAHY wrote one of the ten best suspense novels of the eighties, *Eternal Bliss*, a book overlooked by almost everybody except Stephen King who pronounced Fahy "A wonderful writer." As he is indeed.

B. W. "BUCK" BATTIN is another one of those professional writers whose books disappear far too quickly and are too often overlooked by mystery judges of more epicene (not to say pretentious) tastes. He's one hell of a writer, as the most glancing look at, say, the opening chapter of *The Creep* will prove.

JOAN HESS' novels have won the Agatha and the American Mystery Awards. Even more importantly, she has given her readers many hours of pure hilarious pleasure. She writes novels of manners about a state thought to have none, Arkansas.

NANCY PICKARD'S "Afraid All The Time" is one of the best crime stories ever written, and her novel *I.O.U.* demonstrated that one could write a quite serious suspense novel without a) disemboweling anybody or b) imitating any of the simpering mannerisms of contemporary literary fiction. And she's getting even better.

LES ROBERTS' gifts are probably too quiet and refined for the noisy era of the sociopath, but his literary reticence only enhances the truth of his observations and the wry sad turns of his plots. He's somebody you should be reading.

MARGARET MARON's novels have won her a steady readership that (as one bookstore owner said recently) "respects the verities of the mystery tradition." Her books include *Bloody Kin* and *Corpus Christmas*.

RICHARD LAYMON's novels sell much better in England than they do here. Indeed, in England he's a real—and formidable—star. His new American publisher promises to work hard on duplicating that same success over here. Meanwhile, he continues to favor us with fine stories of nearly every kind.

CHARLOTTE MACLEOD is a graceful stylist, a witty social critic, and a fine mystery writer. Her turf is New England and she prefers the quip to the dagger. She will someday be acknowledged as the very serious writer she also happens to be.

CAROLYN WHEAT's fiction wins both readers and critics over. She does her own work—modern, hard-edged without being hard-boiled, and sound in its attention to craft and structure. She's another one you should be reading.

BILL CRIDER's most popular books are his small-town Texas mysteries about a long-suffering sheriff who deserves a long rest in Mayberry, RFD. But Crider writes westerns and dark suspense with equal care and craft. He also writes literary criticism and is one of the few true historians of the Gold Medal paperback era.

BARBARA COLLINS is just starting out, but already her first handful of stories have editors inviting her into anthologies and publishers curious about when her first novel might be finished. Pay close attention to her.

SHARYN MCCRUMB writes funny mysteries that seem to shoot right to the top of the bestseller lists as soon as they appear. She has been particularly adept at harpooning science fiction fandom.

KRISTINE KATHRYN RUSCH edits (*The Magazine of Fantasy and Science Fiction*) and publishes (Pulphouse Press) and writes (her story here and dozens others). Her work has real charm and real individuality, and she's one of the few writers who can write an action piece with real philosophic depth to it.

JEREMIAH HEALY is one of today's most prominent private-eye novelists, a man using the form to his own ends, and good and true and innovative ends they are, too. His *Blunt Darts* is one of the finest first novels ever published.

CAT
CRIMES II

REMOTE

John F. Suter

So SHE FINISHED PACKING by throwing in her lab coat and the heavy sweater she sometimes wore at work. After all, when Alice Burford had suggested the weekend visit after several years, she had said, "Lois, be sure to bring some old things, in case the weather lets us go outside."

Outside would be welcome. She didn't get enough of it. And she understood that the Burfords had inherited a generous helping of outside in the less-crowded Connecticut countryside, along with a virtual mansion.

After Alice had met her at the train with the station wagon, Lois Humphrey had begun her unwinding. She felt that this excursion would either complete the process or excitement would carry her along on an adrenalin rush.

"Alice, I had no idea!" she said, as they drove up to the large, gabled, weathered-brick house. "Aren't you lucky!"

Alice laughed as she shut off the engine. "Don't be taken in by the view from here. Prepare to adjust your thinking." Lois took another look at her, contrasting their apparel: Alice's white turtleneck, sharply creased green slacks, and bone walkers against her own good-sense tweed outfit and low-heel cream shoes. Adjust in what way?

Alice went briskly to the tailgate and got out Lois's bag before Lois's feet touched ground. The difference between the two friends was apparent, but Lois dismissed it. Although quick and sure in the lab, she was deliberate in other ways.

She hastened to keep up with Alice, who was headed for the front door. She stopped and laughed.

Alice half-turned. "What?"

Lois pointed to a sign fastened to the right of the doorway. It read: THIS HOUSE IS PROTECTED BY A WATCHCAT.

Alice laughed lightly with her. "Oh, that. That's one of Rudy's conceits."

"Actually," said Lois, "I suppose you really have a large, lazy tabby."

"Not exactly," Alice answered. "Ours keeps busy."

She raised her right hand until it covered a glass panel perforated with tiny holes set in the brick by the door. After about thirty seconds, Lois could hear bolts sliding and a latch clicking. The door swung open.

Alice gestured. "After you."

Lois stepped inside, amused. She looked behind the door, but saw nobody. Just like an old Boris Karloff movie.

Alice followed, setting the bag down. Her black eyes were dancing, and roses showed in her fair skin.

Lois looked at the door. It did not disappoint her. It swung shut, the latch clicked, and a heavy bolt slid into a socket. "Now," she said, "where's the trapdoor? When does the nasty laugh come?"

Alice smiled broadly. "Even Rudy would not be that campy. Actually, it's very practical. The mechanism responds only to the scent of certain individuals: Rudy, me, the cook, the maid—"

"Just those who live here, is that it?"

"Only Rudy and I live here. The rest are day help."

Lois's practical sense came to the fore. "Activated by personal scent. Does that mean that you have to use the same perfume all of the time?"

Alice shook her head. "Not at all. I take care not to get any on my hands, and I wash them thoroughly with unscented soap."

No stranger to hand-scrubbing, Lois nodded. A lock of close-cropped brown hair strayed across her forehead. "Is that one of Rudy's ideas? The trick door gimmick?"

"What else? The place is full of them."

"Rudy's still inventing, then," Lois said.

"You can count on it." Alice grasped Lois's bag and directed them down a hall laid in irregular gray stone with an oriental runner down the center. "He's in his workroom, last door on your left. He's expecting you." She stepped aside to let Lois precede her.

Lois reviewed what she knew about Rudy. He had always been ingenious. A few years ago, he had discovered a unique blend of surfactants and microorganisms that promised to solve the problem of extracting petroleum from oil shale. He had sold the patent to a major oil company that had yet to use it. He had also arranged for payment to be made annually and partly in company stock, instead of a lump sum.

Rudy's workroom was controlled clutter: a complete computer setup, a light table, filing cabinets, chairs and stools wherever needed. At the moment, he was sprawled back in a recliner, his feet up.

When Lois entered, Rudy dropped his feet to the floor and rose in one fluid motion. She reflected that he was not the stereotyped mad inventor. In jeans, corduroy jacket, and sneakers, with lumberjack build, coarse black hair, and square jaw, he was more blue collar than ivory tower. Only inquisitive brown eyes hinted at his nature.

"Well, hello, Lois Humphrey!" he said, extending a wide hand. "It *is* still Humphrey, isn't it? My dimwit fellow males haven't caught on. What a pity."

She let her firm hand be engulfed as she looked up at him.

"As our British friends might say, the Rudy Burfords of this world are thin on the ground. You're the only one."

He laughed heartily. "And this one is roped and hogtied. Well, here you are at Burford Base, as I'm tempted to call it. Never thought we'd be living here, but it turned out that Uncle Ralph always liked me and had no one else to leave the place to. House and thirty acres. We love it."

"And your mark's already on it," Lois said dryly.

"What? Oh, the front door. Like that, do you? After Alice gets you settled in, I'll show you more things."

"I saw your sign. I must meet your watchcat."

Rudy's tone changed slightly. "You probably will. Depends on where old Remote is."

"Remote? He's standoffish?"

A reflective look was in Rudy's eye. "I guess we do think of him as *he*. He's no lap kitty."

Alice cleared her throat. "Rudy. We'd better let Lois freshen up. We can talk a little later."

He smiled again. "Yes. I was forgetting my manners. But I do want to show off my toys."

"I'm anxious to see them."

Lois's room, at the head of the stairs next to a small bath, had south-facing windows. She fell in love with her bed at once. It was a walnut three-quarter, with a headboard in a style reminiscent of a Spanish comb. The wallpaper and the bedclothes enhanced the overall impression of sunniness.

After unpacking, Lois studied herself in the antique mirror set in a gold-leaf frame that hung on the east wall. How good of the Burfords to share their luck, even for a short time. She knew she was intelligent—it showed in her gray eyes—but a party girl she was not.

Rudy and Alice were waiting for her downstairs, ready for a tour. They had wisely left the large living room untouched, with some wavery, handmade glass in the windows; the huge fireplace still capable of cooking meals, its hob still available to keep food warm; the tall chairs nearby still protected from heat by tapestried fire screens.

"Rudy's smart enough to know when to leave things alone," Alice laughed as they left the elegant traditional dining room. "But his ideas are coming. Don't worry."

"That they are," Rudy assured them. "That they are. And, not to keep you waiting, let's detour to the utility room. After that, the kitchen."

"Did you design your own security, or is your watchcat a superguard?" Lois asked.

Rudy became thoughtful. "Not trained—but he could."

They came to a medium-size room all in white at the rear of the house. Rudy pointed to an open-top device near the rear window. It resembled a shallow trough about three feet by four, with a thick shell. Water pipes led to the bottom, on either side of an obvious drainpipe.

"Wonder what it is?" he asked Lois. "It's our washer. Adapted from a device conceived by a Japanese inventor. It removes dirt by ultrasound. I'll show you." He bent down and opened the water valves, allowing the chamber to fill. There was no agitator that Lois could see.

"Where are the stirrer and detergent?" she asked.

"Don't need 'em," Rudy said, walking to a heap of disreputable cloths in the corner. He lifted a grimy rag that might once have been white.

"You see how grungy this is," he said, giving them time to inspect. "Now, into the washer—turn the switch on—" He clicked the switch and pointed to the washer.

Lois stared into the chamber. Nothing was moving. The cloth hovered near the surface. Then she noticed a cloud in the water. After a few minutes it was murky. Rudy clicked the switch again and reached into the water. He pulled out a snow-white cloth.

"Voilà!" he said. "All we do now is open the drain." The valve open, the water and the grime rushed away.

"That's fantastic!" Lois exclaimed.

Rudy next demonstrated a dryer vaguely resembling a big microwave that dried the rag in two minutes. "Now, let's go to the kitchen," he said.

As they passed the back door, Lois noticed a hinged panel in the wood of the door, near the bottom.

"Is that to let your kitty-cat in out of the storm?" she asked.

"That's where he can come in," Alice said. "Usually, when we want him to come in. Chiefly when we suspect that there might be vermin. In bad weather, there are other things."

"You don't let him in to feed him? Or pet him?"

"He doesn't need either one," Alice said, her face expressionless. "He's almost self-sufficient."

"But wouldn't that make him almost too independent?" Alice said, surprised. "Isn't he harder to control?"

Rudy cleared his throat. "We can control him."

In the next fifteen minutes in the kitchen, Lois saw that food processors were unique to her: devices that could, efficiently and cheaply, slice any food almost to transparency, make it absorb flavorings almost instantaneously and uniformly, and by computer program and lasers, form it into any desired fanciful shape. Reduced pressure ovens turned out the lightest soufflés—the possibilities dizzied Lois.

She finally threw up her hands.

"I can't take it all in," she groaned.

Rudy grinned. "Let's go into the living room a bit."

"I want to see all you've done," Lois remarked as she sipped her bourbon and water. "Of course, it will kill my soul with envy, but it is fascinating."

"I live to invent," Rudy said. "Now and then, I sell the rights to an idea."

"All kinds of people must try to steal your plans," Lois said. "Does your watchcat guard them?"

Alice laughed. "You're obsessed by trivia, Lois. Remote's job is to keep us free of vermin and rabbits."

"He doesn't like liver or fish?"

Rudy said quietly, "He's not programmed for that. He might hit on squirrels. As rodents, they're on his list."

Lois stared at him. "He ignores milk, too? Only has a diet of rodents and rabbits?"

"That's right, essentially."

"But that must have taken endless patience. Cats do have minds of their own."

"Most of them, I'll agree."

"Well, then—"

He looked at her steadily. "Ever hear of *Robocop*?"

The hairs on her arms rose. "Yes. Yes, I have."

He lifted a hand. *"Robocat."*

Lois's mouth opened wide. "He's not—"

"Flesh and blood? No. I made him."

"A machine?"

"You could call him that."

Lois could not help herself. "A *killing* machine?"

Rudy shrugged. "You might say so. I prefer *nonhuman exterminator.*"

Lois turned to Alice. "How do you square this with your support for animal rights? Or aren't you their local driving force anymore?"

"Nothing has changed," Alice said unemotionally. "If we didn't control vermin and rabbits, we'd be overwhelmed. Look at Australia's rabbit problem."

"But all these creatures are used to solve problems in disease control. You object to that, don't you?"

Alice's calm held. "In that case, they are helpless victims. The things that humans inflict on them, the torture they endure —that's where my heart goes out to them. Out here, they are adversaries, using their guile to outwit us. I see no problem."

Lois swung to Rudy. "How about you?"

He shrugged. "I share her point of view."

"It's hypocrisy!" Lois blurted. "You use a pet—"

"Not even a scrap of cat fur is in Remote," Rudy said. "Maybe I can show you. Come on."

He got up and led her to the laundry room, where he raised the window, leaving the screen in place. He took an object from his pocket and pointed it outside.

"You're right," he said, answering an unspoken question, "it's a remote control." He pushed a stud.

Nothing happened immediately.

"Maybe out by the back fence," he commented.

Lois became aware of a faint disturbance, then suddenly *it* was there, staring up at the window.

It was the size of a large cat, but, other than the silent approach, there was no feature in common with that animal. It was completely metallic, and it moved with the repellent grace of a coiling snake. Its gleaming head, set on a flexible neck, could rotate in a complete circle. The eyes were unblinking lenses. Thin antennae sprouted above the eyes, and stylized, thin alloy ears also swiveled through 360 degrees. It also had a mouth, nostrils, and cat's whiskers.

"It can hear in a wider range than we can. It can see in a broader spectrum. Its sense of smell is acute, somewhat analogous to the front door sensor," Rudy murmured.

He accidentally touched a stud on the control. The creature's mouth opened in a display of gleaming needle-sharp teeth. At a touch of a stud, the mouth closed. Another touch, and the thing stretched on its side; three-inch claws, razor-sharp, emerged from its paws.

Rudy caused it to retract the claws and get up. He pushed another stud, and it bounded away.

"It operates on rechargeable batteries," he said. "There's a place out back where it can go to recharge when it senses that current's starting to decline."

Lois leaned against the washer, feeling weak. She had never looked pure terror head-on before.

"I thought better of you, Rudy," she gasped.

"I didn't mean to shock you, Lois," he said. "I designed this thing for a need. Ordinary measures don't always work in rural conditions. We can always turn it off when we don't need it, and turn it on again, if we have to."

"You ought to take it to pieces completely and give it to the recycle station!"

She turned around. "I'm going up and lie down."

* * *

A while later, after a troubled nap, Lois was awakened by a light tapping at her door.

"Lois?" It was Alice's voice. "Do you feel up to a stroll outdoors? Fresh air might do you good."

She sat up. "Is that thing still out there?"

"I've asked Rudy to deactivate him while you're here."

Lois thought she could hear the rustle of an olive branch. "All right. I really do want to see all of your place."

"Fine. Better bring something old and warm. It's been windy, off and on."

Lois got up and went to the closet. She paused. The sweater or the lab coat? She decided to take both, leaving one behind after she stepped outside.

She went downstairs to meet Alice.

"It looks like rain, but maybe not for a while," said Alice. "I thought we should get out when we can. The rain might be with us tomorrow. Let's go out the back door."

"You lead," Lois answered. "I'll see what to wear and leave the other thing in the laundry room."

As they went, she glanced at the entry port cut in the back door. She shuddered. They allowed that *thing* inside?

She stepped out just as a wind gust subsided. Overall, the sweater might be the better choice. "Excuse me," she said, went back in, and put the coat on a bench in the utility room.

Without the wind, it was too warm for the sweater, so she carried it. It was an old white cardigan, bought several years earlier in Ireland.

"This is a modest place, as these things go," Alice said. "We have a barn, a springhouse, a woodshed, and land, lots of land— for us, at least."

Lois glanced about. "You seem to have it immaculate. Is it hard to hire someone to keep it looking like this? Or do the two of you do it by the sweat of your brow?"

Alice laughed. "A lot of it's done by machines, self-propelled. Rudy, again. He'd rather exercise his brain than any other muscle."

"I wish he hadn't exercised it to create that Remote." Lois shivered. "And it only protects against rodents."

"Would you try to break in if you saw it?"

"No, I wouldn't even knock at the door."

They walked in silence for a time. Lois saw a grove of trees with a gazebo in it, a relaxing sight. Perhaps tomorrow, if the weather permitted—

Alice broke the silence. "I think we'll skip the barn. Remote bothers you, and he might be there, hunting. But I do think your feeling about our apparent ambivalence toward animals is unjustified. After all, you continue working for that laboratory that uses animals in medical research."

"Those animals are all well treated, I assure you. For some, the life span is shortened; others have long, comfortable lives."

"The ones that live are the controls, of course," Alice said, her voice heavy with irony. She turned to face Lois. "What sort of high-paying work could I find you that would persuade you to give up that laboratory?"

"You couldn't. Every time I consider it, I weigh possible faults against possible benefits to us all. After all, we're members of the animal kingdom, too."

"Except that the ones whose rights I try to protect don't abuse tobacco or alcohol or do drugs."

Lois sighed. "All true, but let's not discuss it, Alice. Not if we want to remain friends."

Alice's face became as dark as the sky had suddenly turned. "We *won't* discuss it, Lois. Not any more."

A sudden gust of wind hit them, bearing a sprinkle of hail.

"Oh!" screamed Alice. "I forgot my jacket. This blouse will be ruined!"

"Here," shouted Lois, holding out her sweater, "take this. It can't really hurt what I have on."

Alice donned the sweater hurriedly. "We'd better run. It's going to pour."

Lois looked about, to check the rain's direction. She screamed and began to run for the house as hard as she could, the wind in her face.

Loping behind them came Remote, jaws gleaming in what would have been a snarl in a flesh and blood animal. The sun had dimmed, and bright lamps gleamed in his eye-sockets.

Alice heard Lois scream. She stopped and turned. Lois's mind barely registered that Alice, herself, showed no fright.

The nightmare was at Lois's heels, and she had to will herself not to faint, to go on as long as she could.

Then it overtook her and went past. It leaped, claws extended, and landed at Alice's waist. Slashing as it went, amid increasing red, it climbed and sank its teeth into her throat, cutting off her scream.

Lois's feet went faster. She ignored the dreadful sounds behind her, fearful that the thing would come for her when it had done. Instinct warned her Alice was beyond help.

Suddenly she was at the back door. She ripped it open, darted inside, and slammed it shut.

A short, wiry woman she had never seen came out of the kitchen. Lois realized that she must be the cook.

"What is this? What's happened?" the woman demanded.

"Never mind," Lois gasped. "Just get a hammer and nails and nail this damned thing shut. Tight." She kicked the hinged entry port.

Rudy was hastening from his workroom. "Why—Lois," he said. "What are you doing? What's happened?"

"Alice," she gasped. "It's Alice. Your thing mistook her for a rat and jumped her."

The blood drained from his face. "Alice? We never meant—"

Lois brushed his comments aside. "You'd better get out there and put it out of commission. Not that I think it will do any good—" She broke off, ran into the laundry room, snatched up her coat, and hurried back.

Rudy was about to go out. "Wait," she said, draping the coat around his shoulders. "And you'd better take an axe—a sledge— or a shotgun."

He held up the remote control and pushed it. "Not necessary.

But I'll lay it here on this chair so it won't be activated accidentally."

He put it down and went out. His actions made Lois's subconscious begin to put things together. Remote had ignored her and attacked Alice. It had begun to rain, intensifying some odors. Remote was programmed to zero in on odors of rodents and rabbits. The sweater she had given Alice—

It went farther. He had said, *"Alice?"* Surprised? "We never meant—" Never meant what? Had meant *Lois?*

She had put her lab coat on Rudy's shoulders. Had she known, deep down, that both of them—?

The cook was still hunting hammer and nails.

She picked up the remote control from the chair. She had noticed which stud he had pressed to deactivate Remote. The one beside it must turn it on again. She pressed it.

The scream that overrode the wind was worse than the earlier one, but she could not hear the other noises. She allowed a long interval, then pressed the control again.

She had just put it down when the cook returned with hammer and nails. "You want me to do this? You're sure?"

Lois shivered. "I'm sure."

"I heard screams twice," the cook said. "Do you know what happened?"

"I think so," Lois said slowly. "You know that thing called Remote?"

"I've seen it. Give you bad dreams, wouldn't it?"

"I think it got out of hand—gave Mr. and Mrs. Burford more than bad dreams."

Shocked, the woman stared at her. "You mean—?"

"Yes."

The cook bent over and began to drive nails. "No wonder you want to nail this shut. God help us all, I don't even dare go outside!"

"I'll call the police and have them come over with heavy guns," Lois said tiredly. "They'll see that you get home."

But explain? She could demonstrate the washer and dryer.

The cook could handle the kitchen. Between them, they could paint a reasonable picture of Rudy Burford for the police. Couldn't they? Everything mechanical had a glitch somewhere. Didn't it?

SARATOGA CAT

Edward D. Hoch

AGATHA PERKINS STEPPED CAREFULLY as she alighted from the train at the Saratoga Springs station. It was well past midnight, with no one around, and the gaslights on Railroad Place were barely bright enough to illuminate the front of the depot.

"Isn't anyone around?" she asked the conductor as he handed down her magenta cloth carpetbag and the little carrying case for Oscar.

"Probably a bit late for the carriages," he replied. "We're running an hour behind schedule. You can walk to the United States Hotel, though. The rear entrance is just across the street there."

"Thank you," she replied, deciding she had little choice at nearly one in the morning. She hefted the carpetbag in one hand and got a good grip on Oscar's case with the other.

A sleepy-looking bellboy came forward to take her bags as she entered the hotel lobby. She'd made a reservation at the Grand Union but this was closer and if they had a room she'd take it. The desk clerk peered at her over the tops of his glasses and said, "You're in luck. With the racing getting under way tomorrow this is usually the busiest time of summer, but we've had a couple of cancellations."

"Good! A single room with a view would be nice."

"I'll put you right in front. You can look out at the trees along Broadway and watch the carriages go by. It's on the third floor but that's not much of a walk. The bellboy will show you up."

As she followed him to the sweeping grand staircase at one end of the lobby she noticed a young man with dark hair and a mustache seated in one of the lobby chairs, smoking a cigar. He seemed perfectly at ease, as if it were one o'clock in the afternoon instead of one in the morning.

"That's a nice cat you've got there," he commented as she passed.

"Thank you."

"What's its name?"

"Oscar."

She kept on going, following her bag upstairs to the third floor. The room was flouncy and nice, reminding her of some of the better New York hotels. This would do very nicely for her stay, she decided. In the morning she would stop by the Grand Union and cancel her reservation there.

She bent to let Oscar out of his carrying case.

Shortly after ten o'clock the following morning, Arnie Russell strode through the front door of Morrissey's Club House in Congress Park. The cleaning women gave him barely a glance as he took the red-carpeted stairs two at a time and headed for Kogan's office.

"Come in," a familiar voice said through the half-open door.

Arnie entered respectfully and strode over to Kogan's desk. He had a secret admiration for Bert Kogan, a big, jowly man in his forties who'd managed Morrissey's casino for the past two years. Kogan was the brains. It was only with the ladies that Arnie had the upper hand. "She's at the United States Hotel," he told Kogan. "Checked in just before one this morning."

"You're certain it was her?"

"She had the cat with her. Told me his name was Oscar."

Bert Kogan smiled. "This is going to bring us both a great deal of money." He'd been a captain of Union forces during the Civil War, and now a decade later he still seemed a bit like a military commander at times. "I want you to get back to that hotel and arrange to meet her. Strike up a conversation, buy her a drink, find out what she's doing in Saratoga. If she seems all right, I'll meet with her tomorrow."

Arnie Russell could understand the reason for the older man's precaution. Late last year a man had come to see Kogan and sell him a package. Everything had gone well until the final moments, when the man—whose name was Baxter—drew a revolver and revealed himself to be a government Treasury agent. They'd been lucky that time, and it was spring before the body turned up in Saratoga Lake, but Kogan wanted no repetition. Morrissey made a great deal of money from the race track and the casino, and he didn't like his men running schemes of their own. He'd have fired Kogan in an instant if he knew about the packages.

"I'll check her out," Arnie Russell promised. "Trust me."

The summer of '75 had been a good one for Saratoga Springs. Warm weather and the recent extension of the racing season had done much to help, as had the extra trains on the line from New York City. John Morrissey's first racing card, in 1863, had lasted just four days, with two races each day.

Agatha Perkins knew all this as she gazed out her window that morning, holding Oscar gently to her bosom. The cat purred softly, shifting slightly in her arms, and she let it hop to the floor. "Come on, boy. I'll take you for a walk."

It was the first time she'd visited the spa, and she paused at the desk to ask the location of the nearest spring. "That would be Putnam Spring, ma'am. Just across Broadway behind the Congregational Church. The Bath is further down the block."

"Thank you!"

She had Oscar on a leash, and that in itself created some

notice as she strolled through the lobby and onto the street. She hadn't gone twenty paces before a male voice behind her said, "Pardon me, miss."

She turned to see the handsome young man who'd been smoking a cigar in the lobby when she arrived. "Yes?"

"Would you mind if I walked with you? I do admire that cat. What breed is he?"

"Persian. Are you a cat fancier, Mr.—?"

"Excuse me," he said with a slight tip of his hat. "Arnold Russell, at your service."

"I'm Agatha Perkins, from Atlanta. This is my first trip north."

"The South's loss is our gain. If you'll permit me to say so, you're a charming young lady. Were you much troubled by the recent war between the States?"

"I was still a child ten years ago, but it was a terrible hardship on my people. Did you fight on the Union side, sir?"

"Only in a supply capacity. I would never take up arms against my brothers."

"A noble sentiment."

Oscar was straining at his leash as a robin alighted on a little patch of grass in search of worms. "Let me help you with that cat," he volunteered.

"Oh, I couldn't trouble you. I'm on my way to take the waters at the Putnam Spring. I believe I cross here."

"Might we meet later in the day for a cocktail?"

She hesitated a moment and then smiled. "I think that would be delightful, Mr. Russell, but I assumed you were here for the opening of the racing season this afternoon."

"The card is a short one. I could be at your hotel before five."

"Very well," Agatha told him. "We will meet in the lobby at five."

Shortly after noon Arnie Russell took a carriage out to the race track on the north side of Union Avenue. There were the usual opening-day festivities, with more women in attendance than last year. He liked that. Even in their full-length dresses that swept the ground he found them utterly attractive. He knew Agatha Perkins was not as young as she pretended—certainly in her thirties rather than her twenties—but she was still a woman he wanted to know better. Perhaps after she concluded her business with Kogan she would stay on and let him show her Saratoga by night, when the casinos came alive and there was always a high-stakes game on the second floor of Morrissey's Club House.

While he waited for the racing to begin, he took from his pocket the folded letter that Agatha Perkins had sent to Bert Kogan. Though he knew what it said, he wanted to read her words again:

"Dear Mr. Kogan,

It has come to my attention that your enterprise in Saratoga Springs, New York, has been purchasing large quantities of printed paper for distribution through your private channels there. You must realize that the quantity of such paper is definitely limited and the supply is nearing its end. I can now offer you a method by which you personally may replenish the supply at any time, for a reasonably modest initial investment. I will be in Saratoga Springs at the beginning of this summer's racing season, and I hope you will contact me. I shall be traveling with my cat, Oscar, and should not be difficult to locate.

Yours sincerely,
Agatha Perkins,
Atlanta, Georgia."

She used the language well, and was obviously an intelligent woman. The letter had attracted him as soon as Kogan showed it to him some weeks back. In fact, it had been his idea that he watch the trains and hotels on the day she was expected to arrive. He'd established that she had a reservation at the Grand Union, but when the train was delayed a gut feeling told him she might switch to the United States simply because it was closer to the station.

Arnie won a little on the first race, which was always a good sign. It was after another winner in the second race, while he was chatting casually with one of the Club House dealers, that he noticed a slim man with a walking stick glancing in his direction. When he was alone again the man approached him. "I hope you don't mind the intrusion, but I've noticed you seem to have a knack for picking winners. You collected after both races."

Arnie Russell chuckled. "Those two were favorites. I didn't win much."

"Nevertheless—" The man hesitated. "I should introduce myself. I'm Franklin Longworth from New York City. This is my first time in Saratoga Springs."

"Arnie Russell."

"Are you a visitor or a resident?"

"I work at Morrissey's Club House, in Congress Park."

"I hear that's a good casino."

"The best in town. If you drop in, ask for me and I'll show you around."

"I might do that. Thanks." He consulted the racing card. "Anything good in the next race?"

"Try betting number four to place. He might do something."

"Thanks again."

Number four was a long shot, but it was Arnie's lucky day. He won by a nose and paid ten dollars to place. Arnie looked around for Longworth but didn't see him.

The waters of Putnam Bath were warm and soothing on Agatha's skin. They relaxed her to the point where she didn't really mind the odor of sulphur that hung over the place. Lolling in the bath, it was almost possible to forget the real reason why she'd come north.

Later, the woman at the desk who had been watching Oscar turned the leash over to Agatha with a smile. "Such a good little kitty! I'd like to take him home with me."

"You wouldn't say that after he started pulling on the lace curtains with his claws."

"Oh, my!"

Agatha walked along Broadway for a time, keeping an eye on the clock. She returned to her room shortly before four, after stopping to buy a hat at one of the shops near the hotel. Oscar cavorted about the place, hopping onto the bed and exploring every area of the room in search of treasure. At five o'clock Agatha left Oscar in the room and went downstairs to meet Arnold Russell.

He was waiting in the lobby, seated on the red plush sofa while he glanced through the current issue of *Harper's New Monthly Magazine*, thoughtfully provided for guests. As soon as he saw her descending the staircase he rose to his feet and came to meet her. "I thought you might have Oscar along," he said by way of greeting.

"He usually goes everywhere with me, but I made an exception this time."

Over cocktails on the wide front porch of the hotel, Russell asked, "How was the Spring?"

"Most enjoyable and relaxing. I was amazed at the business those places do. There were all sorts of people lined up for just a glass of the water to drink. I went on to the baths after that."

"If you're free tomorrow I would much enjoy the pleasure of escorting you to the race track."

She merely smiled at the invitation and asked, "Are you employed by the track, Mr. Russell?"

"Not at all." Then, as if to avoid a lie, he added, "I work for John Morrissey, it's true, but in one of his other enterprises. I'm at Morrissey's Club House, our leading casino."

"Now there's a place I'd really like to visit. I've always had better luck with cards than horses."

"I'll take you tonight! We have a fine dining room on the main floor, and we can have dinner before you try your luck."

"Well—" She hesitated. "I do hope Oscar will be all right if I'm away for so long."

* * *

The evening was going so well that Arnie sat across the dinner table from Agatha Perkins and actually found himself imagining that it might end in a romantic interlude. She seemed to enjoy the roast beef that was a casino specialty. "Do you eat this well every night?" she asked as they were having dessert.

"Only on special occasions."

"Exactly what do you do for Mr. Morrissey?"

"Actually I work for his assistant, Bert Kogan, who's manager of the Club House. I make sure things run smoothly and nobody cheats. If you're finished, I'll show you the gaming room."

Though the hour was still early, there was a fair crowd at the roulette and hazard tables. Agatha seemed surprised to see a number of women grouped around a table at the far end of the room. "What's that?" she asked.

"Faro. It seems especially popular with women, and this is one of the first casinos to offer facilities for them. Would you care to try your hand?"

She turned then and looked him in the eye. "Not right now, Arnold. I think it's time we got down to business. I'd like to see Mr. Kogan."

"Well—" She'd taken him off guard and he didn't know quite how to answer her. "Wait here a moment while I see if he's busy."

Morrissey's office downstairs was locked, so he knew Kogan would be in his own office on the second floor. Arnie hurried up the carpeted stairs and crossed the high-stakes room where only a mild game of whist was in progress at the moment. He knocked on Kogan's door and entered at once.

"I saw you arrive," Kogan said. "Did she enjoy her dinner?"

"She enjoyed it. Now she wants to get to the point. She wants to see you."

Kogan considered that, leaning back in his chair and biting the tip off a fresh cigar. "All right," he decided. "It might as well be tonight as tomorrow. Bring her up."

Arnie went back downstairs, feeling important, and escorted

Agatha Perkins up to Kogan's office. After he'd introduced them, he took a chair over on the side, hoping that Kogan wouldn't embarrass him by sending him from the room.

"Is it Mrs. Perkins?" Kogan asked, acting with all the politeness of a Union officer at a formal ball.

"It is. My late husband was killed in the war."

"You hardly seem old enough—"

"We marry young in the South."

"I understand from your letter that you have a proposition to make."

She smiled and crossed her legs beneath her long skirt. "I know you have been receiving packages regularly from certain people in the South."

"What sort of packages?" Kogan asked. He was not about to reveal anything she didn't already know.

She sighed impatiently. "Counterfeit twenty- and fifty-dollar greenbacks, printed on the same presses that turned out Confederate money during the war. As you know, the printing of greenbacks by the North, unsupported by gold or silver, increased inflation, and the South hoped to spur the North's inflation with counterfeit greenbacks. The war ended before much of it gained circulation, and in fact the entire plot remained unknown to government leaders and the general public. During the past decade much of this uncirculated counterfeit money has made its way north, and what better way to put it into circulation than through race tracks and gambling casinos? With or without the knowledge of your employer, Mr. Kogan, you have been buying counterfeit currency in bulk from the South and circulating it through Morrissey's enterprises in Saratoga Springs, at a healthy profit."

Arnie could see that even Kogan was impressed by her knowledge. "And you say the supply of such counterfeit money is now running low?"

"Of course it's running low! None has been printed since the war ended ten years ago. Your profitable little sideline is about to come to an end. That is, unless you're willing to purchase the package I have for sale."

"Which is—?"

Agatha Perkins smiled. "A set of the original steel engravings from which the counterfeit greenbacks were printed. With those you can print your own. All you need is the right grades of paper and ink and you're in business. I needn't remind you that Washington is considering bringing all remaining greenbacks into the regular currency system within the next few years, backing them with gold."

"What's your price for a set of plates?" Kogan asked softly. Arnie could see him weighing the possibilities.

"Fifty thousand dollars in gold certificates."

"Fifty—!"

"For a set of twenties and a set of fifties. That's not much. You know you can make it back in a single day."

Arnie knew she was right. If the plates were as she described them, they were invaluable. Instead of feeding the false greenbacks into the track and Club House payoffs a few at a time, they could do it all through the racing season.

"Let me see them," Bert Kogan said.

"I don't carry them around with me. They're well hidden, back at the hotel. I can bring them tomorrow if you're interested."

"I'm interested," he admitted.

"Then I'll be here at noon tomorrow with the plates. Have your money ready. Five packets of ten thousand each. Gold certificates." She smiled at Arnie as if she'd just remembered his presence in the room.

He cleared his throat and asked, "Would you like to play some faro now?"

"I believe I'll be getting back to my hotel."

"I can escort you."

"No, no. It's only two blocks and this is a lovely evening for walking."

When she'd gone, Kogan said, "She's a clever woman. We might have to pay something for those plates."

"Fifty thousand?"

"We'll see tomorrow."

It was later in the evening, when Arnie was collecting the excess cash from the gaming tables, that he spotted a familiar face. It was that fellow Longworth from the track. "So you took my advice," he said by way of greeting.

Franklin Longworth grinned. "I'm glad I did. I'm a hundred dollars ahead right now. And I had some money down on that horse you mentioned in the third race."

"Good for you!" Arnie accepted a handful of bills from the roulette operator and dropped them into his canvas bag.

"Say, I'm glad I ran into you again. It's none of my business, but I saw you earlier with a lovely young woman. Was that Agatha Perkins?"

"It was. Do you know her?"

"A friend of mine had some dealings with her in Atlanta last year. You did me a favor with that tip this afternoon so I figure I owe you one. Agatha Perkins is on the con."

"What?" Arnie asked, feeling his stomach turn over.

"She's a confidence woman. Been traveling around the South for years fleecing anyone she could. Her favorite trick, the one she used on my friend, is the quick switch. She shows a package full of money or jewelry, gets something from you in return, and then diverts your attention while she switches packages. It works every time."

Arnie's mouth was dry. "That's very interesting."

"Look, if you need me to confront her, or tell the police what I know, I'd be glad to do it. Her kind needs to be locked up."

"Could you be back here at noon tomorrow?"

"I could. What do you want me to do?"

"I don't know yet."

Agatha Perkins took a long time bathing and applying her makeup in the morning. It would be an important day for her, and she wanted to be certain she looked her best. Then she tended to Oscar, feeding him and brushing his fur. "I have to put you in your case for a little bit," she told him, "but I'll take you out as soon as I can." She put his collar and leash into her big purse.

It was exactly noon when she arrived at Morrissey's Club House in the park. The place was not yet open for business, but Arnold Russell must have been watching for her. The front door opened as she started up the steps. "You're right on time," he greeted her. "And you brought your cat!"

"It's bad enough leaving him alone at night. I have to bring him out during the day."

Kogan looked distastefully at the cat case when she entered his office, but she pretended she didn't notice. However, when she opened the case to remove Oscar, he asked, "Is that necessary?"

"It is if you want to see the engravings. They're hidden in the bottom of his case."

While Arnold and Kogan watched, she fitted the collar around Oscar's neck and attached the leash. "Does he know any tricks?" Arnold asked.

"Just one," she answered with a smile. "I'll show you later." She carefully removed the newspaper from the bottom of the carrying case and lifted a small rubber mat beneath it. Two rectangular spaces had been cut into the wood at the bottom, and from these she carefully lifted the engravings for the front and back of a twenty-dollar greenback, followed by a similiar set for a fifty-dollar greenback. "Satisfied?"

Bert Kogan took a magnifying glass from his desk drawer and studied the engravings in some detail before responding. Finally he laid down the glass and said simply, "They're most impressive."

"Then we have a deal?"

"I'll pay you thirty thousand for them both."

Agatha shook her head, feeling very sure of herself. "Fifty thousand or it's no deal." She took the engravings and began wrapping them with the newspaper, forming a neat little package.

Arnold was looking at Kogan. Finally the older man said, "All right. It's a deal, Mrs. Perkins. You drive a hard bargain."

She tapped the package of wrapped engravings. "Give me the money and they're yours."

Kogan opened another drawer and took out a key. He walked to a side cabinet and opened it, revealing a small safe. The key went easily into the lock and turned smoothly. He opened the thick steel door and extracted five bundles of currency. "Ten thousand in each package. Count it if you doubt me."

She chose one package at random and did just that. It was ten thousand on the nose. As she returned the bundle to the desktop, she gave a little tug on Oscar's leash.

Suddenly the cat's neck was free of the collar and he bounded across the room. "Oscar!" Agatha shouted. "Come back here!"

Arnold went after the animal, trying to capture it in his arms, while Kogan headed around the other side of the desk. It took them only a moment to corner him.

"Let me get the collar back on him," Agatha said. "Bad cat! Bad cat! Behave or you'll go in the box!"

Kogan was smiling at her, and there was a look of triumph on Arnold Russell's face. As she reached for the money, Kogan said, "Just one moment, Mrs. Perkins. Your Southern tricks don't work up north."

"What's that?"

Arnold had opened the office door, and she turned to see Franklin Longworth walk in, a smile on his lips and the familiar walking stick in his hand.

"I believe you know each other," Arnie said, glancing toward Agatha. "At least Mr. Longworth knows you from your Atlanta activities."

The young woman looked Arnie straight in the eye and said, "I have no idea what you're talking about."

"We're talking about the switch you just pulled," Bert Kogan said with a growl. "When that cat got loose you used the distraction to substitute false engravings while the real ones went into your purse."

She turned toward Longworth with a helpless gesture. "Perhaps you can straighten this out. These men just offered to sell me some counterfeit greenbacks and the engravings to print more of them."

"What?" Kogan looked thunderstruck at the accusation. "These aren't greenbacks, they're gold cert—"

He'd lifted a packet of currency and turned it over. Even Arnie could see the familiar green backs that gave the wartime money its name. Longworth saw them too, and picked up the packet to study it more closely. "Counterfeit, all right," he decided. "No doubt of it."

"Are you an expert?" Arnie asked him.

"Yes, I am." He was unwrapping the engravings to study them.

Arnie saw the badge appear in his hand. SECRET SERVICE, it read, and somehow he knew it was going to be a long day. He wouldn't be getting to the track in time for the first race, or maybe any of the races.

Kogan's face had turned white. "This is some sort of setup! She didn't switch the engravings, she switched the money! Look in her purse and you'll find my gold certificates."

But Longworth only shook his head, and Arnie began to see that the whole thing had been a trap. The letter she wrote to Kogan had been the bait, and then she appeared with her cat and those engravings. When Longworth approached him, Arnie had played right into their hands by suggesting the Treasury agent confront her at the Club House. He turned to Agatha and said, "I didn't know the Secret Service employed women."

"Her husband was an agent," Longworth explained. "You may remember him. Fritz Baxter? Found his body in Saratoga Lake back in the spring."

Arnie moistened his suddenly dry lips, knowing now what he had to do. "It was Kogan killed him! I just helped dispose of the body!"

That was when Kogan went for the gun he kept in his drawer. Arnie never knew which of them he was intending to shoot. But he saw the little derringer come out of Agatha's purse and heard her say, "Go ahead! Try it, Mr. Kogan! I'd love to shoot the man who killed my husband."

* * *

The following day, Agatha Perkins boarded the morning train for New York. Frank Longworth had to remain in Saratoga Springs for an extra day to appear at Bert Kogan's arraignment on the murder charge. Arnold Russell had promised to testify against him in return for a lighter sentence.

"Have a good trip," Longworth told her. "I'll see you in a few days."

"I have Oscar to keep me company," she replied. "Though I will have to start fastening his collar a bit tighter. He has a terrible habit of slipping out of it lately."

TOM

Bill Pronzini

DECKER WAS SO ABSORBED in the collection of Fredric Brown stories he was reading that he didn't see the cat jump onto the balcony railing. He felt its presence after a while, and when he glanced up there it was, switching its tail and staring at him.

At first he was startled; it was as if the cat had materialized out of nowhere. Then he felt a small pleasure. Except for birds and two deer running in the woods, it was the first living creature he'd seen in two weeks. Not that he minded the solitude here; it was the main reason he'd come to this northern California wilderness—a welcome change from his high-pressure Silicon Valley computer job, and a chance to work uninterrupted on the novel he was trying to write. But after fourteen days he was ready for a little company, even if it was only a stray tomcat.

He closed the well-worn paperback and returned the cat's stare. "Well," he said, "hello there, Tom. Where'd you come from?"

The cat didn't move except for its switching tail. Continued to watch him with eyes that were an odd luminous yellow. Otherwise it was an ordinary *Felis catus*, a big butterscotch male with the unneutered tom's overlarge head. It might have been anywhere from three to ten years old.

A minute or so passed—and Decker's feeling of pleasure passed with it. There was something strange about those steady unblinking eyes, something in their depths that might have been malice . . .

No, that was silly. A product of his hyperactive imagination, nurtured for nearly twenty years now by a steady diet of mystery and horror fiction, his one passion other than microtechnology. A product too, he thought, of the coincidental fact that the cat's sudden appearance had coincided with his reading of a Brown story called "Aelurophobe," which was about a man who had a morbid fear of cats.

He had no such fear; at least he'd never been afraid of cats before today. And yet . . . those funny luminous eyes. He had never encountered a cat quite like this one before today.

His mind conjured up another Brown story he'd read, about an alien intelligence that had come to Earth and taken over the body of the protagonist's pet cat. Then, in spite of himself, he remembered a succession of other stories by other writers about cats who were demons and sorcerers, about human beings who were werecats.

Decker suppressed a shiver. Shook himself and smiled a little sheepishly. "Come on," he said aloud, "that's all pure fantasy. Cats are just cats."

He got up and crossed to the railing. The tom seemed to tense without actually moving. Decker said, "So, guy, what're you doing way out here in the piney woods?" and reached out a hand to pat the animal's head.

Before he could touch it, the cat leaped gracefully to the floor and ran through the open doors into the cabin. He blinked after it for a few seconds, then followed it inside. Where he found it sitting on one arm of the wicker settee, flicking its tail and staring at him again.

For a reason he couldn't explain Decker began to feel apprehensive. "Hell," he said, "what's the matter with me? Tom, you're nothing to be afraid of."

The apprehension did not go away. Neither did the cat. When Decker walked deliberately to the settee, with the intention of either shooing or carrying the tom outside, it bounded off again. Took up another watchful position on top of a battered old bookcase.

"All right now," Decker said, "what's the idea? You want something, is that it? You hungry, maybe?"

The fur along the cat's back rippled. Otherwise it sat motionless.

Decker nodded. "Sure, that must be it. Big old tom like you, you need plenty of fuel. If I give you something to eat, you'll go away and let me get back to my reading."

He went into the kitchen, poured a little milk into a dish, tore two small strips of white meat from a leftover Swanson's chicken breast, and took the food back into the living room. He put it down on the floor near the bookcase, backed off half a dozen paces.

The cat did not move.

"Well, go ahead," Decker said. "Eat it and get out."

Ten seconds died away. Then the tom jumped off the bookcase, walked past the food without pausing even to sniff it, and sat down again in the bedroom doorway.

Okay, Decker thought uneasily, so you're not hungry. What else could you want?

He made an effort to recall what he knew about cats. Well, he knew they had been considered sacred by the ancient Egyptians, who worshipped them in temples, paraded them on feast days, embalmed and mummified them when they died and then buried them in holy ground. And that the Egyptian goddess Bast had supposedly endowed them with semidivine powers.

He knew that in the Middle Ages they had been linked to the Devil and the practice of Black Arts and were burned and tortured in religion-sanctioned witch hunts.

He knew that Henry James (whom he had read in college)

once said about them: "Cats and monkeys, monkeys and cats—all human life is there."

He knew that they were predators with a streak of cruelty: they liked to toy with their prey before devouring it.

And he knew they were independent, selfish, aloof, patient, cunning, mischievous, extra clean, and purred when they were contented.

In short, his knowledge was limited, fragmentary, and mostly trivial. And none of it offered a clue to this cat's presence or behavior.

"The hell with it," he said. "This has gone far enough. Tom, you're trespassing. Out you go, right now."

He advanced on the cat, slowly so as not to frighten it. It let him get within two steps, then darted away again. Decker went after it—and went after it, and went after it. It avoided him effortlessly, gliding from one point in the room to another without once taking its yellow-bright gaze from him.

After several minutes, winded and vaguely frightened himself, he gave up the chase. "Damn you," he said, "what do you *want* here?"

The tom stared, switching its tail.

Decker's imagination began to soar again. All sorts of fantastic explanations occurred to him. Suppose the cat was Satan in disguise, come after his soul? Suppose, as in George Langelaan's story "The Fly," a scientist somewhere had been experimenting with a matter transporter and a cat had gotten inside with an evil human subject? Suppose the tom was a kind of modern-day Medusa: look at it long enough and it drives you mad? Suppose—

The cat jumped off the couch and started toward him.

Decker felt a sharp surge of fear. Rigid with it, he watched the animal come to within a few feet and then sit again and glare up at him. Incoming sunlight reflected in its yellow eyes created an illusion of depth and flame that was almost hypnotic.

Compulsively, Decker turned and ran out of the room and slammed the door behind him.

In the kitchen he picked up the telephone—and immediately

put it down again. Who was he going to call? The county sheriff's office? "I've got a strange cat in my rented cabin and I can't get rid of it. Can you send somebody right out?" Good Christ, they'd laugh themselves sick.

Decker poured a glass of red wine and tried to get a grip on himself. I'm not an aelurophobe, he thought, and I'm not paranoid or delusional, and I'm not—nice irony for you—a 'fraidy cat. Cats are just cats, dammit. So why am I letting this one upset me this way?

The wine calmed him, made him feel sheepish again. He went back into the living room.

The cat wasn't there.

He looked in the bedroom and the bathroom, the cabin's only other rooms. No cat. Gone, then. Grew tired of whatever game it had been playing, ran off through the balcony doors and back into the woods.

That made him feel even better—more relieved, he admitted to himself, than the situation warranted. He shut and locked the balcony doors, took the Fred Brown paperback to the couch, and tried to resume reading.

He couldn't concentrate. It was hot in the cabin with the doors and windows shut, and the cat was still on his mind. He decided to have another glass of wine. Maybe that would mellow him enough to restore his mental equilibrium, even get his creative juices flowing. He hadn't done as much work on his novel in the past two weeks as he'd planned.

He poured the wine, drank half of it in the kitchen. Took the rest into the bedroom, where he'd set up his laptop Macintosh.

The tomcat was sitting in the middle of the bed.

Fear and disbelief made Decker drop the glass; wine like blood spatters glistened across the redwood flooring. "How the hell did you get in here?" he shouted.

Switch. Switch.

He lunged at the bed, but the cat leaped down easily and raced out of the room. Decker ran after it, saw it dart into the kitchen. He ran in there—and the cat had vanished again. He searched the room, couldn't find it. Back to the living room. No cat. Bedroom, bathroom. No cat.

Fine, dandy, except for one thing. All the doors and windows were still tightly shut. The tom couldn't have gotten out; it *had* to still be inside the cabin.

Shaken, Decker stood looking around, listening to the silence. How had the cat gotten back inside in the first place? Where was it hiding?

What did it want from him?

He tried to tell himself again that he was overreacting. But he didn't believe it. His terror was real and so was the lingering aura of menace the tom had brought with it.

I've got to find it, he thought grimly. Find it and get rid of it once and for all.

Bedroom. Nightstand drawer. His .32 revolver.

Decker had never shot anything with the gun, for sport or otherwise; he'd only brought it along for security, since his nearest neighbor was half a mile away and the nearest town was another four miles beyond there. But he knew he would shoot the cat when he found it, irrational act or not. Just as he would have shot a human intruder who threatened him.

Once more he searched the cabin, forcing himself to do it slowly and methodically. He looked under and behind the furniture, inside the closets, under the sink, through cartons—every conceivable hiding place.

There was no sign of the tom.

His mouth and throat were sand-dry; he had to drink three glasses of water to ease the parching. The thought occurred to him then that he hadn't found the cat because the cat didn't exist; that it was a figment of his hyperactive imagination induced by the Brown story. Hallucination, paranoid obsession . . . maybe he was paranoid and delusional after all.

"Crap," he said aloud. "The damn cat's real."

He turned from the sink—and the cat was sitting on the kitchen table, glowing yellow eyes fixed on him, tail switching.

Decker made an involuntary sound, threw up his arm and tried to aim the .32; but the arm shook so badly that he had to brace the gun with his free hand. The cat kept on staring at him. Except for the rhythmic flicks of its tail, it was as still as death.

His finger tightened on the trigger.

Switch.

And sudden doubts assailed him. What if the cat had telekinetic powers, and when he fired, it turned the bullet back at him? What if the cat was some monstrous freak of nature, endowed with super powers, and before he could fire it willed him out of existence?

Supercat, he thought. Jesus, I *am* going crazy!

He pulled the trigger.

Nothing happened; the gun didn't fire.

The cat jumped down off the table, came toward him—not as it had earlier, but as if with a purpose.

Frantically Decker squeezed the trigger again, and again, and still the revolver failed to fire. The tom continued its advance. Decker backed away in terror, came up against the wall, then hurled the weapon at the cat, straight at the cat. It should have struck the cat squarely in the head, only at the last second it seemed to *loop around* the tom's head like a sharp-breaking curveball—

Vertigo seized him. The room began to spin, slowly, then rapidly, and there was a gray mist in front of his eyes. He felt himself starting to fall, shut his eyes, put out his hands to the wall in an effort to brace his body—

—and the wall wasn't there—

—and he kept right on falling . . .

Decker opened his eyes. He was lying on a floor, only it was not the floor of his rented kitchen; it was the floor of a gray place, a place without furnishings or definition, a place where the gray mist floated and shimmied and everything—walls, floor, ceiling—was distorted, surreal.

A non-place. A cat place?

Something made a noise nearby. A cat sound unlike any he had ever heard or could have imagined—a shrill mewling roar.

Decker jerked his head around. And the tom was there, the tom filled the non-place as if it had grown to human size while he had been shrunk to feline dimensions. It loomed over him, its tail switching, its whiskers quivering. When he saw it like that he tried to stand and run . . . and it reached out one massive paw, almost lazily, and brought it down on his chest, pinned him to the floor. Its jaws opened wide, and he was looking up then into the wet cavern of its mouth, at the rows of sharp white spikes that gleamed there.

Cats are predators with a streak of cruelty: they like to toy with their prey before devouring it.

"No!"

Big old tom like you, you need plenty of fuel.

Decker opened his mouth to scream again, but all that came out this time was a mouselike squeak.

And then it was feeding time . . .

THE MALTESE DOUBLE CROSS

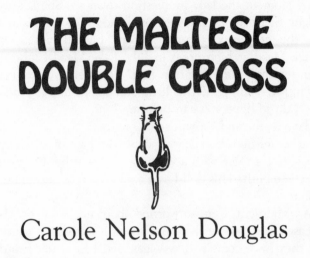

Carole Nelson Douglas

"You ARE GOOD," I tell her in my best Bogart growl. "You are very good."

Sassafras brushes against my shoulder and purrs like a puma on catnip.

She is a long, lean lady in a two-tone autumn haze coat with caramel-colored eyes. She is also my secretary, occasional nurse and gal Friday. And sometimes more than that.

Right now she has just given me the rundown on a new client: sleek number in foreign furs. Might be money in it. Said she was a Miss Wonder Leigh.

I am the unofficial house dick at the Crystal Phoenix Hotel and Casino, the most tasteful joint in Las Vegas. Tasty, too. I keep a private office under the calla lilies out back by the carp pond. The fish add a touch of class to my waiting room, and divert clients while Sassy and I confer. Watching fish can be fascinating, although I prefer catching them. I always was an outdoor dude, when I am not acting as an inside man.

In a moment the lady in question struts in. She is a wonder, all right. Sleek smoke gray fur from head to toe. Legs that do not know the meaning of the word "stop." Limpid eyes as hot blue as Lake Mead at high noon in July. Lake Mead is also quite a haven for carp, did I mention that? I am very fond of carp.

"Oh, Mr. Midnight," this little doll begins in a nervous, high trill, "I do so hope you can help me."

"Have a seat and we will see," say I.

She settles herself delicately upon the base of a nearby bird-bath—I like a room with a view—and pats at her little ears and her little mouth. This doll has a case of nerves laudanum could not cure.

"Mr. Midnight, I am so worried about my sister. She is from the East Coast, where she met this most unsuitable gentleman. Now they have come to Las Vegas, and I have not heard from Whimsy for weeks. I fear that this cad might hurt her."

"Description?"

"My sister's or that of her gentleman friend?"

I eye her sleek, languid length. Inside she might be a nervous Nellie, but outside she is a long velvet glove. I am your ordinary American domestic of immigrant stock, but I recognize breeding when I see it.

"Your sister would of course be your twin," I point out. "It is the looks of the dude in question that are a mystery."

She stretches her lovely neck and tilts her head. "Why, Mr. Midnight, however did you know that my sister and I were twins?"

"Easy. I could see right off that you were not from these parts. Where do you hail from?"

She simpers happily. Every dame likes to think that she is exotic, although this babe definitely proves to have a claim to fame in that department. "Malta."

"Malta? Heard of it. That would make you Maltese, then?"

She shrugs with exquisite indifference, the silver-tipped blue gray fur casually draped over her shoulders shifting as subtly as sand in a dune. I had always thought a Maltese was a breed of dog, but no one in his right mind would apply such a noun to this lady. It crosses my mind to wonder whether Miss Wonder's affections are otherwise engaged.

"Now what does this bad-boyfriend of your sister's look like?" I ask instead.

"He goes by the name of Thursday. I have only seen him once since I arrived. A rude-looking bounder who dresses cheaply. Three colors," she sniffs, "and his shirts are none too white. He frequents the Araby Motel."

I wrinkle my nose at the address, a dive a dog would not touch for sanitary purposes. Things look bad for lost Little Miss Malta.

"Thursday, huh?" An odd name for a lowbrow Romeo, but I cannot fault it. Once in my dimmest youth I was called Friday in honor of my antecedents and my black hair by a little doll in anklets interested in keeping me, but I ran out on that dame. She was more than somewhat underage. Now they call me what I tell them. Usually my friends call me Midnight Louie, though I admit I require a professional pseudonym now and then.

"And where do you hang your collar?" I ask, purely for professional reasons.

"The Cattnipp Inn."

"All right, Miss Leigh." I rise and yawn to indicate the interview is over. "I will have my leg man look into it."

On cue Manny slinks from around a palm tree. He is a cobby tailless dude with an untidy set of whiskers, and his interest in legs is close up and personal. While he is eyeballing Miss Leigh's silken gray hose and generally cozying up to my client, I maintain a businesslike distance. She finally tumbles to my fixed stare and offers me a fistful of legal tender—Tender Vittles coupons.

After she leaves, Manny drools over the cash as well. I tell him to tail this Thursday dude and find out where the sister is. Simple enough. Even a Manx could handle it. Then I go home.

I room with a classy redhead named Miss Temple Barr at the Circle Ritz condominium, a fifties establishment long on vintage charm and short on residents of my particular persuasion. I like to stand out, except when I do not wish to be seen while working, and then I am virtually invisible, especially at night.

Miss Temple Barr and I have a very modern arrangement: she

provides room and board, I am free to come and go and see whom I will. At two A.M. a scratching on the French door to the patio wakes me from visions of sugarpusses kicking in a chorus.

When I pry open the door, I am hit with a blast of hot air and the news from a snitch of mine that Manny has bought a one-way ticket to Cat Heaven, found dead as a dormouse outside the Araby Motel. Hit and run. I tell my informant to find Sassy and have her look in on the unfortunate widow. Then I go to the scene of the crime. An acquaintance of mine, Detective Sergeant Doghouse, is on the case. Below the embankment I see Manny sprawled on his side, legs askew. I do not hang around.

I am in not too good a mood at the office the next day (sure, I can always grab a catnap, but I need my beauty sleep). Then Mrs. Manx trots in, sides heaving and blue eyes large and limpid. She is a white-hot platinum blonde, but a bit on the neurotic side.

That happens to be the side that is all over me before Sassy can make a discreet exit. The widow's long nails clutch my shoulders, putting a crimp in my tailoring.

"Oh, Louie," says she. "You have heard?"

I discourage the Saran Wrap act, peeling free before she can cause any permanent damage. The scene is delicate. Iva Manx and I have been known to share a midnight rendezvous in more ways than one, both before and after she linked up with Manny.

"Be kind to me, Louie," she whimpers, wriggling her rear.

I disengage as gently as possible and tell her to go home until the murderer is caught. She seems less interested in my investigative schedule than in my off-hours plans. I give her a lick and a promise and escort her to the reception room.

After her exit, Sassy looks up with one amber peeper half-cocked and says, "Wherever she has been, it was not at home. They lived under a desert bungalow, and the cupboard was bare —not even a mouse, much less the lady of the house—when I got there at three A.M."

Sassy has never liked Iva, but then Sassy has a distaste for flashy blondes from exotic climes like Turkey. And maybe Malta, too.

This is troubling news. Iva would not be the first dame to hurry hubby off the planet under the mistaken impression that some other dude—say a business associate of the same spouse—might take her for a stroll under the orange blossoms were she free. I would not take Iva for better or worse if she were even $2.98.

Next I report to Miss Wonder Leigh. The Cattnip Inn, however, reports a vacancy at the room number—2001—given me by the lady in question. I look it over anyway, and who should ankle into the landscaping out front but the missing Miss Leigh.

"Oh, Mr. Midnight," says she, widening her azure eyes until her pupils are thin vertical slits and I think I am in blue heaven.

I tell her the news, at which she waxes the usual distraught: much pacing, pausing every now and then to chew her nails. She admits she has taken the room under a false name: Blanche White. Given her coloring, I tell her, Griselda Gray would have been better.

She whines a bit about poor dead Mr. Manx.

I tell her to save the sobs, that Manny had a prepaid plot at Smokerise Farm, no kits, and a wife that would not so much as clean his stockings.

"Oh, be generous, Mr. Midnight," she wheedles, all the while wrapping that soft gray fur around me. "You are so brave, so strong. Help me."

"You are good," I tell her. "You are so good I believe that I can get you a job in the soaps. Especially when you get that little catch in your purr."

"Oh, I deserve that," says she, casting herself away. "I have not been straight with you. My sister is not missing at all."

"Never figured that she was. You cannot hide a Maltese dame in Las Vegas. So are you going to tell me the truth now, Miss White?"

"My name is not White. It is really . . . Blue. Babette Blue."

"And Thursday's your, er, pal?"

"My . . . partner. I met him in Hong Kong. He was escorting a shipment of Siamese back to the States for clandestine breeding purposes. I needed protection—"

"Like Schwarzenegger," I interjected, and she flashes me a pleading look that could wring a filet mignon from a vegetarian.

"It is not what you think. Thursday was big and mean. He had come to Hong Kong as bodyguard for a gambler who had to leave the States. He was always ready for action. He even slept with kitty litter around his bed so no one or nothing could creep up on him. Sometimes he . . . he knocked me around. I was afraid of him, Mr. Midnight, that is all. I thought you and Mr. Manx could scare him off. And now Mr. Manx is dead and—"

"And now we get to the nitty gritty, speaking of kitty litter. Who are you so afraid of, that you would hook up with an ugly customer like Thursday?"

"Oh, Mr. Midnight, I cannot tell you."

I rise to go.

"Please, you must help me. It is a matter of life or death."

"More like death, Miss Blue." I examine the dirt at the base of an oleander bush. This is not an act. I really have to go."

"You are right; I cannot expect a stranger to risk life and limb on my behalf. Go, then. I do not blame you."

I pause to scratch my neck. I do not wish to walk out on a lady at a critical moment, even if it is my own. "Listen. I can look into this without knowing everything, but I need some filthy lucre to fling around if you expect me to keep you out of Thursday's death. How much you got lying around?"

She fluffs her furs and goes huffy, but finally produces a fistful of cash from the kitty. "What will I live on?"

"Got any jewelry?"

"Some . . . genuine faux diamond dollars."

"Hock 'em," say I, giving her back a few coupons for snacks. "Now I really got to go."

After I leave, I check out the facilities behind the azaleas, then I check with a business acquaintance. In such instances it is necessary to consort with the sorry dogs who run the law and order game in this town. It turns out that they are looking for me. Doghouse, the sergeant and my sometimes pal, is all right, but Lieutenant Dandy is a typically tight Scotsman. The pair collar me and tell me that Thursday has been found dead. Did I do it in revenge for Manny? Might have, say I, but did not get around to it. I talk them out of hanging the rap on me and go where I was heading when so crudely interrupted, my lawyer's office. At least I know a legal beagle who knows how to keep his tongue rolled up like a red carpet and his nose relatively snot-free.

I spread most of Miss Blue's kitty litter coupons around— there is a black market in this stuff; apparently people find it conducive to growing seedlings. Then I go back to the office at the Crystal Phoenix.

It has not moved, and Sassy is out front straightening the seams on her stripes. I head for the desk and a short snooze, seeing as how my slumber has been as fitful as that of the fairy-tale princess forced to recline on an illegally concealed legume.

Sassy soon rounds the calla lily curtain marking my inner sanctum and poses artfully. "Mr. Puss-in-Boots to see you, boss." Her pet name is no compliment to the forthcoming visitor.

She admits a stranger broadcasting a distinct odor of baby powder, a fussy sort born to give basic black a bad name. He accessorizes his fine black coat with pristine white gloves and spats. A precious little spot of pure white like a pearl stickpin nestles in his black cravat. Not my type, believe it.

He gives his name as Jewel Thebes. I cannot tell if he is announcing his profession but is lisping, or if he is indeed of Egyptian ancestry. I can certainly picture him mummified.

First he consoles me on Manny's death. Then he announces with the softest of purrs that he is prepared to pay five thousand Fancy Feast coupons with no expiration date for an item, merely ornamental, says he, that he believes I know the whereabouts of: "the black bird."

I cannot quarrel with the quality of the color, nor the amount of the reward: five thousand mackerels is nothing to sniff at. Nor am I normally adverse to a little bird hunting. While I am distracted by the sight of Sassy swaying off to lunch under an archway of calla lily leaves, Thebes pulls a pretty little piece from a discreet pocket and asserts that he is about to search my office.

Go ahead, say I, putting my mitts up. As he is searching me, I pinion his white bootie with my rear foot, pounce, and knock the weapon halfway to the birdbath. One good five-finger exercise on that dainty jaw, and Mr. Thebes is seeing the bluebirds of happiness.

I steel myself and search the dude. A flowered pouch of catnip, a fat wallet and a ticket to *Cats!* is about it. Thebes recovers in time to pout at my inroads upon his person, which also enables him to fork over two hundred clams via my intervention. Clams are not carp, but I remain fond of seafood in all forms. I also choke out of him that the lively Miss Blue is now in Room 635 of the Belle Chat Hotel.

When I get outside the Crystal Phoenix, though, I discover that some alley cat is tailing me, so I hop a ride on a motor scooter and head over to the hotel.

She may no longer be owning up to the name "Wonder," but this gray lady still manages to amaze. When I mention Thursday's death and my visit from Thebes, she goes down on all fours and lifts a dainty paw to her worried brow.

"I have not lived a good life," she confides with a tremor. "I have been bad."

To Midnight Louie this is not necessarily a detriment. I remind her that I find her theatrics good, very good. This is a favorite saying of mine. The ladies like it, yet it leaves me room to be cynical, not to mention mysterious.

"If only," wails she, "I had something to give you. What can I bribe you with?"

I manage a quick pass of the kisser that makes the answer painfully evident. The notion does not seem to dismay her, but then the girl is good. All right, bad.

She also comes clean about the black bird. It will be hers within the week, she says. The late Thursday hid it.

What, I ask, really happened to that late unlamented partner?

"The Fat Cat," says she, employing a thrilling tone.

I am not impressed. I weigh in at eighteen pounds on a good day.

Then who should show up but Thebes, still packing that pretty little piece. We three are at a standoff, when who should arrive but my police pals, Doghouse and Dandy. It is hard to take two guys whose names sound like the title of a television cop show seriously.

They take me into the hall to give me trouble. Now they are thinking I might have killed Manny as well as Thursday. Were Iva and I involved? Nope, say I. I only lie in defense of a lady. And was she trying to divorce Manny, but he was against it? Manny, I say, was not against anything, including fur coats.

A commotion erupts inside. We three burst in and what have we but Jewel Thebes sporting a slash above the right eye and lovely Miss Blue holding the decorative gat on the little Egyptian.

"Please," this Thebes dude whines to the police, "do not leave me or these two will kill me when you go."

Nothing gets the police's goat so much as death threats, and the dogged pair settle in for an inquiry. I turn it all into a joke, for by now both the ex-Miss Wonder and the sniveling Thebes have figured out that the one thing neither of them wants is the police involved in the hunt for this black bird. None of us three is particularly big on sharing with the force.

Things do get ugly, though, and Lieutenant Dandy squeezes up his ugly Scottish mug and wipes my face with a big black-gloved paw.

I hold my temper, mainly because there is a reputed lady present. Doghouse finally herds his inferior superior officer out of the room, along with Thebes.

Babette eyes me with her long mascara-black lashes half-lowered. "You are the most persistent pussycat I have ever known," she coos, stroking an agile extremity over my jaw. "So wild and unpredictable."

I never turn down a compliment, but point out that a little accurate information would soothe my wounded kisser more than this rub-and-tickle game.

So she comes across. Babette, Thursday and Thebes stole the black bird from the dude who owned it because the Fat Cat offered five hundred pounds of prime Venezuelan catnip for it. But Thebes planned to ditch the duo and elope with the black bird on his lonesome, so Babette and Thursday teamed up to do to Thebes what he would have done to them before he could do it. That is what a life of crime will do to your grammar.

Then, she confides, she found Thursday was planning to ditch her and keep the bird all to himself.

"What does this desirable bird look like?" I ask.

Big, she says. So high, and shiny. Has feathers. She only saw it once for a few minutes. I gaze deep into those baby blues and tell her she is a liar.

"I have always been a liar," she purrs.

I suggest that she should find something new to brag about.

"Oh, Louie, I am so tired," she says, leaning listlessly against my shoulder. "I am so tired of lying and not knowing what is a lie and what is true. I wish—"

Well, there is only one way to shut up a lady bent on confessing her sins, and I take it. I could tell you that this is the end of that scene, but you were not born yesterday. Let us just say that talk is cheap after that point.

The Belvedere Hotel, when I get there, is cheesy as usual. I spot several rats on the fringes. I also find Thebes fresh from a long interrogation with Doghouse and Dandy. He looks as if he had been mauled by a rat terrier, but claims he told the cops nothing. He also rags me about my association with Babette, but I tell him I had to throw in with her.

Back at the office, Sassy is full of bad news. A Mr. Spongecake called, says she, and Babette is waiting for me. I am surprised to see her so soon again, but the lady is more ruffled than ever, and it has nothing to do with our private matters.

"Oh, Louie," she says, "my place was mussed up when I returned and I am scared."

I stash her where I always stash disheveled dames, at my gal Sassy's place, which is not too bad. It has a great view on the alley behind Sing Ho's Singapore restaurant. No sooner are the two dames on the way there, but my calla lilies part and Iva Manx pads in. Has a dude no privacy?

She admits that she sent the police to my place.

I reply by asking where she was when Manny was given his fatal shove.

This encourages her to leave in a hurry and brings my first peace of the day, which is interrupted by a call on the blower from this Fat Cat, Spongecake. He is in Room 713 of the Crystal Phoenix and wants the black bird.

There is nothing to say but that I got it and we can talk. Like Miss Blue, I am a liar, too, but purely for professional reasons.

When I arrive I realize that the Fat Cat has great taste. He has taken the ghost suite at the Crystal Phoenix. These rooms feature the same forties decor as when Jersey Joe Jackson lived at the hotel, then known as the Joshua Tree. Some say Jersey Joe still lives there. The rooms are never rented, but we law-bending dudes are not against arranging a private powwow on the premises. As for Jersey Joe, he had proclivities of a criminal nature, to hear tell. If he objects to some larcenous company, he is the last to say so.

The Fat Cat is an oversize bewhiskered gent in a brown striped suit with full sideburns and a stomach pouch that would make the spreading chestnut tree look like a bonsai bush. I have heard this particular breed called a Maine Coon, and he is indeed big enough to pass for a raccoon, or perhaps the state of Maine itself.

An anonymous, almost albino gunsel is hunched in the corner with his eyes hooded. I pay him no mind.

"Are you are here, sir, as Miss Blue's representative," says Spongecake, who tends to talk like a preacher addressing the millionaires' club, "or Mr. Thebes's?"

I pull a pussycat face. "There is me," I say modestly.

The bushy eyebrows frosting Spongecake's fat face lift. "She did not tell you what it is, did she?"

"Thebes offered me ten thousand for it," I return, upping the ante to keep things interesting.

Spongecake arranges himself more comfortably in his chair, which is a green satin upholstered job with wine fringe. There is a lot of Spongecake to rearrange. He offers some coffee for my cup of cream, which I accept. A dash of caffeine adds spice to my day and Spongie is big on formalities.

"Let me tell you about the bird," Spongecake begins, his yellow eyes slit with greed and nostalgia. "It is a songbird of sorts," says he, "but not in the usual sense. It wears a glossy black coat somewhat like your own. I like," he adds, "a gentleman who maintains his grooming. This legendary bird dates from the mid-eighteenth century. Eighteen forty-five, to be precise."

I get the impression that Spongecake is nothing if not precise.

"After a circuitous history beginning in the States, the black bird finally arrived in the possession of a gent of antiquarian nature, a Russian blue, in Istanbul. A general. Then, sir," Spongie adds, "I sent agents to acquire it. They did."

"What can one bird be worth?" I ask.

"That depends upon the buyer. I confess that this globe hosts certain . . . collectors, shall we say? Such individuals would be willing to pay dearly for a rare bird of the proper vintage, much as others would kill for a bottle of Napoleon brandy. Reputedly this bird's craw is crammed with diamonds." Spongie leans back to look down his flowing white cravat. "I can offer you, sir, twenty-five thousand in whatever currency you prefer, or one-quarter of what I realize from the sale, which might be a hundred thousand, or even a quarter of a million."

This is not an insignificant amount of nip. Plans for this pile of affluence are dancing in my head, along with something of a chemical character. It occurs to me that the caffeine I have imbibed is having an effect reminiscent of valium.

The room blurs, which is disturbing. Spongecake blurs, which is an improvement. I rise and spar briefly with the furniture, then conk out on the floor.

I wake to the sound of four-and-twenty blackbirds piping in a pie. They flock away like cobwebs. I find myself alone in the Jersey Joe Jackson suite. Whenever I find myself alone, I make good use of the opportunity, but first I lurch to the nearest mirror, which requires a staggering bound atop a console table covered in snakeskin. Speaking of which, it seems one of the dear recently departed—Spongecake, Thebes or the pale gunsel in the corner—has given my head a parting shot. Four slashes decorate my temple. I clean up by rubbing a wet mitt over them, then search the premises. I find little or nothing, but I feel better.

One of the little nothings I find is yesterday's newspaper listing the schedule of charter flights to Las Vegas. La Paloma Airlines is flying in a raft of eager gamblers from Hong Kong, I read. Those of an Oriental persuasion have a fondness for gaming that is exceeded only by my taste for carp, but I find the name of the charter suggestive. According to a hot-tempered hoofer of my acquaintance, "paloma" means dove in Spanish.

Such irony as a white bird flying in a black bird cannot be merely accidental, but it *is* Occidental: the port of departure is in the right quarter of the globe. I recall that the lovely Babette was definite about needing a week to get her paws on the bird.

By the time I return to the office, the sidewalk has stopped playing spin the bottle. Babette is not there, but Sassy says the lady has called and is now at the Wellington Hotel. That lady changes hotels more frequently than a sheepdog rotates fleas.

So I am sitting at my desk nursing my noggin, which requires me to add a little milk to the Scotch I keep in my drawer, when the calla lily leaves part dramatically. I prepare myself for the entrance of another foxy lady. Instead, a wizened Siamese staggers in, dragging a parcel almost as big as he is wrapped in burlap.

The old dude falls over, and a quick check finds him pumped full of birdshot. Sassy is not amused. She does not do cleanup work.

"Do not blame the poor sap for keeling over on our turf," say I. "He has just come in on a long intercontinental flight."

I pat him down and find his identification tag. "Captain Jack." No doubt his last assignment was the La Paloma.

Sassy agrees to tidy the place.

"You are a good man, sister," I tell her, then take the burlap bundle and scram. I deposit it in one of my favorite stashes, which I am not about to divulge, save that it is under a blackjack table in the Crystal Phoenix. I take a hike to the address of the Wellington, and find a vacant lot. I am not surprised. Napoleon did not do well with Wellington, either. So I return to home, sweet homicide.

Guess who is waiting at my place? It could be the police, but it is Miss Babette, looking, as usual, ravishing.

Unfortunately, she is accompanied by Spongecake and Thebes, neither of whom look ravishing, although Thebes always looks as if he would be amenable to the idea. The nondescript gunsel is in the corner, looking threatening.

Spongie wastes no time.

"You are a most headstrong individual, sir. I see we will have to cut you in on ten thousand for your trouble."

"No trouble," I reply. "I want a much bigger cut than that. What say we feed the gunsel to the police dogs? After all, he did shoot Thursday and Captain Jack."

Here Spongie gets apoplectic, which he reveals by twitching his whiskers. "You cannot have Wilmar. Wilmar is a particular pet of mine."

I cannot say much for Miss Babette's associates; they all appear to have unnatural attachments. Well, say I, give them Mr. Thebes then.

The dude in question's pouty little peke-face whitens before my eyes.

Wilmar erupts from the corner to spit in my face, the whites of his eyes forming a neat circle around his putty-colored orbs. As far as whisker-twitching goes, he has Big Daddy Spongecake beat by a hairsbreadth.

Poor Wilmar is so wrought up that the beauteous Babette slinks up and disarms the poor sap with one practiced swipe of her pretty paw.

Wilmar belly-crawls into the corner in a funk.

"So, Mr. Midnight," Sponge demands affably, which does not fool me a bit. The only thing affable about Spongecake is his vocabulary. "Where is the bird?"

"It will be delivered here. Shortly. Meanwhile, we might as well entertain ourselves. Let me see if I have the playbill down pat. You," I tell Spongie, "killed Thursday because he was in cahoots with Babette. What about Captain Jack?"

"Oh," says Sponge, "that was Wilmar's doing, as was Thursday. I do not descend to dirty work. And it all really was Miss Babette's fault. She had given Captain Jack the bird in Hong Kong, to deliver it to her here. Wilmar—whom I had, er, picked up in the East—and I called upon Thursday and Miss Blue in Malta. I was to pay Babette for the bird when they snatched it. While I went to get the payment, she and Thursday got away. Wilmar and I traced them to Hong Kong, then here. After La Paloma landed, we followed Captain Jack to Babette's apartment. Captain Jack ran with the bird. Wilmar shot him on the fire escape, but the captain managed to get away. That is when I . . . persuaded Babette to call you and say she was at the Wellington. I wanted to search your office."

"Find anything I been missing?"

Spongecake glowers, then pats his enormous stomach until he withdraws ten one-dollar Whiskas coupons.

I take the cash, look it over, and say I want fifteen.

Spongecake and I dance around some more on price. When I hand back the ten, he says I kept one coupon. No, say I, you padded it. In fact it is crumpled tighter than a love note between his front fingernails.

"A word of advice, Mr. Midnight." Sponge narrows his bland yellow eyes. "Be careful." He jerks his head in Babette's direction. It takes a crook to predict another crook. "Now, where is the bird?"

I manage to dial Sassy's number on the vintage rotary phone and tell her to withdraw the bundle from my favorite storage facility. Not much later the ever-efficient Sassy drops off the burlap-wrapped object of all our affections.

Spongecake is so pleased he hyperventilates as he claws away the wrappings. What we see is one large, black bird, its scrawny feet tied with some sort of leather anklet. Over its head is a leather hood like you see on fancy hunting birds like falcons.

Spongecake's long nails tremble as they pluck the bag away.

The big bird is somewhat disoriented, which—given its port of departure—is understandable.

"Hawwwk," this creature declares.

Spongecake recoils as if scratched, and indeed the sound is crude enough to scar the most sensitive ear.

"Fraud," Spongecake declares, still incensed at the idea of criminal doings. "Fakery. This is a genuine, live bird!" he snarls at Babette. "I expected a stuffed specimen—stuffed with diamonds. A live bird could not harbor such treasure for long."

Babette shakes her pretty head. "I did not know—"

"You cheated me," Thebes screams at Spongecake, bristling until his hair stands up all over, even on his white-socked feet. "You promised me riches beyond counting!"

I turn to Babette. "You must have known."

"No, Louie, I did not!" She curls sharply filed fingernails into my lapels. "I never saw the bird for more than a few moments—"

"Peacock feathers!"

"I want my ten coupons back." Spongecake pokes me crudely on the shoulder.

I shrug. "Too bad."

Thebes and Spongecake depart, arguing. Spongecake is threatening to find the Russian blue who pulled the switch in Malta. Thebes is threatening to go along for the ride. That is what you call company that loves misery. No one notices Wilmar hunched quietly in the corner.

I turn to Babette, who is looking nervous.

"All right, baby, time to talk turkey. What exactly is this here bird?"

"I do not know, Louie, truly I do not," she says, barely casting the creature a glance.

"What about Manny?"

"What *about* Manny?" She runs light nails up and down my spine.

"You warned Thursday that he was being followed, hoping he would confront Manny and force him to kill Thursday for you. When that did not work, and Manny went up the alley, just doing his job, you pushed him into the path of an oncoming Brinks truck. You knew the Crystal Phoenix transports the casino take at that hour along that route. So did I. You set Manny up. You killed him."

"Why, why, Louie? Why would I do it?"

"Because you are bad, sweetheart; you said it yourself. And you figured that I would go after Thursday to avenge Manny. You were right, only Wilmar got there first. Do not fret, pet; maybe someone will bail you out of stir. You still have your long legs and eyelashes. They say there is a sucker born every minute. You are a pretty swell-looking purebred, after all, both you *and* your sister."

"S-sister?" She swishes past me nervously, twitching her tail in a way that is not a come-on. "I have no sister, I told you. That was a lie."

"Sure you do." I nod at the subdued gunsel everybody has overlooked. "In that corner, we have Wilma Leigh, aka Whimsy. And here, weighing in at seven pounds soaking wet, is her sister Wonder, aka Babette. No wonder you disarmed 'Wilmar' so easily just now. How long did your sister work for the Fat Cat by posing as a pansy?"

"Louie . . . what are you saying?"

"You gave it away yourself. Came from Malta, you said. Could not help bragging about your exotic origins. That was about the only honest thing you said. See, there is this small oddity about certain types of purebreds that gave you away. If you had not snagged the black bird, your sister would have been around to collect it off Spongecake and Thebes when they got it. She was your ace in the hole. Either way, Midnight Louie would have been out in the cold wailing Dixie, and I do not play the patsy for any dame."

Wilma is ankling over, shaking herself out of the nondescript tan trenchcoat that hid her natural coat of creamy blonde fur. Once Wilma doffs her macho demeanor she proves to be a nubile lady with eyelashes as extenuated as the gams on a daddylonglegs.

"You are both the unacknowledged daughters of the general,

the Russian blue from Malta who owned the bird," I tell them.
"There is something called the Maltese dilution in cat-breeding
circles, with which I am not normally intimate, I admit.

"In the Maltese dilution, a coat that is black dilutes to blue,
and one that is yellow dilutes to cream. The Russian blue was
already one watered-down dude. You two came from the same
litter—twin sisters, only one of you came out cream, and the
other gray. It is a Maltese peculiarity. You remember when I met
you, angel? I said I had heard of Malta. As it happens, the
dilution is the solution."

"Will you turn us in, Louie?" Babette pouts, pressing her warm
soft body close to mine.

"I should."

Wilma presses close to my other side, giving me the eye but
no lip.

"Naw," I decide. "The bird is a family heirloom of sorts. But I
will never turn my back on you two."

As the evening turns out, such a maneuver is not in the least
necessary. I must say that these Maltese dilutions lack for nothing when it comes to nocturnal gymnastics.

As for the bird, the twins insist that it is valuable to their
esteemed daddy for reasons relating not to diamonds, but to
dinner. Some gourmands, they claim, would kill to consume a
rare bird of proper vintage, much as other individuals would sell
their souls for a bottle of Napoleon brandy. I tell the Maltese
sisters that I wish to keep the black bird for a while as a souve-
nir, and they can hardly object.

The next morning—late—I take it over to a friend of mine
who runs a used musical instrument shop off the Strip. This
dude can play a riff on a piano that would have a shar-pei tapping its tail, and that particular breed is notoriously tone-deaf.
My pal is also something of a feather fancier. His moniker is Earl
E. Bird. He shares the same sophisticated coloring I do, only he
happens to be short on hair, long on skin and as bald as an eight
ball on top of it.

I show him the bird.

He jerks off the hood and smiles until he exposes what look like all fifty-two ivories in his mouth.

"Say, Louie, my man! Where did you get this? This here bird is a genuine mynah, or maybe a raven. Or possibly a crow."

Some expert. "Do these mynahs, ravens and crows live for a long time?"

"Some parrots can reach a hundred."

I would whistle if I could; most dudes I know do not make much more than twelve. "I had in mind about a hundred and fifty years."

Earl E. shrugs. "I do not know how well these black birds age, but I know this one to be a mellow fellow, and an oracle of old. Talks, if you know what to say to it. What is the word, bird? Tell me your name. Where are the seven keys to Baldpate? When will the Cubs win the World Series?"

Earl E. can go on like this indefinitely, but at this interrogation the bird finally perks up, cocks its head, flashes a beady eye about the premises and intones, "Nevermore."

I wish that I could say what this means, since I have a feeling that it expresses the dark, brooding soul of mystery itself. But I am a practical dude, not a poet. At that pivotal moment I find the room spinning as if I had imbibed another shot-glass of Spongecake's spiked Coffeemate.

The bird starts flapping its wings and squawking "Nevermores." Brass instruments glitter past like a carousel. Must have been something Maltese I had for dinner the night before.

As my vision clears, I find myself alone in Miss Temple Barr's comfy condominium, stretched out on her batik pillows with one mitt on the television remote control.

Some black-and-white film of days gone by is reeling off the screen. I breathe a sigh of relief. For a moment, in my mental fog, I thought that this vintage classic had been colorized. As anyone of any taste whatsoever knows, the only classic colors in film and real life are black with a dash of white around the whiskers and the incisors.

I still cannot figure out how the bird lasted almost a hundred and fifty years, or who would pay big dough to consume such a senior citizen. I do know one thing: if Midnight Louie keeps snoozing in front of the television set, the Bogeyman will get him.

ALL PLACES ARE ALIKE

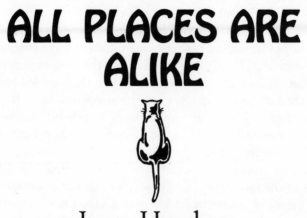

June Haydon

The cat. He walked by himself and all places were alike to him.

—Rudyard Kipling

BETH ADAMS STIRRED in her sleep and turned over. Immediately Tabitha moved from her place on Beth's pillow and purred, ducking her furry gray head under Beth's hand.

"You silly pussums; what woke you up? That's good. Settle down. Good pussums."

With slow gentle strokes, Beth lulled the cat into slumber and the room became quiet once more, as she slipped into sleep.

It was not always so.

When Stratford was home, the Persian was banished to the basement. But, lately, Stratford was out of town on business about half the time. However, there was another, a new interruption to the quiet, predictable tenor of the cat's life. For, when Stratford was gone, there was someone else in Beth's bed.

Kevin Darte, his name was, and he was younger than Beth. Whenever he came to the house, after they had drinks, Beth, with murmured apologies, put Tabitha in the basement. Tabitha would doze, wake to listen until, sometimes as late as dawn, she would hear the front door open and close.

Then Beth, padding about barefoot, her long dark hair spilling over her shoulders, her revealing nightgown clinging, would call Tabitha and carry her upstairs for the rest of the night. Together mistress and cat would settle into the rumpled bed and sleep until midmorning. Or, until the telephone rang. It would be Stratford, calling from out of town, to tell his darling how much he missed her and how he longed to see her. Beth would sleepily murmur to him approximately the same words.

Stratford would soon return and Tabitha would spend her nights in the basement. She knew it was useless to complain or hide. Stratford always found her and dumped her unceremoniously on the basement steps and shut the door before she could escape.

One Saturday Beth said she was going shopping. She had to choose a dress for a wedding they were attending, and such shopping always took a long time. Also, she and Kay, her best friend, were having lunch. So, she would be gone for a while. Was that all right?

"Of course, darling. Take your time. I'm going to use the Jacuzzi, listen to *La Bohème*. Then Dave and I are playing tennis. Is our date with the Martins still on for tonight?"

"Yes. They said something about having dinner at the country club but I'm tired of it. We agreed to decide where to eat when we pick them up."

Kevin worked at the country club.

"We're picking them up?" asked Stratford, amused. "So you can show off your BMW?"

"Certainly not."

"Go on to your shopping, hon. I'm teasing you."

"Goodbye," she said, turning her head so that Stratford's kiss landed on her cheek. "Goodbye, Pussums. You be a good kitty."

"Does she still resent it that I kicked her out of our bed?" wondered Stratford, not caring very much.

"No, she's of a forgiving nature," replied Beth as she stooped to pet the cat.

Stratford and Beth did not keep their appointment with their friends that evening.

After Beth left, Stratford, leaving the bathroom door ajar, turned on the radio, slid happily into the Jacuzzi and relaxed. He did not notice a bored and restless Tabitha wander into the bathroom, jump on the shelf where the radio blared, become entangled in its cord, right herself quickly and jump down. As she did so she bumped the radio, it fell into the Jacuzzi and the last thing Stratford heard was his own scream. The cat fled and, hours later, Beth, after confronting horror in the bathroom, found Tabitha in a square, asleep in the middle of the blue silk coverlet in the master bedroom, the overhead fan barely fanning the cat's gray fur.

The police came. The man in charge, Frank Davis, later told an associate that Mrs. Adams put on the best act he had ever seen.

"But it didn't save her," continued Frank. "No, she had no alibi, she saw no one the day of the murder, the day she was supposed to be shopping. We found out about her lover and Mr. Adams' life insurance policy, very large it was, made out to her. It was an open-and-shut case."

"And the lover?"

"He got life. He helped, he had to have. Mrs. Adams was so squeamish, she couldn't have done it alone. No, he helped and then they had planned to skip the country. The boyfriend had already bought the tickets. She vowed she knew nothing about them. He said they were to be a surprise. But people will say anything when they're trying to save their skins."

Beth Adams went to the electric chair, protesting her innocence to the end. Sometime before the execution, but after the appeals had been denied, Kay, who had forgotten the lunch date on the day of Stratford's death, came to see Beth. There was little to say. After several interminable silences, Kay rose to go and cast around nervously for something to say.

"Tabitha seems to have adjusted well to living with us. But we have a fuss every night when she tries to sleep with us. Don won't have it and stashes her in the kitchen. We can't let a cat run our lives. But, other than that, the kitty is very comfortable with us." Her face crumpled and she stood quickly and took a step backward. "Well, Beth, er, goodbye."

Beth watched as Kay left the visitors' room, her heels tapping lightly on the linoleum-covered floor.

HUNGER

Christopher Fahy

GREAT, JUST WHAT I NEED, Dillon thought.

The guy ahead of him—the only other patron in the tiny store—was truly pathetic. He was bent and bald, with a stubble of mangy gray whiskers, a grubby blue short-sleeved shirt with a missing right armpit, and watery eyes behind sagging glasses patched with electrical tape. To top it all off, he stank—the odor was sour and musty both. He fussed with his tattered wallet, his withered hands shaking.

With a sniff of disgust, Dillon looked at the rack of gum and candy bars. It had rained from Atlantic City to Pittsburgh, a tire had given out before Cleveland, a cop had made him move on when he tried to camp out in his car. He'd smoked the last of his cigarettes an hour ago, had run in here to get a new pack, and—this is the way it was going—had gotten behind Mr. Slow.

"So how are the cats, Mr. Logan?" the man at the register said. He was middle-aged, jowly, with dark blue suspenders.

The customer's voice was phlegmy and loose as he piped, "Getting old, I'm afraid."

"Aren't we all?"

The man didn't respond to this. A coupon slipped out of his wallet and fell to the floor.

"You drop something, Mr. Logan?"

"What?" The old man looked up with a frown. "Oh," he said, and then slowly bent down for the coupon. "Tissues," he said, coming up again. "I forgot them."

"Allow me," the cashier said, and, locking the register, walked away.

Terrific, Dillon thought.

The old man kept fooling around with his wallet, and when he at last latched onto something, Dillon's eyes narrowed. The bill those feeble fingers held bore the face of Benjamin Franklin.

"Here we go, Mr. Logan," the cashier said smiling, dropping the tissue box in the old man's cart. He rang up the item, deducting the coupon. "Twenty-three fourteen out of a hundred," he said as he took the money. "Oops, here's an extra." He held up a crisp new bill.

The old man stared at it. "What?"

"Two hundreds were stuck together."

"Oh."

The cashier counted out the change, placing it in the old man's palm on top of the extra hundred. Laying his wallet down on the counter, the old man picked up the coins in slow motion, depositing them in his pocket. He took up his wallet again and opened it wide and began to insert the bills.

Dillon watched. And there was another hundred, another, a fifty . . .

The old man at last got his things in order and shuffled off, dragging his cart.

"Sorry to keep you waiting," the cashier said.

"No problem. I just want a pack of Marlboros."

"Sure."

Dillon paid and went out the door.

The old man was lugging his cart down the sidewalk. Dillon tore open the Marlboros, lit one, got into his car and watched.

At the corner the guy stopped and looked both ways, craning

his scrawny neck left, then right, then all the way back to the left again before crossing.

The street was industrial, tired and bleak, in a lost hopeless pocket of urban decay. A car without tires, its windshield cracked, squatted next to the opposite curb. Except for the feeb, there was no one in sight.

Dillon smoked, thinking: still Indiana, right? Yeah, had to be. He pressed on the gas and turned the key and started down the street.

Surely the guy didn't live far away, and the chances were very good that he lived alone. And he had money—possibly *lots* of money. Some of these characters lived like paupers and had thousands stashed in their cookie jars.

Dillon pulled to the side as a white truck with STANTON'S PRIME CUTS painted on it went by, and the old geezer rounded the corner.

The block was dead. A factory with its windows shattered took up the street's south side, while the north side held rubble-strewn lots and a trio of row houses covered with asphalt: fake stone and fake brick.

Dillon parked on the corner, breathing out smoke and squashing his Marlboro butt in the car's ashtray. The dude hauled his cart up the granite step of the middle house—the one that was covered in fake yellow brick—then reached in his pocket. After a while he found the key and fumbled it into the lock. His door opened up and he hoisted his groceries inside.

Dillon lighted another Marlboro, thinking: Give him some time to take a leak, unpack, then go for it.

He finished the Marlboro, started another, and thought of Atlantic City; of how, in the very near future, a guy would show up out of nowhere, demanding the money. Five thousand bucks, and he'd better have it—or else.

He opened his door and got out of the car and flicked what was left of his Marlboro into the weeds in the empty lot on the corner. The air was damp and the lot smelled of plaster dust.

The houses on either side of the old coot's place were boarded up and the sidewalk was covered with garbage: smashed bottles, old rags, scraps of paper, a hubcap, some stained white acoustical tiles. He mounted the granite step and pushed the black button on the doorjamb.

He heard no ring inside the house, and pushed again. Still nothing, so he knocked.

He waited awhile and knocked again. Come on, old man, he thought, don't make me break your damn door down.

A scratching sound, the click of the latch, and the door came open a crack. The man's face, puzzled, fearful, looking up.

In his mind Dillon saw himself shoving the door open, knocking the guy to the floor and grabbing the wallet. But Christ, it could kill the old fart. That, he certainly didn't need. No violence if he could help it. And maybe that wallet was only the tip of the iceberg, after all.

"I was thinking you might like some help around here," he said. "I could clean up your sidewalk. Your yard, your cellar, I'm fast and I'm cheap."

The old man stared with a dense, opaque look. "What?"

"Clean up," Dillon said a notch louder. "This mess on the sidewalk."

"Oh." The man squinted. "I saw you in Russell's, right?"

So he wasn't completely unconscious after all. "The store?" Dillon said.

"Russell's Market."

"Yeah. I was there."

"I thought so."

Not good, Dillon thought. The cashier could tell cops important stuff if the geezer blabbed. "Your name's Mr. Logan, right?" he said.

"How'd you know that?" The old face was pinched and suspicious.

"The guy in the store called you that."

"Yeah. Logan's my name."

Dillon stuck out his hand. "Mine's Stanton. Bill Stanton."

The old man ignored Dillon's hand. He kept squinting. "So what do you want?"

"I do odd jobs."

"You live near here?"

"Across town."

"Where?"

"Lawrence Street."

"Never heard of it."

"I never heard of your street either until today," Dillon said, looking down at the sidewalk. "It sure is a mess. Trash like this can attract rats, you know."

"Rats?" said Logan. He shook his frail head. "I got no rats; my cats make sure of that."

"Uh-huh," Dillon said.

Then the old man surprised him. "I got an old stove in the hallway," he said. "If you take it outside, I'll give you a dollar."

"A dollar. Sure," Dillon said.

Logan opened the door, and Dillon stepped into a vestibule tiled in brown. The odor he'd smelled in the store was heavy in here. Did this guy ever shower?

"This way," Logan said.

They went into the hall, where a low wattage bulb wrapped in cobwebs hung down on a cord. "That's it right there."

It was buried in bundles of old newspapers, and so was the hallway floor. "Gotta move all these papers to get to it," Dillon said. "So you want me to stick 'em outside?"

"While you're at it, sure," Logan said.

Dillon thought: While I'm at it. Clean out the hallway *and* move the stove for a buck. Quite a deal.

As he picked up some bundles of papers, the smell hit him hard. The place *reeked*. Cats, he thought. That's what that odor was. Cats.

He carried the papers out to the sidewalk. Compared to the house, the stale city air smelled sweet. In the hallway again he said, "You got a real fire hazard here. You oughta get rid of *all* these papers, you know?"

Logan didn't respond for a moment. Then, nodding, he said, "I suppose you're right. Well, I'll give you another dollar."

"For what's in the hallway?"

"No, no, for the living room, too. And I got some out in the dining room and the kitchen."

The dingy living room was crammed so full there was barely space to walk. "It'd take me a couple of hours to get all this out," Dillon said. "I'll have to ask for five bucks."

"Make it four," Logan said.

Dillon looked at him hard. He imagined his fist smashing into that sallow face, those glasses splintering. "Four bucks," he said. "Not much for all that work."

"Well, take it or leave it," Logan said. "I have to check something out back; you decide what you want to do."

He made his way down the hall past the piles of paper. As Dillon watched, he thought: I've decided to take it, old man. I've decided to take it *all*.

He made five more trips to the sidewalk before he had cleaned out enough to be able to move the stove. He thought he'd get used to the sickening odor, but no, and now *he* stank; the cat smell covered his sweaty skin, was in his shirt, his hair. But where the hell *were* the things? He hadn't seen one of them yet, and you'd think that with a stench this bad the place would be crawling with them.

The stove was so old it was probably worth some money: a green enameled gas job on slender black legs. Dillon grabbed it and pulled.

Heavy sucker, for Christ's sake. He pulled on its opposite side and it moved a few inches—and something fell onto the floor.

Dillon stared at it. Money, a roll of bills. He reached down and snatched it up.

"Having problems?"

The old man was down at the end of the hall by the door that led into the kitchen. Slipping the roll of bills into his shirt, Dillon said, "This baby's heavy."

"Of course," Logan said. "If it wasn't, I'd move it myself."

"Right."

Inch by inch, Dillon wrestled the stove toward the door. Finally he got it outside on the step, then yanked it down onto the sidewalk and out to the curb. Out of breath, sweating hard and his shoulders aching, he stood with his back to the house and reached in his shirt.

He took the rubber band off the bills and unrolled them. Ten twenties. Two hundred bucks. If he had any luck this would just be the start. He went back inside.

He cleaned out the rest of the hallway while Logan watched. "I haven't seen this much floor in years," the old man said. "It sure makes a difference, all right."

Dillon found no more money. At the living room doorway he said, "Where's the light switch in here?"

"The bulb's dead," Logan said. "I don't use the living room much anymore, I pretty much stay in the kitchen. Just take out the papers now, don't touch those baskets."

"You don't have an extra bulb?"

"Maybe somewhere."

"Uh-huh."

Dillon had cleared out half the room before Logan said, "I'll be back in a while," and left.

The baskets were stacked at the foot of the bookshelves, most of them peach baskets made out of wood. Dillon went to them quickly, leaned down. The room was so dark he could hardly see. An iron without any cord, a few broken light fixtures, rusty stuck hinges, screwdrivers—just worthless junk. Three whole baskets of empty jars.

A toilet flushed, and Dillon stood up. On the dark marble mantel some lighter fluid, a bar of soap, and a carved wooden box. Dillon opened the box.

More bills. Two rolls. He shoved them into his pocket and closed the lid.

"How's it going?"

The old man was there in the doorway, his features in shadow.

"You sure have a mess here," Dillon said, lifting more papers.

"I know," Logan said. "You save a little here, a little there, and the next thing you know . . ." He shrugged.

Dillon went through the hallway and out to the curb. The sidewalk held a wall of papers now.

As he looked at the house again, he gagged. His throat was itching, burning with that awful smell. For a minute he thought he should quit right now and be happy with what he had. Then he said to himself: Are you nuts? This guy is the next best thing to Fort Knox. Gagging again, he took a deep breath of foul air and went back inside.

"Just the newspapers," Logan said again. "I could probably do without some of the other stuff too, but I'd have to go through it first. You get old and forget what you have." He waved his shriveled hand and said, "You wouldn't know. You're young and strong and your mind's okay, you wouldn't know what I mean."

Dillon lifted more papers. His ribs and arms were aching now. When he went back into the house, Logan was gone.

Dillon went to the bookshelves. He leafed through the dusty volumes quickly, alert for the sound of Logan's slow feet. The books yielded nothing, nothing, nothing—then a bill floated onto the floor.

A hundred. All *right*. Dillon went through more books. A twenty, a ten and a fifty came out, and he stuffed them away in his pocket.

"So, Mr. Stanton, you like to read?"

Dillon broke into sudden sweat. "Oh, yeah," he said as he put the book back.

"Books are wonderful friends," Logan said. "Next to my cats, they're the best friends I have."

"Uh-huh," Dillon said. He bent over and lifted more papers.

"I'd hate to lose even a one of them," Logan said. "I'd miss them so. Funny, since I haven't been able to read in a long time now." He touched his glasses. "These things don't work anymore."

Dillon grunted and carried the newspapers out the door.

Logan watched as he finished the living room. But when Dillon attacked the dining room, the old man went off again.

A tureen on the dark ornate sideboard. Dillon went to it, lifting its china lid with the utmost caution. Paper clips and rubber bands and matches and stubs of old pencils, old gas bills, a few rolls of cellophane tape—and no money. He put the lid down again, holding his breath. It made a tiny clink as it touched the bowl.

He looked over his shoulder—no Logan—and opened the sideboard's top drawer.

He rummaged through playing cards, yellowed receipts, a lace tablecloth, white linen napkins. A handful of pennies. No bills. He shoved the drawer closed and opened the bottom drawer. No money. Behind the cabinet door on the right, more papers. He pushed them aside. No bills. Wiping sweat off his forehead, he opened the door on the left.

More papers, some plastic place mats—and then, beneath the place mats, a metal box. Dillon opened it quickly, hands shaking.

His breath stopped. Good God. It was filled to the brim with hundreds. Quickly he shoved them down into his pockets, sweating. Thousands of dollars here, *thousands*. Closing the box, he put it back under the place mats and shut the door.

"Problems?"

Sudden cold sweat and his chest felt numb. Standing, rubbing his shoulder, Dillon said. "Yeah, pulled my back. I'm afraid that's all for today. I can come back tomorrow, though, if it eases up."

"Fine," Logan said. "I'll pay you tomorrow, then."

"I'd like to get paid for today's work now," Dillon said.

Logan nodded. "I understand. In case you can't make it tomorrow."

"Right."

"So how much you want?"

"Three dollars."

"Oh? You did three quarters of the job?"

Dillon narrowed his eyes and thought: Come on, old man, don't push your luck. He said, "I think three bucks is a bargain for what I did."

Logan didn't respond to this. He said, "Before you go, do one more thing for me."

"What's that?"

"There's a broken TV in the yard that I'd like you to take out front. It's small, not heavy, it won't hurt your back."

"Where is it?"

They walked through the kitchen, where fat flakes of cream-colored paint curled away from the ceiling and walls. The table was piled with magazines. A path through the newspapers led to the cast-iron sink, where a faucet dripped; another path led to the door, which was steel, like something you'd find in a warehouse or store. The window beside it was covered with metal mesh. Logan pushed back two bolts on the door, turned the knob.

The yard was bordered by high wooden walls that were smothered in dark lush vines. Its grass was knee-high, yellow and brown, and, down at the far end, a tangle of bushes with flat broad leaves obscured a wrought-iron gate.

An old refrigerator stood against one wall, vines spilling across its door. Beside it, a rickety table, its legs lost in grass, held three cans of paint and the TV set.

"Just put it out front with the papers," Logan said.

Dillon entered the grass. He had just about reached the table, when Logan laughed. Then the kitchen door slammed and the bolts clicked shut.

Dillon whirled. "Hey!" He waded across to the door again, grabbed the knob. "Hey!"

Then Logan was at the window, behind the mesh.

"What the hell's going on?" Dillon said.

Logan held up a finger. "I knew," he said. "From the very first moment I saw you at Russell's, I said to myself: I've got one."

A nut, Dillon thought. The old man's a friggin psycho!

"And then when you walked in the house and the cats went wild, I *really* knew."

"Open up this door," Dillon said.

"Oh, I'm not always right," Logan said, "but with you I was certain. Your hunger was just so *obvious*."

Sweat was pouring down Dillon's neck. "You open this goddamn door right now or I'll smash it down," he said.

"You can't," Logan said. "And you can't get the mesh off this window, either; don't think others haven't tried. What I need you to do now is go to the table and put my money on it."

A setup. The old man had set him up. But why? "What money?" Dillon said. "You didn't pay me yet."

Logan barked a curt laugh. "Put it all on the table right now, Mr. Stanton—if that's your name."

Dillon went to the window. Grabbing the metal mesh, he said, "Now listen, Logan, and listen good. You call the cops and I'll get you. I'll come back someday and I'll get you, you understand?"

Logan's face was devoid of expression. "I won't call the cops. Just do what I say. Put the money on the table. *Now*."

Cursing under his breath, Dillon went through the tall yellow grass. He reached in his pockets and took out the bills and laid them next to the paint cans.

"All of it, Mr. Stanton."

"That *is* all of it, damn it."

"Good." Logan's shadow was barely visible through the mesh. "It never fails," he said. "When I ask them to take out the TV set, they never turn me down. Perhaps there's more money in there, they think. And then when they see the old icebox they think, I bet that's *jammed* with bills, it's the old guy's safe."

He laughed again. "They'll never have enough, you see, their hunger knows no bounds. You took ten thousand dollars of mine but you wanted more, and more, and *more*. And there *is* more. You know where I got all that money? You want to guess?"

"Deposit bottles?" Dillon said, sneering.

"Good to see you're retaining your sense of humor," Logan said. "No, I was a prospector, Mr. Stanton, up in the Arizona hills. I lived thirty years in those hills, and I know about hunger, I've seen what greed does to men. It was rugged up there, but I loved that life. When I got my cats I figured I'd stay forever, but no, it was not to be. My sister took sick and I had to come home. I was all she had left in the world. She died six years ago."

"I gave you your money back," Dillon said. "Let me out of here now."

"Let you out?" Logan said. "Without punishment? You think you can steal from me and not pay the price?"

"So you *are* going to call the cops," Dillon said.

"Oh, no," Logan said. "I'm a man of my word. I promised you that I wouldn't do that, and I won't. You see, I don't trust the legal system—too many loopholes. And bringing police out here would be very unwise. My cats wouldn't like it, and what they don't like, I don't do."

He paused for a moment, then said, "Well, I pamper them, yes, I admit it. I worried about them so when I moved back here. City air, my damp cellar, this cramped little yard. But they've thrived! And you know why? The extras! The once-a-year extras!"

"So why don't you clean up their shit," Dillon said, "so your house doesn't smell like a zoo?"

Logan said: "But I *like* that smell. I love my cats and I *like* that smell. You see, they were born in captivity, bottle fed, given meat in a bowl, it's not good. If they don't have to hunt, they can lose their edge, their zest for life."

Dillon frowned. "What the hell are you talking about?" he said.

"The kill!" Logan said. "I'm talking about the thrill of the chase and the kill!"

This time his laugh was hoarse, high, crazed. And a panel below his window slid open, a steel panel set in the brick foundation.

Darkness, then motion, a flash of tan. Then the head of a cat coming out of the cellar, a head both fierce and huge.

"Good God!" Dillon said, stumbling backward.

Another maniacal laugh, and, "You're not the only one who's hungry, Stanton! You're not the only one!"

Dillon ran through the tangled grass. It tripped him up; he fell; sprang instantly to his feet again and ran with his blood roaring loud in his ears. "For God's sake, Logan, no!" he cried. He grabbed the iron gate.

And then they were on him.

AILUROPHOBIA

B. W. Battin

"HERE, KITTY, KITTY, KITTY," he said, holding his hand out palm down and wiggling his fingers. "Come to me, kitty, kitty."

The cat simply sat there, looking off to its right, as if unaware of the man's presence. She was a small calico, white with brown and black splotches. Her fur was filthy and matted, and she was nothing but bones, another of the world's castoffs that had made its way to Jason Harker.

"What's your story?" he asked the cat. "What kind of bad things has the world done to you?"

The cat sat in Jason Harker's driveway, ignoring him. The animal, of course, was quite aware of Jason's presence. It was just being cautious, and maybe a mite arrogant in the manner of its species. But the tired and thin calico had come to him, as so many others had, because it needed him.

Although people sometimes dumped them off here, knowing that he'd take them in, most of his cats had come of their own accord, drawn here by some sense that let them know this was a place of sanctuary.

A silver tabby walked by, glancing first at the new arrival, then at the man, and disappeared around the corner of the house.

"Come on, kitty, kitty," Jason Harker said, wiggling his fingers. "You know you can trust me."

The cat's green eyes momentarily met his, a silent communication passing between them, and then the calico walked slowly over to him, turning just as it reached him, so that it gently touched his leg with the tip of its tail. In cat body language, it meant Jason had been accepted—at least for the moment.

"You're probably not ready to come inside," Jason said. "So I'll bring some food and water out to you. Just watch the others. They know what to do."

After she'd learned to trust him, Jason would check her over for injuries and parasites and the like, but the immediate concern was getting her rested up, and getting some meat on those bones. He stepped to the front door, opening it just as Midnight, a shiny black tom, was about to use one of the two pet doors cut into its bottom. The cat looked up at Jason as if to say, *How dare you do that just as I'm about to go out?* And then he leaped through the cat-sized door, which swung back and forth from its top-mounted hinges.

Eyes, green and brown and hazel and amber, watched as Jason Harker stepped inside. Three cats were stretched out on the couch, one on a cushion, one on an arm, one on its back. Another lay in the easy chair. Still others occupied bookshelves, the center of a small oval throw rug, the top of the old black-and-white Philco TV set that had quit working five years ago.

Or was it more like a dozen years ago?

Jason Harker scratched his head. Twenty years ago?

It was getting harder and harder to remember things. But then that was natural, he supposed. He was seventy-eight, and when you got that old you were expected to be forgetful.

He worried about what would become of his cats if something were to happen to him. Actually he was pretty sure he knew what would occur, and he didn't want to think about it.

The house was a small, two bedroom home in the woods, sort of a glorified summer cabin that he lived in year-round. Close enough to town for him to get what he needed, far enough from the nearest neighbors so that no one complained about his cats.

He put food and water outside for the new arrival; then, gently easing an orange tabby named Amber off the cushion, he sat down in the easy chair. Running a thin hand through his wispy white hair, Jason Harker stared at the seventeen-inch TV set, wondering how long ago it had quit. His thoughts were interrupted by Mismatch, who jumped into his lap and made herself at home. She was white, with one blue eye, one green. She began to purr as he absently stroked her.

Jason remembered working for thirty-six years at Neusome Enterprises, which made replacement automobile parts, things like fuel pumps and starters and distributors. He recalled Myra dying the year before he retired, the memory making his eyes misty, as it always did. He recalled selling his place in town and buying this one, in part because he just wanted to be by himself and in part because the other place was just too full of reminders of Myra.

So why couldn't he remember when the TV had quit?

A cat brushed up against his leg, and he decided a better question was why he hadn't gotten rid of the TV set if it didn't work. The answer, he realized, was that it was just too much bother. Mismatch purred loudly, sending gentle vibrations of contentment into Jason Harker's lap.

"No."

"Hey, Mike, come on," Damon Carswell said, "it's not like those other times. This is different. This is a real emergency. Pat's operation . . . if she doesn't get it . . ."

Michael Olson was studying him as if he were looking at a malignant tumor. Damon Carswell thought: Where do you get off looking at me like that? Just because you're my brother-in-law doesn't mean you don't have to show a little respect.

The two men were sitting at a booth in a dingy bar, draft beers in front of them on the chipped Formica table. Electric signs promoting various brands of beer were mounted on the walls, glowing and winking.

"It figures you'd want to meet me in a place like this," Michael Olson said. He had on an expensive-looking double-breasted suit, charcoal gray with chalk stripes. Onyx cuff links. Patterned tie in rust and white. Linen pocket square folded so that four white points protruded from the suit's breast pocket. Elegant. Michael Olson was a lawyer, a partner in the most prestigious firm in town. Damon Carswell's sister had done well. She was the pride of the family.

Damon Carswell was its black sheep.

"It's a quiet place to drink a beer," he said. "What's wrong with that?"

The attorney didn't answer. An errant strand of dark hair had dropped onto his forehead. He absently pushed it back into place. It had always amazed Damon Carswell that two men as different in most respects as he and his brother-in-law could look so much alike. Both were tall and broad shouldered with thick dark hair, wide-set brown eyes, square jaws, noses that were just a touch too large, heavy beards that sprouted into five-o'clock shadow.

"Little Patty needs the operation," Carswell said. "If it was just for me, I wouldn't ask—not after all the money you've already lent me."

"Given you."

"No, no, lent me. I'll pay it all back as soon as I can."

"Uh-huh."

"Hey, I wouldn't—"

"Yes, you would."

"Mike, you've got me all wrong. I—"

"You don't even know where Nancy and the kids are. Patty could be dead for all you know—for all you'd care."

"Mike, how can you say a thing like that?"

"What's wrong with Patricia?" Michael Olson asked wearily.

"Leukemia. She needs a bone marrow transplant."

"Where is she?"

"Chicago. You can check it."

"I did. I talked to Nancy this morning."

"You did?"

"Yes, I did. She's not in Chicago. And she asked me to make sure you didn't learn where she really is."

"Well, uh . . ."

"And both your kids are fine—now that they're away from you."

"Mike, look—"

"No. Whatever you were going to say, I'm not interested. I've given you money because you're my wife's brother, because I thought a little help might get you going in the right direction. But all you did was waste it drinking and gambling."

Well, there was that drug deal, Damon Carswell thought. If that hadn't fallen apart, I'd be sitting real pretty right now. But the attorney was basically right. What Damon needed the money for was to pay off some debts to people who had a very nasty way of collecting what was owed them.

"These guys," he said beseechingly, "they'll kill me if I don't get the money."

"I can't help you."

"Can't or won't?"

"Both, actually. The firm's being sued. I won't bother you with the details, but we're apparently going to settle for six million and nondisclosure of the terms."

"Lawyers suing lawyers?"

"Happens all the time."

"Don't you have insurance?"

"Only up to three million."

It won't come out of your pocket, personally, he thought. No, no, you guys never pay out of your own pockets. You'll keep right on belonging to the country club and driving that fancy imported car and taking my sister to the symphony and the ballet—so the family can keep on being so damned proud of her. Meanwhile I'll be lying in an alley somewhere with two broken legs.

"Mike, look, I admit I lied to you. But this is a true emergency. I will truly be in a ton of shit if I don't get three thousand by the end of the week."

"In that case, you're in a ton of shit."

"Mike, Jesus, how can you—"

"The only reason I came here is to tell you that we've decided not to give you any more money. Not now. Not ever. Janice agrees with this decision completely, so please don't call her and give her a hard time about it."

Damon just stared at him. His own sister didn't care if he got beaten or murdered. What kind of a thing was that? His own sister!

Two men wearing blue bowling shirts were sitting at the bar. A silence had settled over the booth where Damon Carswell and his brother-in-law sat, and the conversation of the other two men drifted in to fill the void.

"I tell you the old guy's got millions stashed out there," one of them said. He wore his hair in a short ponytail. His companion was bald.

"I heard the guy used to work in a factory. How could he have millions?"

"I don't know how he got the money," Ponytail said. "But you hear about stuff like that all the time. Guy dies, and they find his mattress is filled with money."

"Just stories."

"No, no, this is for real. A friend of Jake's is a TV repairman. Went out there to fix the old man's TV, and when he took the back off, there was money in there. The old man got real scared and gathered it up, and took it into the next room."

"No kidding—in a TV set?"

"That's what he said. And he figured there was a lot more of it stashed out there. The old guy's loaded. Never used a bank, I guess. Probably lived through the Depression and doesn't trust them." He gulped some of his drink. "TV set was an old black-and-white. Couldn't be fixed. Couldn't get the tubes for it. And you know what else? The house was full of cats. Must have been thirty of them, lying wherever there was room. Place gave the TV guy the creeps, let me tell you."

The bald man said, "Come to think of it, I've heard about a guy like that. Weird old dude living with about a jillion cats. In a little place on Grantley Road, right?"

The thought of all those cats sent a little icy lump sliding down Damon Carswell's spine. He didn't like cats, didn't like being around them. They looked at you with those vertically slitted eyes, and you had the feeling they were looking inside you, knowing your most secret thoughts. One had clawed him badly when he was a boy. He'd been catching stray cats and dropping the animals off a bridge into Thompson Creek, just to see whether they could swim. The first five had drowned. The sixth had realized in time what was happening and fought for its life. But it hadn't just wanted to escape, that cat. Instead of fleeing, it had gone crazy, seeking retribution in a hellish, sanguinary frenzy.

When it was over, eight-year-old Damon Carswell's eyes were burning and so full of blood he was unable to see. Certain he was permanently blind, he'd run screaming through the street, holding his hands over his eyes, falling, bumping into things. He hadn't known he still possessed his sight until an emergency room doctor made him open his eyes an hour later.

Ever since then, he'd been afraid to so much as touch one of the animals (although he had deliberately flattened a few with his car). Ailurophobia, it was called. Fear of cats.

"Even before I heard about the money in the TV set," Ponytail was saying, "I heard that the old man had a lot of bread stashed out there, so I figure it's gotta be true."

The attorney rose, bringing Damon Carswell's attention back to his more immediate surroundings. "I guess we have nothing further to say to each other," the lawyer said.

"When they find me dead, what will you think then?" Damon Carswell asked.

"That you brought it on yourself, Damon. No more money. Not now. Not ever." He laid a ten on the table. "For the drinks." And then he turned and strode from the bar.

Fuck you and the horse you rode in on, Damon Carswell thought.

"Guy with all that money, living out there with a bunch of cats," the bald man said, shaking his head.

"Something, ain't it?" Pigtail said.

Yeah, Damon Carswell thought. Ain't it, indeed. He stood up, picking up the ten, and he spotted something lying in the seat his brother-in-law had just vacated. The object was light green, about the size and shape of a credit card. Damon Carswell bent down to look at it, some instinct telling him not to pick it up, not yet. In large letters were the words FIDELITY PARKING, ANNUAL PERMIT. Then there was some smaller print stating that Fidelity Parking, Incorporated was not liable for theft or damage, and that the card was the property of the company. Below that was a bar code. It was Michael Olson's pass to leave his fancy German car in that big multitiered parking structure downtown. Stick the card in the slot, and the gate opens. Everything automatic.

My, my, Damon Carswell thought, carefully picking the card up by its edges, I do believe that fate has just smiled on me.

Two days after the conversation with his brother-in-law, Damon Carswell drove his rusty vintage Toyota into a clearing filled with tire tracks, beer bottles, and used condoms. It was a safe place to leave the car, for it was only used at night. He made his way through the quarter mile or so of woods that separated the teenagers' parking spot from the home of Jason Harker.

It was a small house, white with peeling paint, shingles that were starting to curl at the edges. The place wasn't exactly what you'd call rundown, but it was hurting for routine maintenance. The only car in sight was in a detached garage with badly weathered siding, a Buick station wagon with faded blue paint, one of the old gas guzzlers that contained as much steel as a destroyer.

As he approached the door, a cat lazily crossed his path, stopped, and turned its amber eyes on him, golden orbs that seemed to say, *I know why you're here*.

"Scram," he hissed, kicking some gravel at it, and the cat scurried away.

The door was opened by a scrawny old man with white hair.

He had a large, bulbous old-person's nose, filled with little dents. His hands were covered with brown blotches. He wore thick glasses that made his eyes look like a pair of pale blue dots, and yet they were clear and bright, those eyes, filled with warmth and intelligence.

"What do you want?" the old man asked.

Damon Carswell put a gloved hand on Jason Harker's chest and pushed him into the house. "I want the money."

"I . . . I don't have any money. Only a few dollars."

Damon almost didn't hear him. The stench washed over him, enveloping him as if he were a surfer who'd just been eaten up by a big howler. The place smelled like a menagerie. And there were cats. Everywhere. Inwardly he cringed. He'd known they were here, of course, but realizing it in the abstract and experiencing the reality were two different things.

The cats eyed him balefully. A big brownish-gray one arched its back and spat at him. And a voice somewhere deep within Damon Carswell was whispering, *Get away from here—before they go for your eyes!* He forced himself to remain calm. His ailurophobia was controllable. He could prevent its getting out of hand through willpower, by being stronger than it was.

"I want the money," he said. "You tell me where it is, and this will be much easier on everybody."

"I . . . I don't have any money," the old man said, his voice barely a whisper.

A touch of claustrophobia swirled through Damon, and he struggled to fight it off. It was the smell. That was all. Just the smell.

"How can you stand it?" he asked.

"What?" the old man asked, staring at Damon with terror-filled eyes.

"The smell."

"The cats are my friends. I don't mind their smell."

Damon Carswell decided it was time to stop fooling around. He pulled an automatic from his coat pocket and pressed it into the soft flesh of the old man's neck. "Where's the money?"

What the old geezer did at that point was the last thing

Damon Carswell would have expected. The scrawny coot pulled his hand back and punched Damon in the belly. Though not a forceful blow, it had come as a complete surprise and packed enough wallop to take away some of Damon Carswell's wind.

"Jesus," he said, struggling to find his breath. He looked up in time to see the old man emerging from the kitchen, coming at him with an enormous knife of the variety chefs on TV always used to chop stuff up faster than Aunt Sadie could do it with her Vegamatic.

Damon shot him, the noise sending the cats scattering.

The old man lay on his back, his eyes open, looking normal-sized without the glasses, which rested on the floor beside him with a diagonal crack running through one of the thick lenses. His eyes were dull, lifeless.

As soon as Damon collected his thoughts, he realized his mistake. The old man was dead, unable to tell him where the money was. Well, he decided, I'll just have to find it.

He cut open the mattress, took out all the stuffing.

He went through every drawer.

He ripped the innards from the vintage TV set.

He found a crowbar and pried up the floorboards.

It took him three hours to do it, and when he was done there wasn't much left of the house or the garage. He stood in the middle of the living room, breathing heavily, pretty sure the old man's money had just been a story, a tall tale that had somehow become a small bit of local folklore.

Well, he thought, so be it. Finding the money wasn't his only reason for being here.

In the corner of the room, a cat made a low growling noise, a sound he'd never heard from a cat before. It was one of those pinto cats—calico or whatever they called them—and it was staring at him. No, not just staring, but hating him with an intensity that made him take a step backward. Its green eyes seemed aglow with it, gleaming with the notion of leaping at him and ripping his eyes out. Another cat joined it, a big gray one with a piece missing from its ear. A third slunk along the wall to his left.

Until now, Damon had shoved his fear of cats into a compartment somewhere in the deepest reaches of his mind and locked the door. The cats had stayed out of his way. Suddenly they were showing interest, and a prickly uneasiness churned in his gut.

"Scat!" he hollered.

But the cats didn't budge. There were more of them now. About half a dozen. He hurled the crowbar at them, and the animals scattered, three of them dashing out the pet door, the others disappearing into other parts of the house.

"Stupid cats," he muttered. But it was bravado. Inwardly he was trembling, recalling the terror of a boy who believed his eyes had literally been scratched out.

Forcing the memory from his thoughts, Damon took an envelope from his pocket, turned it upside down so the green rectangular object inside fell out. With his foot he pushed it under the easy chair. Or what was left of the easy chair. In his search for the apparently nonexistent money, he'd reduced it to a wooden frame and tatters.

He left the door open when he left. The electrician he'd called would come tomorrow, and Damon wanted to be sure he found the body.

That evening Damon Carswell slipped into the parking structure used by his brother-in-law, the tightwad rich lawyer. Michael Olson parked on the third level, so that's where Damon hid the gun. On a wide metal beam that could only be reached by a tall man standing on his tiptoes. Damon was six-one, just about the same height as Michael Olson.

There was nothing to connect the gun with Damon. He'd wiped it clean of fingerprints. And it was registered to a doctor who lived on the east side of town. Damon had taken it from the doctor's house when he and Larry Deemis burglarized the place.

He'd give the police a few days to find it on their own. If they failed, well, there was always the anonymous tip: I saw this guy hiding a gun in the parking structure. Got out of an expensive German car.

Though a little upset that the old man hadn't had any money, Damon felt pretty good about things. He whistled as he walked into the cool evening.

The day after Damon Carswell murdered the Cat Man, as he now thought of him, the evening news carried the story of the old man's body having been found by an electrician who'd been asked to estimate the cost of upgrading the home's wiring. The pretty blonde reporter told of all the cats the victim had kept, described him as a recluse, made him sound peculiar. The police declined to say whether they had any suspects, but they did have some "promising leads."

Two days later, Damon phoned his sister, asked her how things were going.

"Terrible," she said. "Just terrible."

Michael, it seemed, had been taken in for questioning in connection with the murder of a strange old man who had about thirty cats.

"They can't be serious," Damon said.

"They found his parking pass at the murder scene."

"He must have lost it somewhere. The real murderer picked it up."

"But the police don't believe that. They think he did it."

"How could they?" Damon asked, his voice full of indignation.

His sister started to cry. "I don't know. I just don't know. They keep asking him about our financial situation."

"Why on earth would they want to know about that? Surely they don't think some weird old cat fancier was killed for his money."

"Apparently there were rumors that old guy had millions stashed out there."

"You're kidding. A crazy old recluse like that!"

"And . . . and, well, things aren't going too well for us now financially. You see, there's this lawsuit, a former client of Mike's . . ."

Gee, that's too bad, Sis, Damon thought, thoroughly pleased with the way things were working out. He wasn't trying to hurt his sister. But on the other hand, he didn't have any misgivings about what he was doing either. All the time he'd been growing up, Janice was the good one, setting the example he could never live up to, his parents always making it clear they thought they had one good kid and one lemon. He shrugged. There was no harm in Janice's being brought down a peg or two. Might even do her some good.

He went to bed that night, feeling content, at peace with the world. A noise intruded into his slumber, and he incorporated it into a dream. He was back in high school, and Dean Iverson was drawing his fingernails along a blackboard, making Damon and everyone else in the classroom cringe. It was one of Dean's tricks, doing that; he thought it was clever.

And then Damon Carswell jerked bolt upright in bed. The noise was real, not a dream. And it was coming from the window. Taking a few seconds to round up a good supply of courage, he went to investigate.

There was nothing at the window. No monsters or bogeymen grabbed him. And yet, as he looked out into the night, he was unable to stop trembling.

He studied the neighborhood, seeing only shadows, the silhouettes of darkened houses, the glow of an occasional streetlight. It was a working-class neighborhood, home to welders and truck drivers and factory workers. Damon's house was a lot like the Cat Man's place, a small two-bedroom home that was suffering from lack of maintenance. Although the rent was quite reasonable, Damon was often behind on it, as he was at this particular moment.

Abruptly he found himself staring at the bottom-center pane of the wooden-sash window. It was covered with tiny scratches. Then he saw something move in the shadows, about half a block away. Two glowing golden dots appeared, fixed on him, and then a large gray cat darted beneath a streetlight and vanished into the night.

Damon refused to accept what a part of his brain wanted to conclude. No, no, he thought. No way.

He went back to bed, tossed and turned for the rest of the night.

In the morning, when he opened the door to get the paper, a white cat darted out from under the bushes that ran along the front of the house, and ran across the tops of his slipper-clad feet, sending an icy jolt of terror through him, momentarily paralyzing him as totally as if he'd been shot with a stun gun.

"Shit," he muttered as he regained his composure.

When he was able to move, he grabbed the newspaper, which lay in the grass about three feet from the front door, and hurried back inside. For a few moments, he simply stood in the living room, convincing himself that it was just a neighbor's pet, that there could be no connection with the Cat Man.

One of the front-page headlines cheered him up. It read, PROMINENT LOCAL ATTORNEY QUESTIONED ABOUT SLAYING. The story made no mention of the gun having been found. He'd give it another day or two, then present the cops an anonymous tip.

That afternoon, Damon Carswell was watching television when he saw a calico cat sitting on the outside sill of the living room window, looking at him through the glass.

For a moment, he stared at it, transfixed, fear gripping his insides like an invisible icy hand. Then he found his voice. "Get out of here!" he screamed. "Get away from me!"

The cat watched him, its eyes both mocking and accusing. *I know what you did*, they seemed to say. *And you won't get away with it*. Damon grabbed the first thing he could find, which turned out to be a heavy ceramic ashtray, and hurled it at the cat, which leaped out of the way a fraction of a second before the glass pane shattered.

Damon hurried to the window. At first he didn't see the cat, but then he spotted it standing at the edge of the yard, studying him. It was joined by an orange tiger-striped cat, both of them watching him with unwavering, malevolent stares.

He shrieked obscenities at them through the broken window,

but the cats simply watched, unperturbed. It was the feline equivalent of giving him the finger.

Calm yourself, he thought. So there're cats out there. So what? Sure, some of them look like the old man's cats, but to you all cats look pretty much alike. I mean, hey, cats wouldn't track you all the way from the outskirts of town. They don't do things like that. Whoever heard of a cat as a bloodhound? Or a drug-sniffing cat? It simply wasn't their style to do stuff like that.

Okay, smartass, so why are those cats out there, and where did they come from?

The only answer he could come up with was that they were just neighborhood cats and their presence was just a coincidence. He told himself he believed that.

He tried to eat a bowl of cereal because there was nothing much else in the house, but his eyes kept drifting over to the window. Before long the cereal was a soggy, unappetizing mess, and he poured it down the drain. He checked the cabinet to the left of the sink, which was where he stored liquor. The only booze in the house was a quarter-full bottle of whiskey. In the refrigerator he found some whiskey-sour mix and made himself one. An hour later, the booze was gone. He considered going out for more, but he didn't feel like leaving the house. Though uncertain why he did so, he switched on the lights. Maybe he was hoping they'd keep the monsters away, as they did at night. Sitting down on the couch, he used the remote control to switch on the TV set.

The combination of booze and a restless night caused him to drift into an uneasy sleep. He awoke with a start when someone touched him, his first thought being that this wasn't the world's greatest neighborhood, that maybe he was about to be robbed, maybe even murdered.

Then he saw the striped cat in his lap.

He leaped up, swinging his fist at the animal all in one jerky, terror-driven movement, and the cat leaped nimbly out of the way. It retreated to a safe distance and turned around to watch him. Damon Carswell stared at it, shaking, trying to find a logical thread of thought he could follow back to reality like a spelunker's string.

The cat hissed at him, and Damon gave in to the fear-driven emotions swirling through him in a mental maelstrom. He heard a high, piercing wail, a sound that didn't seem human, and yet he knew it had come from him.

In the next instant he was dashing into the kitchen, fumbling in the knife drawer. Finally he simply dumped its contents onto the floor, shoving cutlery aside until he located the Chinese cleaver. He'd shoplifted it just because it caught his eye and then never used it. Until now. He picked it up.

"Here, kitty, kitty, kitty," he whispered, heading toward the living room. The cat was in the same spot. Damon charged it, raising the cleaver. The animal adroitly moved out of the way, trotted to the window, and leaped through the pane Damon had broken out with the ashtray. He hurled the cleaver at it, missing by a good three feet.

Looking out the window, Damon was taken aback to find it was night. With the lights on, he hadn't noticed. Had he slept all afternoon? The answer was unimportant. The cats were his immediate concern. Although he couldn't see them, they were out there, lurking in the shadows. From the shelf that made up the lower portion of the roll-away TV stand, he got his only book, a hardbound collegiate dictionary, and leaned it against the broken pane, blocking the opening. Boarding it up would be better, but he had no wood, so the dictionary would have to do.

For dinner, he heated a can of chili with beans, which he scorched because he got impatient and turned the heat up too high. Then he watched TV until he started drifting off to sleep again. He thought about simply getting out of there, spending the night at someone else's place. But he really had nowhere to go. Most of the people he knew considered him a deadbeat and a leech. And, in truth, he really didn't want to go outside right now. Not with the cats out there. He'd wait for daylight, when he'd be able to see what was waiting for him.

Finally he went to bed, leaving the lights on. Shortly after he drifted off, a thump had him sitting up, wide awake. He knew what it was without looking. The sound of a book falling. Through the bedroom door, he could see the dictionary lying on the living room floor.

Then he saw the big gray tomcat sitting next to the bed, looking up at him. Before Damon could decide how to react, the cat leaped onto the bed. Instantly Damon pulled the covers over his head, drawing up his knees, his fingers finding the pillow so he could use it to protect his eyes.

The cat was on top of him, walking around. Then something else landed on top of the bed. Followed by another one. Then another. There was an army of cats, crawling all over the bed. A scream, a primal shriek of pure terror, welled up from somewhere deep within him, but it died in his throat, which seemed incapable of making a sound.

Abruptly the small paws pressing on him through the covers were gone. He waited, listening intently, hearing nothing but the silence of the room and the distant night sounds. Finally, he peeked out from under the covers, sure it was a trick, certain a deadly feline claw would instantly attempt to rip out his eyes. But nothing happened. The room was empty. The dictionary lay on the living room floor, the curtain swaying in the night breeze.

Did he imagine it?

Did the curtain knock the book from the sill?

He let the questions swirl away unaddressed, for terror told him that the cats had been real, and terror was far too powerful to be mitigated by mere reason.

Scrambling out of bed, he rushed into the living room, located the Chinese cleaver and backed into a corner, holding the weapon out in front of him as if he were warding off vampires with a cross. For a few moments, he simply stood there, confused and afraid. Then his mind began to work. The cleaver was next to useless against an army of cats. He needed a gun.

Damon had about fifteen dollars in his wallet. How was he going to get a gun? For ten bucks he could buy a hot credit card from a guy he knew. He dismissed the idea. There was a waiting period for a handgun in this state, and Damon needed one now.

A hot piece would cost a good bit more than fifteen dollars, and —and he knew where there was a gun just waiting for him.

All he had to do was go get it. He could clean his prints from it, put it back in its hiding place, and everything would be just as it had been.

Yes.

Shortly after dawn he retrieved the automatic. Next he stopped by a gun shop and bought a box of ammunition.

Returning home, he spent the day waiting. He paced through the house with the weapon in his hand, thinking, *Come on, cats. I dare you. Come on in and let's play, whaddya say?*

And that night they came.

First a gray one leaped through the window, then an orange one, then a brown one, followed by countless others, until they were nothing but a blur. And every time one of them came through the broken window, Damon shot it. Cat bodies were littering the floor. Damon reloaded so many times he lost count. But he was fast, too fast for the cats to get him.

He only distantly heard the siren. He was vaguely aware of someone taking the gun from his hand, leading him from the house, worried neighbors watching as he was put in the rear of the police car, a distant voice saying, "Be sure to run a complete check on that gun. Have ballistics test-fire it, see if it matches anything outstanding."

"Could you make any sense out of what he was saying?" another voice asked.

"He kept going on about all the cats he'd just killed."

"What cats?"

"I don't know. I didn't see any cats."

But Damon Carswell saw one. Across the street, a dark shadow by the Sandowskis' hedge, its eyes glowing yellow-orange dots, watching him, mocking him.

THE MAGGODY FILES: HILLBILLY CAT

Joan Hess

I WAS REDUCED to whittling away the morning, and trying to convince myself that I was in some obscure way whittling away at the length of my sentence in Maggody, Arkansas (pop. 755). Outside the red-bricked PD, the early morning rain came down steadily, and, as Ruby Bee Hanks (proprietress of a bar and grill of the same name, and, incidentally, my mother) would say, it was turning a mite crumpy. I figured the local criminal elements would be daunted enough to stay home, presuming they were smart enough to come in out of the rain in the first place. This isn't to say they rampaged when the sun shone. Mostly they ran the stoplight, fussed and cussed at their neighbors, stole such precious commodities as superior huntin' dawgs, and occasionally raced away from the self-service station without paying for gas. There'd been some isolated violence during my tenure, but every last person in town still based their historical perspective on before-or-after Hiram Buchanon's barn burned to the ground.

I suppose I ought to mention that my sentence was self-imposed, in that I scampered home from Manhattan to lick my wounds after a nasty divorce. In that I was the only person stupid enough to apply for the job, I was not only the Chief of Police, but also the entirety of the department. For a while I'd had a deputy, who just happened to be the mayor's cousin, but he'd gotten himself in trouble over his unrequited love for a bosomy barmaid. Now I had a beeper.

That October morning I had a block of balsa wood that was harder than granite, and a pocket knife that was duller than most of the population. I also had some bizarre dreams of converting the wood into something that remotely resembled a duck—a marshland mallard, to be precise. Those loyal souls who're schooled in the local lore know I tried this a while back, with zero success. Same wood, for the record, and thus far, same rate of success.

So I had my feet on the corner of my desk, my cane-bottomed chair propped back against the wall, and an unholy mess of wood shavings scattered all over the place when the door opened. The man who came in wore a black plastic raincoat and was wrestling with a brightly striped umbrella more suited to a swanky golf course (in Maggody, we don't approve of golf—or any other sissified sport in which grown men wear shorts). He appeared to be forty or so, with a good ol' boy belly and the short, wavy hair of a used car salesman.

Strangers come into the PD maybe three times a year, usually to ask directions or to sell me subscriptions to magazines like *Field and Stream* or *Sports Illustrated*. I guess it's never occurred to any of them that some of us backwoods cops might prefer *Cosmopolitan*.

He finally gave up on the umbrella and set it in a corner to drip. Flashing two rows of pearly white teeth at me, he said, "Hey, honey, some weather, isn't it? Is the chief in?"

"It sure is some weather," I said politely, "and the chief is definitely in." I did not add that the chief was mildly insulted, but by no means incensed or inclined to explain further.

This time I got a wink. "Could I have a word with him?"

"You're having a word with *her* at this very moment," I said as I dropped my duck in a drawer and crossed my arms, idly wondering how long it'd take him to work it out. He didn't look downright stupid like the clannish Buchanons, who're obliged to operate solely on animal instinct, but he had squinty eyes, flaccid lips, and minutes earlier had lost a battle to an umbrella.

"Sorry, honey." His shrug indicated he wasn't altogether overwhelmed with remorse. "I'm Nelson Mullein from down near Pine Bluff. The woman at the hardware store said the chief's name was Arly, and I sort of assumed I was looking for a fellow. My mistake."

"How may I help you, Mr. Mullein?" I said.

"Call me Nelson, please. My great-grandaunts live here in Maggody, out on County 102 on the other side of the low-water bridge. Everybody's always called them the Banebury girls, although Miss Columbine is seventy-eight and Miss Larkspur's seventy-six."

"I know who they are."

"Thought you might." He sat down on the chair across from my desk and took out a cigar. When he caught my glare, he replaced it in his pocket, licked his lips, and made a production of grimacing and sighing so I'd appreciate how carefully he was choosing his words. "The thing is," he said slowly, "I'm worried about them. As I said, they're old and they live in that big, ramshackle house by themselves. It ain't in the ghetto, but it's a far cry from suburbia. Neither one of them can see worth a damn. Miss Larkspur took a fall last year while she was climbing out of the tub, and her hip healed so poorly she's still using a walker. Miss Columbine is wheezier than a leaky balloon."

"So I should arrest them for being old and frail?"

"Of course not," he said, massaging his rubbery jowls. "I was hoping you could talk some sense into them, that's all, 'cause I sure as hell can't, even though I'm their only relative. It hurts me to see them living the way they do. They're as poor as church mice. When I went out there yesterday, it was colder inside than it was outside, and the only heat was from a wood fire in a potbelly stove. Seems they couldn't pay the gas bill last month and it was shut off. I took care of that immediately and told the gas company to bill me in the future. If Miss Columbine finds out, she'll have a fit, but I didn't know what else to do."

He sounded so genuinely concerned that I forgave him for calling me "honey," and tried to recall what little I knew about the Banebury girls. They'd been reclusive even when I was a kid, although they occasionally drove through town in a glossy black Lincoln Continental, nodding regally at the peasants. One summer night twenty or so years ago, they'd caught a gang of us skinny-dipping at the far side of the field behind their house. Miss Columbine had been outraged. After she'd carried on for a good ten minutes, Miss Larkspur persuaded her not to report the incident to our parents and we grabbed our clothes and high-tailed it. We stayed well downstream the rest of the summer. We avoided their house at Halloween, but only because it was isolated and not worth the risk of having to listen to a lecture on hooliganism in exchange for a stale popcorn ball.

"I understand your concern," I said. "I'm afraid I don't know them well enough to have any influence."

"They told me they still drive. Miss Columbine has macular degeneration, which means her peripheral vision's fine but she can't see anything in front of her. Miss Larkspur's legally blind, but that works out just fine—she navigates. I asked them how on earth either had a driver's license, and damned if they didn't show 'em to me. The date was 1974."

I winced. "Maybe once or twice a year, they drive half a mile to church at a speed of no more than ten miles an hour. When they come down the middle of the road, everybody in town knows to pull over, all the way into a ditch if need be, and the children have been taught to do their rubberneckin' from their yards. It's actually kind of a glitzy local event that's discussed for days afterwards. I realize it's illegal, but I'm not about to go out there and tell them they can't drive anymore."

"Yeah, I know," he said, "but I'm going to lose a lot of sleep if

I don't do something for them. I'm staying at a motel in Farberville. This morning I got on the phone and found out about a retirement facility for the elderly. I went out and looked at it, and it's more like a boardinghouse than one of those smelly nursing homes. Everybody has a private bedroom, and meals are provided in a nice, warm dining room. There was a domino game going on while I was there, and a couple of the women were watching a soap opera. There's a van to take them shopping or to doctor appointments. It's kind of expensive, but I think I can swing it by using their social security checks and setting up an income from the sale of the house and property. I had a real estate agent drive by it this morning, and he thought he could get eight, maybe ten, thousand dollars."

"And when you presented this, they said . . . ?"

"Miss Columbine's a hardheaded woman, and she liked to scorch my ears," he admitted ruefully. "I felt like I was ten years old and been caught with a toad in the pocket of my choir robe. Miss Larkspur was interested at first, and asked some questions, but when they found out they couldn't take Eppie, the discussion was over, and before I knew what hit me, I was out on the porch shivering like a hound dog in a blizzard."

"Eppie?"

"Their cat. In spite of the sweet-sounding name, it's an obese yellow tomcat with one eye and a tattered ear. It's mangy and mean and moth-eaten, and that's being charitable. But they won't even consider giving it away, and the residence home forbids pets because of a health department regulation. I went ahead and put down a deposit, but the director said she can't hold the rooms for more than a few days and she expects to be filled real soon. I hate to say it, but it's now or never." He spread his hands and gave me a beseeching look. "Do you think you or anybody else in town can talk them into at least taking a look at this place?"

I suspected I would have more luck with my balsa wood than with the Banebury sisters, but I promised Nelson I'd give it a shot and wrote down the telephone number of his motel room. After a display of effusively moist gratitude, he left.

I decided the matter could wait until after lunch. The Banebury sisters had been going about their business nearly four score years, after all, I told myself righteously as I darted through the drizzle to my car and headed for Ruby Bee's Bar & Grill.

"So what's this about Miss Columbine and Miss Larkspur being dragged off to an old folks' home?" Ruby Bee demanded as I walked across the tiny dance floor. It was too early for the noon crowd, and only one booth was occupied by a pair of truck drivers working on blue plate specials and a pitcher of beer.

"And who'd pay ten thousand dollars for that old shack?" Estelle Oppers added from her favorite stool at the end of the bar, convenient to the pretzels and the rest room.

I wasn't particularly amazed by the questions. Maggody has a very sturdy grapevine, and it definitely curls through the barroom on its way from one end of town to the other. That was one of the reasons I'd left the day after I graduated, and eventually took refuge in the anonymity of Manhattan, where one can caper in the nude on the street and no one so much as bothers with a second look. In Maggody, you can hear about what you did before you're finished planning to do it.

"To think they'd give up their cat!" Ruby Bee continued, her hands on her hips and her eyes flashing as if I'd suggested we drown dear Eppie in Boone Creek. Beneath her unnaturally blond hair, her face was screwed up with indignation. "It ain't much to look at, but they've had it for fourteen years and some folks just don't understand how attached they are."

I opened my mouth to offer a mild rebuttal, but Estelle leapt in with the agility of a trout going after a mayfly. "Furthermore, I think it's mighty suspicious, him coming to town all of a sudden to disrupt their lives. I always say, when there's old ladies and a cat, the nephew's up to no good. Just last week I read a story about how the nephew tried to trick his aunt so he could steal all her money."

I chose a stool at the opposite end of the bar. "From what Nelson told me, they don't have any money."

"I still say he's up to no good," Estelle said mulishly, which is pretty much the way she said everything.

Ruby Bee took a dishrag and began to wipe the pristine surface of the bar. "I reckon that much is true, but Eula said she happened to see him in the hardware store, and he had a real oily look about him, like a carnival roustabout. She said she wouldn't have been surprised if he had tattoos under his clothes. He was asking all kinds of questions, too."

"Like what?" I said, peering at the pies under glass domes and ascertaining there was a good-sized piece of cherry left.

"Well, he wanted to know where to go to have all their utility bills sent to him, on account of he didn't think they had enough money to pay 'em. He also wanted to know if he could arrange for groceries to be delivered to their house every week, but Eula stepped in and explained that the church auxiliary already sees to that."

I shook my head and made a clucking noise. "The man's clearly a scoundrel, a cad, a veritable devil in disguise. How about meatloaf, mashed potatoes and gravy, and cherry pie with ice cream?"

Ruby Bee was not in her maternal mode. "And wasn't there an old movie about a smarmy nephew trying to put his sweet old aunts in some sort of insane asylum?" she asked Estelle.

"That was because they were poisoning folks. I don't recollect anyone accusing the Banebury girls of anything like that. Miss Columbine's got a sharp tongue, but she's got her wits about her. I wish I could say the same thing about Miss Larkspur. She can be kind of silly and forgetful, but she ain't got a mean bone in her body. Now if the cat was stalking me on a dark street, I'd be looking over my shoulder and fearing for my life. He lost his eye in a fight with old Shep Humes's pit bull. When Shep tried to pull 'em apart, he liked to lose both of his eyes and a couple of fingers, and he said he cain't remember when he heard a gawdawful racket like that night."

"Meatloaf?" I said optimistically. "Mashed potatoes?"

Still wiping the bar, Ruby Bee worked her way towards Estelle. "The real estate agent says he can sell that place for ten thousand dollars?"

"He didn't sound real sure of it, and Eilene said Earl said the fellow didn't think the house was worth a dollar. It was the forty acres he thought might sell." Estelle popped a pretzel in her mouth and chewed it pensively. "I took them a basket of cookies last year just before Christmas, and the house is in such sad shape that I thought to myself, I'm gonna sit right down and cry. The plaster's crumbling off the walls, and there was more than one window taped with cardboard. It's a matter of time before the house falls down on 'em."

Aware I was about to go down for the third time, I said, "Meatloaf?"

Ruby Bee leaned across the bar, and in a melodramatic whisper that most likely was audible in the next county, said, "Do you think they're misers with a fortune buried in jars in the back yard? If this Mullein fellow knows it, then he'd want to get rid of them and have all the time he needs to dig up the yard searching for the money."

"Them?" Estelle cackled. "There was some family money when their daddy owned the feed store, but he lost so much money when that fancy co-op opened in Starley City that he lost the store and upped and died within the year. After that, Miss Larkspur had to take piano students and Miss Columbine did mending until they went on social security. Now how are they supposed to have acquired this fortune? Are you accusing them of putting on ski masks and robbing liquor stores?"

"For pity's sake, I was just thinking out loud," Ruby Bee retorted.

"The next thing, you'll be saying you saw them on that television show about unsolved crimes."

"At least some of us have better things to do than read silly mystery stories about nephews and cats," Ruby Bee said disdainfully. "I wouldn't be surprised if you didn't have a whole book filled with them."

"So what if I do?" Estelle slapped the bar hard enough to tump the pretzels.

It seemed the only thing being served was food for thought. I drove to the Dairee Dee-Lishus and ate a chilidog in my car while I fiddled with the radio in search of anything but whiny country music. I was doing so to avoid thinking about the conversation at Ruby Bee's. Nelson Mullein wasn't my type, but that didn't automatically relegate him to the slime pool. He had good reason to be worried about his great-grandaunts. Hell, now I was worried about them, too.

Then again, I thought as I drove out County 102 and eased across the low-water bridge, Estelle had a point. There was something almost eerie about the combination of old ladies, cats, and ne'er-do-well nephews (although, as far as I knew, Nelson was doing well at whatever he did; I hadn't asked). But we were missing the key element in the plot, and that was the fortune that kicked in the greed factor. Based on what Estelle had said, the Banebury girls were just as poor as Nelson had claimed.

The appearance of the house confirmed it. It was a squatty old farmhouse that had once been white, but was weathered to a lifeless gray. What shingles remained on the roof were mossy, and the chimney had collapsed. A window on the second floor was covered with cardboard; broken glass was scattered on the porch. The detached garage across the weedy yard had fared no better.

Avoiding puddles, I hurried to the front door and knocked, keenly and uncomfortably aware of the icy rain slithering under my collar. I was about to knock a second time when the door opened a few cautious inches.

"I'm Arly Hanks," I said, trying not to let my teeth chatter too loudly. "Do you mind if I come in for a little visit?"

"I reckon you can." Miss Columbine stepped back and gestured for me to enter. To my astonishment, she looked almost exactly the same as she had the night she stood on the bank of Boone Creek and bawled us out. Her hair was white and pinned up in tight braids, her nose was sharp, her cheekbones prominent above concave cheeks. Her head was tilted at an angle, and I remembered what Nelson had said about her vision.

"Thanks," I murmured as I rubbed my hands together.

"Hanks, did you say? You're Ruby Bee's gal," she said in the same steely voice. "Now that you're growed up, are you keeping your clothes on when you take a moonlight swim?"

I was reduced to an adolescent, "Yes, ma'am."

"Do we have a visitor?" Miss Larkspur came into the living room, utilizing an aluminum walker to take each awkward step. "First Nelson and now this girl. I swear, I don't know when we've had so much company, Columbine."

The twenty years had been less compassionate to Miss Larkspur. Her eyes were so clouded and her skin so translucent that she looked as if she'd been embalmed. Her body was bent, one shoulder hunched and the other undefined. The fingers that gripped the walker were swollen and misshapen.

"I'm Arly Hanks," I told her.

"Gracious, girl, I know who you are. I heard about how you came back to Maggody after all those years in the big city. I don't blame you one bit. Columbine and I went to visit kin in Memphis when we were youngsters, and I knew then and there that I'd never be able to live in a place like that. There were so many cars and carriages and streetcars that we feared for our very lives, didn't we?"

"Yes, I seem to recall that we did, Larkspur."

"Shall I put on the tea kettle?"

Miss Columbine smiled sadly. "That's all right, sister; I'll see to it. Why don't you sit down with our company while I fix a tray? Be sure and introduce her to Eppie."

The room was scantily furnished with ugly, battered furniture and a rug worn so badly that the wooden floor was visible. It smelled of decay, and no doubt for a very good reason. Plaster had fallen in several places, exposing the joists and yellowed newspaper that served as insulation. Although it was warmer than outside, it was a good twenty degrees below what I considered comfortable. Both sisters wore shawls. I hoped they had thermal underwear beneath their plain, dark dresses.

I waited until Miss Larkspur had made it across the room and was seated on a sofa. I sat across from her and said, "I met

Nelson this morning. He seems concerned about you and your sister."

"So he says," she said without interest. She leaned forward and clapped her hands. "Eppie? Are you hiding? It's quite safe to come out. This girl won't hurt you. She'd like the chance to admire you."

An enormous cat stalked from behind the sofa, his single amber eye regarding me malevolently and his tail swishing as if he considered it a weapon. He was everything Nelson had described, and worse. He paused to rake his claws across the carpet, then leapt into Miss Larkspur's lap and settled down to convey to me how very deeply he resented my presence. Had I been a less rational person, I would have wondered if he knew I was there to promote Nelson's plan. Had I been, as I said.

"Isn't he a pretty kitty?" cooed Miss Larkspur. "He acts so big and tough, but him's just a snuggly teddy bear."

"Very pretty," I said, resisting an urge to lapse into baby-talk and tweak Eppie's whiskers. He would have taken my hand off in a flash. Or my arm.

Miss Columbine came into the room, carrying a tray with three cups and saucers and a ceramic teapot. There were more chips than rosebuds, but I was delighted to take a cup of hot tea and cradle it in my hands. "Did Nelson send you?" she said as she served her sister and sat down beside her. Eppie snuggled between them to continue his surly surveillance.

"He came by the PD this morning and asked me to speak to you," I admitted.

"Nelson is a ninny," she said with a tight frown. "Always has been, always will be. When he came during the summers, I had to watch him like a hawk to make sure he wasn't tormenting the cat or stealing pennies from the sugar bowl. His grandmother, our youngest sister, married poor white trash, and although she never said a word against them, we were all of a mind that she regretted it to her dying day." She paused to take a sip of tea, and the cup rattled against the saucer as she replaced it. "I suppose Nelson's riled up on account of our Sunday drives, although it seems to me reporting us to the police is extreme. Did you come out here to arrest us?"

Miss Larkspur giggled. "What would Papa say if he were here to see us being arrested? Can't you imagine the look on his face, Columbine? He'd be fit to be tied, and he'd most likely throw this nice young thing right out the door."

"I didn't come out here to arrest you," I said hastily, "and I didn't come to talk about your driving. As long as you don't run anybody down, stay on this road, and never ever go on the highway, it's okay with me."

"But not with Nelson." Miss Columbine sighed as she finished her tea. "He wants us to give up our home, our car, our beloved Eppie, and go live in a stranger's house with a bunch of old folks. Who knows what other fool rules they'd have in a house where they don't allow pets?"

"But, Columbine," Miss Larkspur said, her face puckering wistfully, "Nelson says they serve nice meals and have tea with sandwiches and pound cake every afternoon. I can't recollect when I last tasted pound cake—unless it was at Mama's last birthday party. She died of influenza back in September of fifty-eight, not three weeks after Papa brought the new car all the way from Memphis, Tennessee." She took a tissue from her cuff and dabbed her eyes. "Papa died the next year, some say on account of losing the store, but I always thought he was heart-sick over poor—"

"Larkspur, you're rambling like a wild turkey," Columbine said sternly but with affection. "This girl doesn't want to hear our family history. Frankly, I don't find it that interesting. I think we'd better hear what she has to say so she can be on her way." She stroked Eppie's head, and the cat obligingly growled at yours truly.

"Is Eppie the only reason you won't consider this retirement house?" I asked. I realized it was not such an easy question and plunged ahead. "You don't have to make a decision until you've visited. I'm sure Nelson would be delighted to take you there at tea time."

"Do you think he would?" Miss Larkspur clasped her hands together and her cloudy eyes sparkled briefly.

Miss Columbine shook her head. "We cannot visit under false pretenses, Larkspur, and come what may, we will not abandon Eppie after all these years. When the Good Lord sees fit to take him from us, we'll think about moving to town."

The object of discussion stretched his front legs and squirmed until he was on his back, his claws digging into their legs demandingly. When Miss Columbine rubbed his bloated belly, he purred with all the delicacy of a truck changing gears.

"Thank you for tea," I said, rising. "I'll let myself out." I was almost at the front door when I stopped and turned back to them. "You won't be driving until Easter, will you?"

"Not until Easter," Miss Columbine said firmly.

I returned to the PD, dried myself off with a handful of paper towels, and called Nelson at the motel to report my failure.

"It's the cat, isn't it?" he said. "They're willing to live in squalor because they won't give up that sorry excuse for a cat. You know, honey, I'm beginning to wonder if they haven't wandered too far out in left field to know what's good for them. I guess I'd better talk to a lawyer when I get back to Pine Bluff."

"You're going to force them to move?"

"I feel so bad, honey, but I don't know what else to do and it's for their own good."

"What's in it for you, Nelson?"

"Nothing." He banged down the receiver.

"My shoe's full of water," Ruby Bee grumbled as she did her best to avoid getting smacked in the face by a bunch of soggy leaves. It wasn't all that easy, since she had to keep her flashlight trained on the ground in case of snakes or other critters. The worst of it was that Estelle had hustled her out the door on this harebrained mission without giving her a chance to change clothes, and now her best blue dress was splattered with mud and her matching blue suede shoes might as well go straight into the garbage can. "Doncha think it's time to stop acting like overgrown Girl Scouts and just drive up to the door, knock real politely, and ask our questions in the living room?"

Estelle was in the lead, mostly because she had the better flashlight. "At least it's stopped raining, Miss Moanie Mouth. You're carrying on like we had to go miles and miles, but it ain't more than two hundred feet to begin with and we're within spittin' distance already."

"I'd be within spittin' distance of my bed if we'd dropped in and asked them." Ruby Bee stepped over a log and right into a puddle, this time filling her other shoe with cold water and forcing her to bite her tongue to keep from blurting out something unseemly. However, she figured she'd better pay more attention to the job at hand, which was sneaking up on the Banebury girls' garage through the woods behind it.

"I told you so," Estelle said as she flashed her light on the backside of the building. "Now turn out your light and stay real close. If that door's not locked, we'll be inside quicker than a preacher says his prayers at night."

The proverbial preacher would have had time to bless a lot of folks. The door wasn't locked, but it was warped something awful and it took a good five minutes of puffing and grunting to get it open far enough for them to slip inside.

Ruby Bee stopped to catch her breath. "I still don't see why you're so dadburned worried about them seeing us. They're both blind as bats."

"Hush!" Estelle played her light over the black sedan. "Lordy, they made 'em big in those days, didn't they? You could put one of those little Japanese cars in the trunk of this one, and have enough room left for a table and four chairs. And look at all that chrome!"

"This ain't the showroom of a car dealership," Ruby Bee said in the snippety voice that always irritated Estelle, which was exactly what she intended for it to do, what with her ruined shoes and toes nigh onto frozen. "If you want to stand there and admire it all night, that's fine, but I for one have other plans. I'll see if it says the model on the back, and you try the interior."

She was shining her light on the license plate and calculating

how many years it had been since it expired when Estelle
screamed. Before she could say a word, Estelle dashed out the
door, the beam from the flashlight bobbling like a ping-pong
ball. Mystified but not willing to linger on her own, Ruby Bee
followed as fast as she dared, and only when she caught Estelle
halfway through the woods did she learn what had caused the
undignified retreat.

According to Estelle, there'd been a giant rat right in the
front seat of the car, its lone amber eye glaring like the devil's
own. Ruby Bee snorted in disbelief, but she didn't go back to
have a look for herself.

The next morning, sweet inspiration slapped me up the side of
the head like a two by four. It had to be the car. I lunged for the
telephone so hastily that my poor duck fell to the floor, and
called Plover, a state cop with whom I occasionally went to a
movie or had dinner. "What do you know about antique cars?" I
demanded, bypassing pleasantries.

"They're old. Some of them are real old."

"Did you forget to jump start your brain this morning? I need
to find out the current value of a particular car, and I assumed
you were up on something macho like this."

He let out a long-suffering sort of sigh. "I can put gas in one at
the self-service pump, and I know how to drive it. That's the
extent of my so-called macho knowledge."

"Jesus, Plover," I said with a sigh of my own, "you'd better get
yourself a frilly pink skirt and a pair of high heel sneakers. While
you're doing that, let me talk to someone in the barracks with
balls who knows about cars, okay?"

He hung up on what I thought was a very witty remark. State
cops were not renowned for their humor, I told myself as I
flipped open the telephone directory and hunted up the number
of the Lincoln dealer in Farberville. The man who answered was
a helluva lot more congenial, possibly (and mistakenly) in hopes
he was dealing with a potential buyer.

Alas, he was no better informed than Plover about the current market value of a '58 Lincoln Continental, but his attitude was much brighter and he promised to call me back as soon as possible.

Rather than waste the time patting myself on the back, I called Plover, apologized for my smart-mouthed remark, and explained what I surmised was going on. "It's the car he's after," I concluded. "The house and land are close to worthless, but this old Lincoln could be a collector's dream."

"Maybe," he said without conviction, "but you can't arrest him for anything. I don't know if what he tried to do constitutes fraud, but in any case, he failed. He can't get his hands on the car until they die."

"Or he has them declared incompetent," I said. "I suppose I could let him know that I'm aware of his scheme, and that I'll testify on their behalf if he tries anything further."

We chatted aimlessly for a while, agreed to a dinner date in a few days, and hung up. I was preparing to dial the number of Nelson's motel room when the phone rang.

The dealer had my information. I grabbed a pencil and wrote down a few numbers, thanked him, and replaced the receiver with a scowl of disappointment. If the car was in mint condition (aka in its original wrapper), it might bring close to ten thousand dollars. The amounts then plummeted: sixty-five hundred for very good, less than five thousand for good, and on down to four hundred fifty as a source for parts.

It wasn't the car, after all, but simply a case of letting myself listen to the suspicious minds in Ruby Bee's Bar & Grill. I picked up the balsa wood and turned my attention to its little webbed feet.

It normally doesn't get dark until five-thirty or so, but the heavy clouds had snuffed out the sunset. I decided to call it a day (not much of one, though) and find out if Ruby Bee was in a more hospitable mood. I had locked the back door and switched off the light when the telephone rang. After a short debate centering around meatloaf versus professional obligations, I reluctantly picked up the receiver.

"Arly! You got to do something! Somebody's gonna get killed if you don't do something!"

"Calm down, Estelle," I said, regretting that I hadn't heeded the plea from my stomach. "What's the problem?"

"I'm so dadburned all shook up I can barely talk!"

I'd had too much experience with her to be overcome with alarm. "Give it your best shot."

"It's the Banebury girls! They just drove by my house, moving real smartly down the middle of the road, and no headlights! I was close enough to my driveway to whip in and get out of their way, but I'm thanking my lucky stars I saw 'em before they ran me over with that bulldozer of a car."

I dropped the receiver, grabbed my car keys, and ran out to the side of the highway. I saw nothing coming from the south, but if they were driving without lights, I wouldn't be the only one not to see them coming . . . relentlessly, in a great black death machine.

"Damn!" I muttered as I got in my car, manuevered around, and headed down the highway to the turnoff for County 102. Miss Columbine couldn't see anything in front of her, and Miss Larkspur was legally blind. A dynamite duo. I muttered a lot more things, none of them acceptable within my mother's ear-shot.

It was supper time, and the highway was blessedly empty. I squealed around the corner and stopped, letting my lights shine down the narrow road. The wet pavement glistened like a snakeskin. They had passed Estelle's house at least three or four minutes ago. Presuming they were not in a ditch, they would arrive at the intersection any minute. Maybe Nelson had a justifiable reason to have them declared incompetent, I thought as I gripped the steering wheel and peered into the darkness. I hadn't seen any bunnies hopping outside my window, and if there were chocolate eggs hidden in the PD, I hadn't found them.

It occurred to me that I was in more than minimal danger,

parked as I was in their path. However, I couldn't let them go on their merry way. A conscientious cop would have forbidden them to drive and confiscated the keys. I'd practically given them my blessing.

My headlights caught the glint of a massive black hood bearing down on me. With a yelp, I changed the beam to high, fumbled with a switch until the blue light on the roof began to rotate, grabbed a flashlight, and jumped out of my car. I waved the light back and forth as the monster bore down on me, and I had some sharp insights into the last thoughts of potential roadkill.

All I could see was the reflection on the chrome as the car came at me, slowly yet determinedly. The blue light splashed on the windshield, as did my flashlight. "Miss Columbine!" I yelled. "Miss Larkspur! You've got to stop!" I retreated behind my car and continued yelling.

The car shuddered, then, at the last moment, stopped a good six inches from my bumper (and a six-hour session with the mayor, trying to explain the bill from the body shop).

I pried my teeth off my lower lip, switched off the flashlight, and went to the driver's window. Miss Columbine sat rigidly behind the wheel, but Miss Larkspur leaned forward and, with a little wave, said, "It's Arly, isn't it? How are you, dear?"

"Much better than I was a minute ago," I said. "I thought we agreed that you wouldn't be driving until this spring, Miss Columbine. A day later you're not only out, but at night without headlights."

"When you're blind," she said tartly, "darkness is not a factor. This is an emergency. Since we don't have a telephone, we had no choice but to drive for help."

"That's right," said Miss Larkspur. "Eppie has been catnapped. We're beside ourselves with worry. He likes to roam around the yard during the afternoon, but this evening he did not come to the back door to demand his supper. Columbine and I searched as best we could, but poor Eppie has disappeared. It's not like him, not at all."

"Larkspur is correct," Miss Columbine added. Despite her

gruff voice and expressionless face, a tear trickled down her cheek. She wiped it away and tilted her head to look at me. "I am loath to go jumping to conclusions, but in this case, it's hard not to."

"I agree," I said, gazing bleakly at the darkness surrounding us. It may not have been a factor for them, but it sure as hell was for me. "Let's go back to your place and I'll try to find Eppie. Maybe he's already on the porch, waiting to be fed. I'll move my car off the road, and then, if you don't object, I think it's safer for me to drive your car back for you."

A few minutes later I was sitting in the cracked leather uphol-stery of the driver's seat, trying to figure out the controls on the elaborate wooden dashboard. There was ample room for three of us in the front seat, and possibly a hitchhiker or two. Once I'd found first gear, I turned around in the church parking lot, took a deep breath, and let 'er fly.

"This is a daunting machine," I said.

Giggling, Miss Larkspur put her hand on my arm and said, "Papa brought it all the way from Memphis, as I told you. He'd gone there on account of Cousin Pearl being at the hospital, and we were flabbergasted when he drove up a week later in a shiny new car. This was after he'd lost the store, you see, and we didn't even own a car. We felt real badly about him going all the way to Memphis on the bus, but he and Cousin Pearl were kissin' cousins, and she was dying in the Baptist Hospital, so—"

"The Methodist Hospital," Miss Columbine corrected her. "I swear, some days you go on and on like you ain't got a brain in your head. Papa must have told us a hundred times how he met that polite young soldier whose mother was dying in the room right next to Cousin Pearl's."

"I suppose so," Miss Larkspur conceded, "but Cousin Pearl was a Baptist."

I pulled into the rutted driveway beside their house. The ga-rage door was open, so I eased the car inside, turned off the ignition, and leaned back to offer a small prayer. "Why don't you wait in the house? I'll have a look out back."

"I can't believe our own kin would do such a thing," Miss

Columbine said as she took Miss Larkspur's arm. I took the other and we moved slowly toward the back porch.

I believed it, and I had a pretty good idea why he'd done it. Once they were inside, I went back to the car, looked at the contents of the glove compartment to confirm my suspicions, and set off across the field. I'd had enough sense to bring my flashlight, but it was still treacherously wet and rough and I wasn't in the mood to end up with my feet in the air and my fanny in the mud. I could think of a much better candidate.

I froze as my light caught a glittery orb moving toward me in an erratic pattern. It came closer, and at last I made out Eppie's silhouette as he bounded past me in the direction of the house. His yowl of rage shattered the silence for a heart-stopping moment, then he was gone and I was once again alone in the field with a twenty-year-old memory of the path that led to Boone Creek.

Long before I arrived at the bank, I heard a stream of curses and expletives way too colorful for my sensitive ears. I followed the sound and stopped at a prudent distance to shine my light on Nelson Mullein. He was not a pretty picture as he futilely attempted to slither up the muddy incline, snatching at clumps of weeds that uprooted in his hands. He was soaked to the skin. His face was distorted not only by a swath of mud across one cheek, but also by angry red scratches, some of which were oozing blood.

"Who is it?" he said, blinking into the light.

"It's traditional to take your clothes off when you skinny-dip in the creek."

"It's you, the lady cop." He snatched at a branch, but it broke and he slid back to the edge of the inky water. "Can you give me a hand, honey? It's like trying to climb an oil slick, and I'm about to freeze to death."

"Oh, my goodness," I said as I scanned the ground with the light until it rested on a shapeless brown mound nearby. "Could that be a gunny sack? Why, I do believe it is. I hope you didn't put Eppie in it in an unsuccessful attempt to drown him in the creek."

"I've never seen that before in my life. I came down here to search for the cat. The damn thing was up in that tree, meowing in a right pitiful fashion, but when I tried to coax him down, I lost my footing and fell into the water. Why don't you try to find a sturdy branch so I can get up the bank?"

I squatted next to the gunny sack. "This ol' thing's nearly ripped to shreds. I guess Eppie didn't take kindly to the idea of being sent to Cat Heaven before his time. By the way, I know about the car, Mr. Mullein."

"That jalopy?" he said uneasily. He stopped skittering in the mud and wiped his face. "I reckoned on getting six, maybe seven thousand for it from an ol' boy what lives in Pine Bluff. That, along with the proceeds from the sale of the property, ought to be more than enough to keep my great-grandaunts from living the way they do, bless their brave souls."

"It ought to be more than enough for them to have the house remodeled and pay for a full-time housekeeper," I said as I rose, the gunny sack dangling between my thumb and forefinger. "I'm taking this along as evidence. If you ever again so much as set one foot in Maggody, I'll tell those brave souls what you tried to do. You may be their only relative, but someone might suggest they leave what's going to be in the range of half a million dollars to a rest home for cats!"

"You can't abandon me like this." He gave me a view of his pearly white teeth, but it was more of a snarl than a smile. "Don't be cruel like that, honey."

"Watch me." Ignoring his sputters, I took my tattered treasure and walked back across the field to the house. Miss Columbine took me into the living room, where her sister had swaddled Eppie in a towel.

"Him was just being a naughty kitty," she said, stroking the cat's remaining ear and nuzzling his head.

I accepted a cup of tea, and once we were settled as before, said, "That polite young soldier gave your papa the car, didn't he?"

Miss Columbine nodded. "Papa didn't know what to think, but the boy was insistent about how he'd gone from rags to riches and how it made him feel good to be able to give folks presents. Papa finally agreed, saying it was only on account of how excited Mama would be."

"It was charity, of course," Miss Larkspur added, "but the boy said he wanted to do it because of Papa's kindness in the waiting room. The boy even told Papa that he was a hillbilly cat himself, and never forgot the little town in Mississippi where he was born."

Eppie growled ominously, but I avoided meeting his hostile eye and said, "He was called the Hillbilly Cat, back in the earliest stage of his career. The original paperwork's in the glove compartment, and his signature is on the bill of sale and registration form." I explained how much the car would bring and agreed to supervise the sale for them. "This means, of course, that you won't be driving anymore," I added.

"But how will we get to church on Easter morning?" Miss Larkspur asked.

Miss Columbine smiled. "I reckon we can afford a limousine, Larkspur. Let's heat up some nice warm milk for Eppie. He's still shivering from his . . . adventure outside."

"Now that we'll be together, will you promise to never run away again?" Miss Larkspur gently scolded the cat.

He looked at her, then at me on the off chance I'd try to pet him and he could express his animosity with his claws.

I waved at him from the doorway, told the ladies I'd be in touch after I talked with the Lincoln dealer, and wished them a pleasant evening. I walked down the road to my car, and I was nearly there before I realized Eppie was a nickname. Once he'd been the Hillbilly Cat, and his death had broken hearts all around the world. But in the Banebury household, Elvis Presley was alive and well—and still the King.

"Give me that shovel," Estelle hissed. "All you're doing is poking the dirt like you think this is a mine field."

Ruby Bee eased the blade into the muddy soil, mindful of the splatters on the hem of her coat and the caked mud that made her shoes feel like combat boots. "Hold your horses," she hissed back, "I heard a clink. I don't want to break the jar and ruin the money."

Estelle hurried over and knelt down to dig with her fingers. "Ain't the Banebury girls gonna be excited when we find their Papa's buried treasure! I reckon we could find as much as a thousand dollars before the night is out." She daintily blotted her forehead with her wrist. "It's a darn shame about the car, but if it ain't worth much, then it ain't. It's kinda funny how that man at the Lincoln dealership rattled off the prices like he had 'em written out in front of him and was wishing somebody'd call to inquire. Of course I wasn't expecting to hear anything different. Everybody knows just because a car's old doesn't mean it's valuable."

A lot of responses went through Ruby Bee's mind, none of them kindly. She held them back, though, and it was just as well when Estelle finally produced a chunk of brick, dropped it back in the hole, stood up, and pointed her finger like she thought she was the high and mighty leader of an expedition.

"Start digging over there, Ruby Bee," she said, "and don't worry about them seeing us from inside the house. I told you time and again, they're both blind."

EVERY WEDNESDAY (A Novel Idea for a Short Story)

Nancy Pickard

CHAPTER 1

MURIAL AND HENRY FRANKLIN are the apparent "perfect couple," living in an attractive ranch house in a suburb outside of Kansas City, Mo. They have no children, but they own a feline, an enormous white Persian named Copycat, which sheds like a cloud in a snowstorm and which sleeps on its own pillow between them. Murial, thirty-five, is a tall, slim woman who is a mid-level executive at a branch office of an international insurance company. She's a nine-to-five sort of person of precise habits and unfailing routine, who suffers from allergies. Her husband, Henry, forty, is much the opposite, which their friends say is probably the secret of their apparently successful marriage.

Henry's a writer, a bit of a slob, drinks too much, indulges himself, prefers to work any hours *but* nine-to-five. While Murial goes to the office every weekday, Henry lounges over three cups of coffee, in his bathrobe, before padding into his home office to tap away at a few chapters on his computer, with Copycat on his lap, and a cigarette burning in his ashtray.

As the chapter opens, we see that Henry and Murial have a conflict that is threatening their marriage. To wit: the house is a mess. There's so much dust that it's causing Murial's allergies to act up. She itches, she sneezes. Murial says that since Henry's home all day, it's his job to clean the house. Henry, who doesn't want to, says he won't. Stalemate. Threat to "perfect" marriage. Can this marriage be saved?

CHAPTER 2

Henry, the creative one, comes up with the perfect solution: hire a housekeeper. Murial agrees, although she demands that he do the interviewing and hiring, and that he accomplish it before mold grows on the pile of damp towels on the bathroom floor. He agrees. They tumble into bed and have sex, a regular morning occurrence, although Murial complains, as she always does, that she'll muss her hair.

CHAPTERS 3 & 4

We see Henry having humorous encounters with various unsuitable "domestics," and then Henry having less humorous encounters with an increasingly impatient Murial. Finally, Murial issues an ultimatum: hire somebody, or I will go to work with perfect hair from now until you do. Henry is so upset he can't write a word that day.

CHAPTER 5

Henry finds somebody. She's a strong, lithe, beautiful young woman who is, he feels, much more intelligent than her lack of formal education suggests. For one thing, she has heard of him. (As a local author, Henry's been featured several times in area media, so he's a minor celebrity.) She has even read one of his books, an erotic fantasy novel that sold quite well at science fiction conventions. Her name, as graceful as the young woman herself, is Etheria Moore. Henry is quite attracted to her references. She says she can work every Wednesday, although Henry presses for twice a week. No, she says firmly, once a week is all I need. Henry, gazing at her shiny brown hair which is severely restrained by barrettes, and at her pert little nose and her sexy brown eyes, and the firm shape beneath the stretch pants she has worn to the interview, wonders how many weeks it will take him.

CHAPTER 6

All appears to go well. Etheria Moore appears at the Franklins' door the very next day, which is a Wednesday. That very morning Murial has gone to work with every hair in place, having not believed Henry's claim that he's found "a girl," so Henry feels this day has not come a moment too soon. Already, he is looking forward to a clean house, as well as to a grateful and compliant Murial. He follows Etheria around the house while she cleans, admiring her thoroughness, her professionalism, her perfectionism, her astonishingly trim little behind which displays itself to him so nicely when she bends over to turn on the vacuum cleaner. Copycat's hairs are sucked off the carpets like magic. Dust balls vanish from beneath the furniture. Sheets whisk off beds and slide back on, miraculously clean and fragrant. Kitchen counter tops to which dishes had begun to stick now shine and glow. So does Murial's face when she arrives home from work that night. Until she begins to sneeze and itch again. What is this? Murial and Henry ask themselves. The housecleaning should have solved that little problem. Shouldn't it? Murial resolves to make an appointment with an allergist. Distracted, she pushes Henry away when he tries to glide her toward the bedroom. Maybe, he suggests grumpily, she's allergic to him?

CHAPTER 7

The house stays pretty clean for the rest of the week. But Murial's allergies worsen. She sees the allergist, who guesses hay fever, asthma and eczema. He starts her on a series of tests to determine exactly what she's allergic to. In the meantime, he suggests that she be careful to keep her house immaculately clean and free of dirt and dust which might exacerbate her problems. Does she do the housecleaning? he asks. No, she says. Well, *don't*, he emphasizes. Make sure somebody else does it. Does she have central air conditioning? Yes. Shut the windows, he tells her, and turn the air conditioner on, and keep it on all the time, but first make sure the filter's clean. He prescribes some low-wattage decongestant and antihistimine, and says, let's see if it helps.

Murial stops by a pharmacist to buy the drugs.

When she gets home, she immediately turns on the air conditioner and tells Henry what the doctor said. "All the time?" he whines. "But I like fresh air!"

"Do you want me to be sick?" she retorts.

Murial takes her pills and half an hour later she is asleep, with Copycat beside her. She sleeps until morning, drags herself out of bed, says to her husband, "The way I feel? Are you crazy?" and then is late to work anyway. Henry is beginning to feel disgusted by all the partially used tissues he is finding around the house. Can't Murial use one tissue several times instead of ten tissues once? He complains bitterly to Copycat, who meows in apparent sympathy. "Can't she pick up after herself, does she have to leave tissues lying on chairs and tables and even on the bed!" He could wait for the cleaning lady to pick them up, he thinks, but no, they're everywhere, and even he can't stand it. Wrinkling his nose in distaste, he picks each one up with the thumb and forefinger of his right hand and drops them delicately into wastebaskets. Copycat bats one about the living room with her front paws. Henry snatches it away from her just as she begins to eat it. For the first time in his married life, Henry does not look forward to his wife coming home from work.

Henry is glad that tomorrow is Wednesday.

CHAPTER 8

Etheria Moore wears silver stirrup pants to work the next day, along with a sleeveless, scoopneck, ribbed teddy that shows off her strong little biceps which Henry thinks are just about the cutest things he's ever seen, apart from her adorable little behind. He's grateful to Etheria for distracting him from his many problems. The book's not going well, he tells her. His wife is seeing a doctor. No, not that way. She's seeing him because of her allergies. This Wednesday, Henry again follows Etheria around the house while she cleans, although this time he talks the whole while, telling her everything that's bugging him. "You're a wonderful listener," he tells her. "Please, call me Henry."

CHAPTER 9

The results of Murial's tests come back, and they're grim. Over the phone from her office, she ticks them off to Henry: "The doctor says I'm allergic to dust, animal dander, plant pollen, wheat products, corn products, dairy products, perfumes and other fragrances, dyes, artificial flavorings and food colorings, chemical preservatives, cigarette, cigar and pipe smoke, and air pollution."

"What does that mean?" Henry asks, cautiously.

"We'll talk about it when I get home," Murial says, ominously.

Henry looks around his clean house and wishes it were Wednesday so he could talk to Etheria Moore again. He looks down at the cat, who is lying in his lap. "Copy, I think you and I are goners." With every stroke of his hand on her back, dozens of silky white hairs flutter to the carpet, where they pile up like snowdrifts, awaiting the gentle suction of Etheria's vacuum cleaner. Henry spends the rest of the afternoon thinking about Etheria's gentle suction action.

CHAPTER 10

Murial comes home wearing a determined look and carrying bags. "Hypoallergenic makeup," she says, as she pulls blusher, lipstick and eye shadow out of one bag. "Hypoallergenic shampoo," she says, as she pulls that, plus conditioner and vials of other kinds of soaps, out of another bag. Henry twists the tops off the first three, but quits when he can't find a single fragrance in any of them. From now on, his wife will smell like . . . nothing . . . he realizes, sadly . . . like no woman he's ever smelled before.

"What's that stuff?"

"Soy flour."

"And that?"

"Sunflower oil."

Henry peeks at the price stamp, and recoils. "My God, you could buy an acre of sunflowers—hell you could buy van *Gogh's Sunflowers*—for what this cost!" He begins to help her empty the sacks, pulling out items faster and faster until he resembles a groundhog frantically digging himself a hole. Several times he stops to look at prices. He asks her about the costs of her tests, of her doctor's appointments, of her prescriptions. Murial informs him that she must shop for a brand new wardrobe, bed linens and bath towels, all natural fibers. Henry is beginning to understand that allergies can be very, very expensive.

"You don't mind, do you?" Murial starts to wrap her arms around his waist. "For my own good?"

"Of course not, darling . . ."

But when he purses his lips pursuant to kissing his wife, she pushes him away, and sneezes.

"Henry!"

"Bless you."

"Aftershave."

For a moment, he confuses this with a German word, a polite response, perhaps, to gesundeit. "You're welcome."

"No, Henry, you'll have to stop wearing aftershave."

Henry's heart sinks as he anticipates the next prohibition to fall from the chapped lips of his beloved. He asks himself why he has failed to notice until this moment how blotchy her skin looks—eczema, did the doctor say?—and how red her nose, how puffy her eyelids, how bloodshot her eyes.

"You'll have to stop smoking," she says, confirming his worst fear.

He pulls back his lips in what he hopes is a reasonable facsimile of a smile. "Anything for your health, darling." He reaches for one of the bottles she has purchased, then turns and walks quickly into their bathroom, where he removes his clothes, turns on the shower, and steps in to shampoo himself, hair to toenails, in hypoallergenic soap. When he steps out of the tub, he sniffs the air. Nothing.

He detects no trace of himself.

CHAPTER 11

The next day is Wednesday, thank God, thinks Henry. Now he can tell the ethereal Etheria all about it. He tags after her all day long, complaining about how Murial is so allergic to dust that *he* is going to have to vacuum the carpets and drapes and upholstery in between Etheria's weekly visits.

"Can't you come more often?" he pleads.

But no, she has other clients, and she cannot.

"We're going to have to buy a new furnace, with special filters; can you imagine how much *that's* going to cost? And we can't go on camping trips anymore, because she's allergic to the whole outdoors. And forget patio barbecues!"

Henry subsides into an injured sulk as he follows Etheria into a bathroom. He loves to cook outdoors, it's the only cooking he ever does, and he's especially good at getting the insides of hot-dog buns crisp and toasty.

"She can't take out the trash anymore. I'll have to do it. She can't ride in a car with the windows down. Forget convertibles."

He'd had his heart set on a snappy little red BMW ragtop for next summer, but now he envisions it filled to the roof with half-used tissues.

"I've got to quit smoking. I *can't* quit smoking! Somehow, I've got to quit smoking."

Morosely, he shuffles into the bedroom, trailing along like one of her vacuum attachments.

"Etheria? Did I tell you my last book got a movie option?"

The lovely, lithe Etheria looks up from her work.

"Really?" she says. "How much?"

"Money?" It's wonderful, Henry thinks, how sharp this girl is, how quick to go to the very heart of the matter that also most concerned him. "Only a little up front, a couple of thousand for a six-month option, but if they go with it, I'll get a minimum of $50,000 and probably a lot more than that, especially if it becomes a feature film or goes into television syndication."

"You're so talented, Henry."

"More than you know," he says, and moves toward her.

Etheria drops her vacuum cleaner hose, and walks into his arms.

This week she has rather more reason than usual to wash the sheets.

CHAPTER 12

Every Wednesday becomes Henry's secret delight from then on. Etheria is so efficient that she can clean the entire house and cleanse Henry's soul, as well, all before Murial gets home. Henry feels embarrassed now, handing Etheria her pay envelope, but she accepts it sweetly, sometimes even turning it into their own private little erotic joke. Henry is so happy he hardly notices that Murial isn't, actually, getting any better.

In fact, her allergies are getting worse.

Murial makes another doctor's appointment.

CHAPTER 13

"The doctor says we have to move Copycat out of the bedroom," Murial tells Henry. That's all right, he thinks, anything's okay as long as I can keep moving Etheria into the bedroom.

CHAPTER 14

Murial suffers an asthma attack that sends her to a hospital emergency room in the middle of the night. "This is serious," an intern tells Henry, as Murial gasps oxygen and medication through a clear plastic facemask. Her eyes, when she rolls them up at Henry, look panic-stricken. They are, he notices, a bleary blue. "We almost lost her this time."

Murial recovers.

"We have to get rid of Copycat," she tells Henry.

He hates to do it, but Etheria agrees to take the cat.

"Anything for you, my love," he tells Murial.

As Etheria tells him.

CHAPTER 15

In September, Kansas City experiences its worst allergy season in decades. Murial makes another doctor's appointment, and when she comes home from this one, she says to Henry, "Darling, I have to quit my job. The air at the office is impure. It's making me sick. All those perfumes and colognes, the cleaning sprays, all those smokers, the pollution from the parking lot. I'll move home with you, Henry, and pick up some freelance work, and we'll be happy together."

"In our vacuum-sealed house," he says, staring in horror at his wife, this woman he hardly recognizes anymore, what with her ugly rashes and her swollen, red, runny nose and the perpetual sneezing which has turned into wheezing that keeps him awake at night. On the few occasions when her tortured snoring doesn't. She has been so grateful to him for not "bothering" her for sex anymore. It's difficult for Murial to breathe while kissing, so he's stopped even that—to his great relief, as well. His voice shakes as he paints a word picture from a Stephen King novel: "We'll shut ourselves in, lock out the world, stock up on nose sprays and decongestants, and get matching laser printers."

"It'll be cody," Murial predicts.

"It'll be what?"

"Cody, you know, cody!"
"Ah, cozy," he says.
Etheria! he thinks.

CHAPTER 16

Henry's novel moves beyond the option stage.

Production is to begin in six months.

The check is to arrive within thirty days.

"Idn't dat grade diming?" Murial says.

Henry has learned to translate her clogged speech. He recognizes the phrase, "Isn't that great timing?"

"Why is that?" he inquires.

"Why, now we can afford for me to start up my own consulting business, silly! I'll give the office two weeks notice, and then I'll move home fulltime with you! I know I'll feel better here."

"You'll need a hobby," Henry suggests.

"Like whad?"

"Bridge, bingo, like that. Once a week. Maybe Wednesdays."

"But, Henry, the point is for me not to ever leave the house."

"Never? Ever?"

Murial moves in close enough for him to count the red lines in her left eyeball. She attempts a seductive smile, but it's not quite successful, as her lips gum together. "Never. It'll be just the two of us, forever, Henry."

He feels a suffocating congestion in his chest, and wonders if he's catching something from her.

CHAPTER 17

On their last Wednesday together before Murial moves home, Henry tells Etheria they won't be able to do this anymore.

"That's too bad," she says, rolling efficiently off of him.

Henry also tells Etheria about the movie deal.

Etheria sits up in bed.

So graceful, Henry thinks.

"Henry," she says, "next Wednesday, go someplace. Leave me alone in the house with Murial so that she and I can get to know each other." With a long, thin, well-scrubbed forefinger, she traces a delicate circle around Henry's left nipple. "I believe I can think of something to get Murial out of the house, so that you and I can be together again."

"You're a darling." Henry closes his eyes as she moves efficiently back onto him again. "A darling girl, that's what you are."

Her tongue flicks in his right ear as she whispers, "Leave the house before I get here next week. Be gone, Henry, even before I arrive."

"But I'll miss you. You'll never know how much."

"You'll never know," she echoes.

Henry is flattered that she liked that line enough to repeat it; he rather liked it, too.

CHAPTER 18

The next Wednesday boasts one of the highest pollen counts of the season. People who suffer from allergies are advised to stay in air conditioning. Henry removes himself from the house early, leaving a note saying he's gone out for breakfast and then he'll be at the library all day. When Murial wakes up, she's groggy and wheezy, and barely manages to toddle down the hall to admit Etheria, whom she's never actually met before.

"I'm the cleaning lady."

"It's all yours."

"I'll try not to disturb you, Mrs. Franklin."

Murial laughs, a phlegmy sound. "Don't worry, once I take my medicine, you couldn't wake me with a sledgehammer. Ha! Did that make sense? I mean jackhammer. Clean your little heart out, I'll be dead to the world."

Murial staggers back to bed.

Etheria cleans the rest of the house and then walks back to the master bedroom, where she cracks the door and peeks in. She doesn't actually have to see Murial to know she's asleep; every time Etheria switches off her vacuum cleaner, she can hear Murial's snores rattling through the walls.

Seeing that Murial is, indeed, out cold, Etheria brings her cleaning equipment and supplies into the bedroom and sets to work. She empties her vacuum bag onto the carpet below Murial's nose. She sprays furniture polish into the air above Murial's head. Etheria opens all the windows, admitting into the room the soft breeze that carries its record load of pollen. She sits down on the bed to smoke a cigarette, which she exhales in smoke rings which land daintily atop Murial's stringy, uncombed hair.

Next, Etheria leaves the bedroom and walks back down the

hall, pausing only long enough to turn the air conditioner to OFF. She returns to her car and brings into the house a cardboard box with slits cut in it. Back in the bedroom, Etheria opens the top of the box. Out jumps Copycat, who is delighted to be back home again. The cat bounds to the bed, where she snuggles against Murial's face, purring happily. The sound of their duet—snoring and purring—follows Etheria back down the hall to Henry's office.

She kills an hour reading Henry's new manuscript.

It isn't, Etheria decides, very good.

Finally, she lays it aside and goes back down the hall, pausing to turn the air conditioner back to ON. In the bedroom, Etheria closes the windows, gathers her cleaning supplies and vacuums the floor. The racket alarms Copycat, who makes a dash for the cardboard box.

Murial, however, doesn't stir.

After stowing her supplies in her car, Etheria returns to the bedroom to give it one last, appraising examination.

Very clean, very efficient, she decides.

Etheria picks up the phone and dials 911.

EPILOGUE

Henry and Etheria honeymoon in Los Angeles, where his novel is being filmed. His agent calls to say that the rest of his novels have been bought for television syndication. They all agree that Murial would have been miserable in L.A., what with the smog and all.

THE SCENT OF SPICED ORANGES

Les Roberts

HE'D BEEN PLAYING bumper tag with the blonde in the old tan Subaru with California plates for over an hour on Interstate 70, starting about noon east of Denver and continuing on across the state line into the middle of Kansas. That particular stretch of highway is probably the dullest in the world, a drive-through sensory deprivation experience, flat and brown and lonely, and before the blonde he'd found himself wondering how many miles it was going to be until the next tree.

He'd noticed her when she came down the on-ramp to the interstate, a sexy-looking woman in her late twenties, wearing a big straw sun hat with a curly blond ponytail threaded through the open back of it, and a maroon halter top. As he sped by her he noticed that every inch of the Subaru was packed with clothes, books and blankets—probably everything she owned. It looked like one of those cars from *The Grapes of Wrath*.

What really got his attention was the cat. It was an orange tabby with eyes the same color, and it prowled atop the blonde's

belongings like a sentry, easily keeping its balance in the speeding car. The summer highways of the United States normally
carry the cars and RVs of senior citizens who have an unlimited
amount of time and a limited amount of money for their vaca-
tions; a pretty blonde with an orange cat was enough of a rarity
to attract his notice. And he was the kind of man who always
noticed good-looking women, wherever they were.

A few minutes after she'd integrated into the stream of traffic
she roared past him on the left and, aware of his gaze, glanced
over at him, a small smile on her lips. He noticed that the car
windows were open just a hairline crack at the top. She must
not have an air conditioner, he thought, but she has to keep the
windows shut because of the cat.

When she'd gotten about twenty yards ahead of him she
drifted back into the right lane, and they drove along like that
for about five minutes while he wondered idly what a California
woman was doing in the middle of Kansas with all her worldly
goods and a muscular-looking orange tabby.

There were two slow-moving trucks and a camper ahead of
her, and she pulled out into the left lane, accelerating to at least
ten miles over the speed limit as she passed them. He followed
her, noticing as he swept by the camper that it was being driven
by an elderly woman with a face like a persimmon, wearing a
baseball cap. As the blonde moved back into the right lane
ahead of the camper, he went by her too, and as he looked over
at her she gave him a radiantly mischievous smile, acknowledg-
ing that they were hopscotching each other every few minutes
and that she was enjoying the game. The cat just glared.

As he returned to the right lane he saw in his mirror that she
was still smiling. She was pretty cute, he thought, and in the
manner of some married men away from home he began
fantasizing about her, about how he could get to meet her, how
he could make his move.

He tapped the brake until he was doing about sixty-two miles
an hour and cruised there awhile, waiting for her to pull up
beside him. When she did he tried to catch her eye, drinking in
dumbshow, hoping she'd get off at the next exit and have a

Coke with him, but this time she didn't make eye contact or even slow down, and at that speed he couldn't keep looking over at her without swerving onto the gravelly shoulder of the road.

He watched helplessly as she pulled far ahead of him. When they reached the next exit, a small town called Victoria, he noticed she didn't pull off. She hadn't seen his pantomime.

They continued their little game for another half-hour or so, until the blonde developed a heavy foot and disappeared ahead of a long line of semis and pickups and he lost interest.

The station he'd found on the radio was fading in and out on him now, the curse of the traveling man while driving in remote rural areas. He had a tape player in the car but he never used it. He didn't care that much about music anyway—all that interested him were the weather and traffic advisories and the sports scores. He punched angrily at the "Seek" button until he found another clear station—country music, which he loathed, but they'd probably do a newscast on the half-hour.

He started thinking about the sales he'd made in Denver yesterday, and the call he would make tomorrow afternoon in Indianapolis. That he'd sell them was a given; he always sold this particular company. The only thing in question was the amount. In his head he was calculating the various commissions he had earned and might earn, depending on the mood of the buyer, and he figured he'd have to spring for a high-priced lunch before getting the order and heading home to Columbus and his wife.

He passed the flattened carcass of what used to be a dog. He refused to look at it, and shuddered. He never got used to seeing dead things, even though roadkill was as much a feature of the scenery as wheat fields. Kansas, it seemed to him, was the dead dog capital of the world.

The sun was high and relentless, giving the landscape the look of a color snapshot that had been overexposed, and the pavement ahead of him shimmered, mesmerizing him. He'd been fortunate on this trip not to have run into too much road construction, those orange barrels blocking one of the two lanes that slowed him down and left him drumming his fingers on the steering wheel in frustration. It was bad enough driving through the endless monotony of the Great Plains at top speed, but to crawl along eating the dust of the car in front of him was intolerable.

He checked his watch to find he'd been on the road for nearly three hours without a break, and then glanced down at the fuel gauge, which was only one-quarter full. He decided to make an all-purpose pit stop at the next town—gasoline, the rest room, and a cold drink.

He rolled into a Shell station in Russell, Kansas at about three o'clock, and when he got out of the car the heat struck him like a fist. He stuck the gas nozzle into the tank and leaned against the fender as the numbers clicked off on the pump. When it stopped automatically he returned the hose to its niche, screwed the cap back on the tank, and went inside to pay and to use the john. On the way out he pulled a can of Pepsi out of the cooler.

When he got back to his car the blonde in the Subaru was just pulling up to an adjacent pump. She rolled her window down, glancing over her shoulder to make sure the cat didn't jump out. But it was resting sphinxlike atop a wicker basket and seemed disinterested in the whole thing.

"Well, hello," he said.

Her laugh tinkled like wind chimes. "Oh, hi," she said. "I thought we'd lost each other." She extended a languid arm out of the window, and when he moved to shake it he could see she was wearing loose-legged white shorts. "I'm Rose."

The restaurant across from the Shell station was almost empty in the midday lull between late lunch and early dinner, and the waitress was trying hard to talk them into trying the buffet dinner for $5.95. They resisted, ordering only iced tea for him and herbal tea for her. She squeezed lemon into hers while he loaded his glass with sugar.

"Actually I'd passed this exit," she was saying, "and then I looked down and realized I needed some gas and Widget needed some water."

"Widget?"

"My kitty," she explained. "I got off a few miles down the road but there were no stations, so I just took the service road and doubled back here." Her eyes twinkled as she looked at him from beneath the visor of her sun hat. "Now I'm glad I did."

"Where you headed, Rose?" he said.

"I'm going to Lee's Summit. It's just the other side of Kansas City."

"What's in Lee's Summit?"

"Peace, I hope. I'm a healer."

"You're a doctor?"

"No, no. A healer. Laying on of hands, meditation, that kind of thing."

He sipped his iced tea and nodded thoughtfully, trying to look interested, thinking it was just his luck to pick up a nut case. Well, if his luck was running, perhaps he could talk her into laying some hands on him. And vice versa.

"I've been living in L.A. for the past three years and I got to hating it a lot," she said. "But you know how it is—you want to get out but you've got no place to go. Finally, I just ran out of money. So I wrote this friend of mine in Lee's Summit and she invited me to come and stay as long as I liked." She shrugged, her breasts lifting in their halter, and his eyes followed their rise and fall, the delicate tracery of blue veins beneath tanned skin. Her perfume rose from them, and he leaned forward to get a better whiff. He couldn't quite place it, but it seemed appropriate on her somehow, a California kind of smell.

"I've got a great idea," he said, consulting his watch. "Let's drive on for another couple of hours until we get to Kansas City, and have dinner together. On me."

"Don't you have to be somewhere?"

"As long as I hit Indianapolis before five o'clock tomorrow I'll be fine," he said.

She chewed on her lip. "I don't know. I really need to be focused on what I'm going to do in Lee's Summit—I shouldn't let anything distract me."

"You've got to eat anyway, don't you? Look, it'll be a nice change for me. I'm always on the road—I spend my whole life eating alone in restaurants." He gave her his best little-boy-lost look. "I'd really like the company." He didn't add that since she'd run out of money she ought to jump at the chance of a free meal, but he was thinking it.

She brushed the hair out of her face. She'd taken off the sun hat, and at close range he could see the network of tiny lines around her eyes and at the corners of her mouth; she was older than he'd thought, maybe late thirties. But she was still pretty cute, and a married guy couldn't be too choosy.

She gave him that tinkly laugh again. "Well—I guess that'd be all right."

He gulped down the rest of his tea and slurped the sugar at the bottom of the glass, glowing with satisfaction and anticipation. He'd always been good at closing a sale.

They crossed the state line some four hours later. As a traveling man it always amused him that each state you enter by car has an enormous sign that bids you welcome to their friendly scenic wonders, and a hundred yards further another sign advising what they'll do to you if you break the traffic laws. He hoped Rose had noticed the second sign; he'd been following her long enough to know that she drove pretty fast when she thought no one was watching, and he certainly didn't want her stopped for a speeding ticket. He had other plans.

The steak house on the Missouri side of Kansas City was one he'd heard of but had never visited before. He wanted to be sure he didn't run into anyone he knew who might also know his wife. It was unlikely in Kansas City, but there was no such thing as being too careful.

He had two martinis before dinner and they both ordered T-bone rib steaks with baked potato. He selected a medium-priced Saint Emilion to go with the meal; he'd never heard of the wine before but he figured it would impress her. She took desultory sips of hers and he wound up finishing the bottle. It made him bold. All during dinner he kept dropping not so subtle double entendres, and she laughed dutifully at each of them. He figured he was a pretty funny guy.

When they'd finished eating he suggested coffee and a brandy.

"I don't drink either one," she said. "But you go ahead, have what you want."

"I always do," he leered, taking her hand in his and giving it a little squeeze, then running up her bare arm with his fingers. She giggled, batting her lashes. He wound up having two brandies and barely touching the coffee, and Rose asked the waitress for a "kitty bag" and inserted the steak bone into it with long, slim fingers.

Before paying the bill he went to the men's room, feeling more than a little woozy. In the stall he checked the cash in his pocket. Two hundred sixty-seven dollars. That was good. He had a company credit card in his wallet, and two of his own, but he didn't want to leave any sort of paper trail that could be questioned by his boss or his wife.

When he got back to the table, Rose said, "I didn't know it was so late. Oh, this is terrible."

"Why?"

"It's almost eleven. I can't walk in on my friend at nearly midnight, not when she's being kind enough to put me up."

He sat back, his full belly pushing against the front of his white shirt, visions of sugar plums dancing drunkenly in his head. "No problem," he said, throwing three twenties and a few singles onto the table next to the bill. "I have to get a motel room anyway."

He had the motel picked out ahead of time. It was in Independence, Missouri, and he had passed it a hundred times on the way through, although he'd never stayed there. Their sign proclaimed rooms from fifteen dollars up, and since the company paid his expenses he always stayed somewhere a little more posh. But tonight was going to be out-of-pocket, and he was nothing if not frugal. After all, he'd already blown more than sixty dollars on dinner.

It was a big motel, more than a hundred units, and he pulled up to a parking spot on the side of the building, noting with satisfaction that she was right behind him.

He climbed out of his car, a wave of dizziness making him stumble a little. He really did have a lot to drink with dinner. "I'll go register," he said.

She nodded her acquiescence and started to gather whatever she'd need for the night from the jumble of belongings on the seat beside her. Despite the heat he rubbed his hands together in anticipation.

"A room for two," he told the clerk, a young girl who looked to be just out of school. "King-size bed if you got one." When she pushed the registration card toward him, he signed it "Richard Thompson, Akron Ohio," which was neither his name nor his home town. He put down a false license number, too. And he paid in cash.

The room was down toward the far end of the building, and he thought about driving down there, but his head was buzzing and he didn't feel like getting into the car again. He grabbed his overnight case and locked the car. Rose stood waiting for him, a large purse her only luggage, the cat cradled in her arm against her breasts.

"You're not bringing him in with us?" he said.

Her eyes widened. "You don't expect the poor kitty to stay in that stuffy car all night, do you?"

He didn't like cats. He'd never trusted them, and he didn't like the way they smelled. But the heat in his loins was his priority right then, so he shrugged and took her arm to lead her down the walkway.

The room was virtually indistinguishable from ten thousand other such rooms lining the interstate highways of America— gray carpeting, off-white walls, imitation blond veneer dresser, too-thin towels and miniature rectangles of Dial soap. The loudly humming air conditioner was blasting icy air, and his damp shirt turned instantly cold and clammy. He shut the door and put his arms around her, nuzzling in her neck. Her perfume made him giddy, and he thought he identified the scent now— she smelled like spiced oranges. She tried to squirm away but he forced his tongue into her mouth, one hand behind her head and the other cupping her buttocks. He ground his body against her.

"I've been wanting to do this since the first time I saw you on the highway," he said. He could hear the slurring of his own words.

"Take it easy, lover," she said finally, out of breath. She pushed him away. "So have I, but I've been on the road all day. A girl needs to freshen up a little, you know?"

She caressed his face with one hand and gave him a fleeting kiss as she disappeared into the bathroom.

He stood in the middle of the room, swaying a bit, tasting the brandy at the back of his throat. He went over and stood directly in front of the air conditioner, letting it blow on his face until he got his bearings again. Widget, the cat, rubbed itself against his leg, and he moved away, startled. The cat prowled the room, sniffing, its tail an orange question mark above its back.

He heard the water running in the bathroom, and a loopy smile twisted his mouth. He turned down the bed; the sheets were stiff with sizing, a drab institutional white, and had seen better days. He stripped off all his clothes, leaving them in a pile on the floor, and after a quick look in the mirror on the dresser and sucking in his gut to its flatness of twenty years ago, turned off the light and slipped under the covers, appropriating both pillows to put beneath his head.

He lay there for a while, impatient for her to finish. He closed his eyes, fantasizing. In his imaginings he wasn't drunk any more, and he imagined how she'd come out of the bathroom, how she'd look, what she'd do, what he would do to her. It was a delicious dream, at first almost violent in its passion and then slow and sensuous and lazy. So lazy . . .

A sudden weight on his feet brought him out of it; the cat had jumped up on the bed and was kneading the blanket with its sharp little claws. He could hear the gentle, soft rhythm of its purring. His eyelids were heavy from the alcohol, and with great effort he forced them open.

She was at the foot of the bed, fully dressed except for the straw hat, with her purse over one arm. She was holding his trousers, going through the pockets, and as though he was viewing a movie that had nothing to do with him, he watched as she extracted what was left of his money.

It wasn't until she scooped the cat off the bed with her free hand and started for the door that he really woke up and achieved full cognizance that he had been suckered. Set up like some small-town chump away from home for the first time. Naked, he vaulted out of bed and across the floor in one motion, his hands reaching for her, pawing at her, but there was nothing erotic about it any more. He wanted what she'd taken from him. "Hey!" he said.

She dropped the cat and tried to struggle out of his grasp. She was quicksilver to hold onto, all elbows and knees, as he tried to wrench the money from her fist. "Let go!" he rasped through teeth clenched so tight that it gave him a headache.

One of her knees pistoned up hard between his legs, making him grunt, and in pain and anger he hurled her away from him. She staggered a few steps, her feet tangling in his trousers on the floor, and she fell, the back of her head striking the sharp corner of the dresser on the way down.

He pounced on her, prying her fingers apart and snatching the money away from her. Then he straightened up, his chest heaving with the unaccustomed exertion. He turned back to her. "Get up," he panted. "And get out."

She didn't move. The cat prowled around her, nudging her with its nose.

"Come on, Rose."

She still didn't stir, and all at once the goose flesh on his bare chest wasn't from the chill of the air conditioner any more.

He knelt down beside her, brushing the cat roughly away from her with the back of his hand. A faint glow from the lights in the parking lot was seeping through the drape on the window, but it was enough for him to see the dark pool spreading beneath her head. He was careful not to touch it. He didn't have to; he knew what it was. Her eyes stared sightlessly at the pebbled ceiling, her mouth an O of horror. He put his palm on her chest just under her left breast and didn't feel a heartbeat. He hadn't expected to. The cat, not minding the rebuff, licked at the puddle beneath the blonde's head.

He leaped upright again, his heart like a hammer in his chest, and ran for the bathroom, his insides contracting violently. Before he was finished his stomach was completely empty and he was bathed in sweat again.

He went back into the room. He couldn't catch his breath, and for a few moments he moved frantically around, gasping like a beached fish. Uncomfortable with his nakedness, he pulled on his trousers, and leaned against the wall next to the bed, the love handles of middle age spilling over his waistband. He made a conscious effort to relax, willing himself to, and after a time he was able to breathe again.

He hadn't meant to kill her, of course. He hadn't even meant to hurt her. She'd hustled him, tried to rob him, and all he'd wanted was to stop her and get his money back. Killing her was an accident. Everyone would understand that.

He went to the telephone on the nightstand, next to the imitation leather-covered Bible thoughtfully provided by the Gideons. He figured the police emergency number was 911, as it was in most cities. But his hand hovered over the receiver and finally fell to his side.

He was in trouble.

Even if no criminal charges were filed against him, this would certainly cost him his marriage. His wife would understand him trying to save his money, but after twelve years of marriage to a man who had been known to stray before she wouldn't be quite so accepting about what he was doing in a motel room with Rose in the first place.

And there went his house, his car, and half his income.

He was also sure his job would evaporate like raindrops in a summer heat; his boss was a straitlaced type, a pillar of the Methodist Church, and would take a pretty dim view of what happened. If he called the police now, he would be ruined twenty ways from Sunday.

He sank down on the bed and rubbed his eyes with his fingers, trying to ease the savage pounding behind them so he could think. He kept his eyes averted from the woman's body on the floor, just as he had with the dead dog on the highway, as though if he didn't look at it, didn't acknowledge it was there, it wouldn't be, and he would be alone in the room, no Rose and no Widget, watching a movie on cable and nodding off before the last reel. Just an ordinary stopover between Denver and Indianapolis.

Then he started to think about it. No one had seen him with the woman except the waitress in Kansas City. He had paid cash for both dinner and the room and falsified the registration card in the motel office. He was practically untraceable.

Spirits soaring, he rushed into the bathroom where the lingering smell of her spiced orange perfume was a silent rebuke. He washed away the vestiges of his sickness with the motel wash cloth, then rinsed it out in hot water and laid it over the shower rod to dry. With a towel he wiped down almost every surface in the room, even though he'd undressed and gotten into bed immediately and couldn't remember touching anything. The heady jolt of fear kept him moving quickly, despite the fact that he was exhausted and still half-drunk.

He had pulled his trousers on quickly, and now he took them off and put on his underwear, his shirt, and the rest of his clothes. They were damp and sweaty, but he didn't care. He put the roll of bills into his pocket, picked up his wallet from the floor where she'd dropped it during her search, grabbed his overnight case and went out, being careful to wipe off the door handles and jamb. He thought about looking back at the woman's body one last time, but fought the impulse off.

When he got into his car he didn't look over at her Subaru, either. He was going to put the whole episode out of his mind, he thought.

It was quiet in the parking lot and almost all the rooms were dark behind their drapes. He started the engine, turned on the air conditioner, and drove out of the lot with his lights off. He almost didn't remember to turn them on when he went down the ramp onto Interstate 70 half a block away. Heading west—back the way he'd come.

He was going to get a hotel room back in Kansas someplace, maybe in Lawrence or Topeka, just in case. Then he could say he hadn't even reached Independence at the approximate time the woman was killed. It was a ruse that could easily be broken by a relentless police investigator, but he didn't think it would even come to that. There was no way anyone could connect a traveling salesman from Columbus, Ohio with a whacked-out cat-loving faith healer from Los Angeles. It would mean an extra-long drive in the morning, but he'd get an early start.

The fact that he'd snuffed out a human life was not lost on him; it lay heavy in his stomach like a cold smooth stone. But like an alcoholic in denial he manufactured a whole set of excuses for himself. If she hadn't smiled so radiantly at him on the highway he never would have bothered with her. She had probably seen him leave the interstate back at the Shell station and had doubled back to find him, larceny in her heart from the very beginning. Healer, my foot, he thought—hustler is more like it.

She'd been good at it, he had to give her that. She'd beaten him out of an expensive meal, tried to steal his money while he slept, and perhaps worst of all, had not delivered the reward he'd been expecting. She probably did this all the time, made her living at it. She deserved what she got.

He had driven about fifteen miles before the anxiety attack hit, and he had to pull off onto the right shoulder until he stopped hyperventilating and his hands quit shaking. He would have been happy to stay there all night, safe in his little steel cocoon while traffic roared by him, but he didn't want a state highway cop stopping by to see what the trouble was. With enormous effort he got control of himself and resumed his westward trek.

He switched on the radio, twisting the dial until he could get clear reception, but he was unaware of the music, "Judy's Turn to Cry" on a rock oldies station. His eyes kept flickering up to the mirror, but there was no one following him, very little traffic of any kind after midnight. Every once in a while a big semi would rumble past him, spouting diesel fumes, its side lights and taillights and running lights like a kid's carnival ride in the blackness.

As he negotiated the interstate where it threaded its way directly through downtown Kansas City and across the Missouri River for the second time that day, he kept a worried eye on the speedometer. Most highway cops gave you a five-mile grace, but he kept the needle at fifty-five. He didn't want to chance getting stopped, still under the influence of alcohol.

And he was exhausted too, wrung out; he nodded at the wheel, his head falling forward on his chest and then snapping up again. He rubbed his eyes and slapped his own face gently. He was too experienced a long-distance driver to go on like that much longer; he had seen too many twisted, burned wrecks at the side of the road. He had to get some sleep.

A green sign told him that Lawrence, Kansas was twelve miles ahead. He'd stopped there for lunch once or twice, a nice quiet college town a few miles south of the highway, with several motels cheek-by-jowl with the truck stops and gasoline stations and ubiquitous fast-food restaurants. He turned up the music and the cold air and took a deep breath. He could make it.

Twenty minutes later he was driving the main drag of Lawrence, batting his eyes to stay awake and gritting his teeth at the proliferation of NO VACANCY signs at all the motels. What was the big deal about Lawrence, Kansas on this particular evening? he wondered. It was midweek, midsummer, no homecoming weekend or football game. He tried not to take it personally, but then he tended to take everything personally, as if society in general had teamed up with the gods to make his life tough.

At the end of the strip he found a Best Western whose red sign told him there was a room available, and he docked his car in front of the office. Not a moment too soon, either, he thought. His eyelids were heavy and his brain was dangerously overloaded.

The kid behind the desk was obviously clerking as a summer job, and he handed him a registration card and a pen, watching while he used his real name and address.

"Credit card, sir?"

"Sure," he said, rotating his head around until his neck popped. He could never remember being so wiped out. All he could think of was the crisp white sheets and the air-conditioned room he had just signed for. He pulled out his wallet and flipped it open, and his stomach wrenched inside him as if someone had pulled taut a rawhide cord around his large intestine.

The credit cards were gone.

That's why she'd dropped the wallet on the floor—she'd removed the credit cards before she went into his pants pockets for the money. They were probably in her own pocket or purse right now where she lay on the institutional gray carpet of the Independence motel.

He heard a sound coming out of his throat that he tried to cover with a cough. "No, ah—never mind, I changed my—"

He snatched the registration card from the startled clerk, crumpled it up and jammed it into his hip pocket, and rushed out the door to his car.

He had to get back to Independence before anyone found her, had to get those credit cards and whatever else she might have removed from his wallet that had his name on it.

This time he didn't worry about holding down his speed on the highway, he wasn't worrying about anything except getting back to that motel room. His head bobbed with exhaustion, but his foot remained steady on the accelerator pedal. He was angry with himself—he had nearly blown it.

As he was driving through Kansas City a horrifying thought struck him. How was he going to get back into the room? Sweat pouring off his face and chest heaving with the effort to breathe, he squirmed around in the seat and plunged his hand deep into his pocket, touching the large flat plastic disc attached to the key. He sighed. One less thing to worry about.

Relief flooded over him and the tension ebbed away. He leaned his head back on the headrest, taking his first relaxed breath in more than two hours, no longer fighting the fatigue and the alcohol, no longer firing all cylinders in panic. Everything was going to be fine.

Just fine . . .

That's when he felt the little needle claws digging into his shoulder and the back of his neck, and he sucked in his breath. The damn cat had followed him out of the motel room and sneaked into his car when he wasn't looking. Startled and in pain, he twisted the wheel frantically. The last sound he heard was the soft, rattling purr just next to his ear.

When the Rescue Squad cut him out of the wreckage of his car with the Jaws of Life, one of the men fished the frightened and trembling orange cat from where it huddled on the floor of the back seat. He took it home that night, and in the morning his little daughter, delighted with her new pet, decided to name it Lucky.

THE BEAST WITHIN

Margaret Maron

EARLY SUMMER TWILIGHT had begun to soften the city's harsh outlines as Tessa pushed aside the sliding glass doors and stepped out onto the terrace. Up here on the twenty-sixth floor, dusk blurred the sharp ugly planes of surrounding buildings and even brought an eerie beauty to the skeletal girders of the new skyscraper going up next door.

Gray-haired, middle-aged and emotionally drained by her last confrontation with Clarence, Tessa leaned heavily fleshed arms on the railing of their penthouse terrace and let the warm night air enfold her.

From the street far, far below, muffled sounds of evening traffic floated up to her and for a moment she considered jumping. To end it all in one brief instant of broken flesh while ambulances screamed and the curious stared—what real difference would it make to her, to Clarence, to anyone, if she lived another day or year or twenty years?

Nevertheless, she stepped back from the railing unconsciously, the habit of life too deeply rooted in her psyche. With a few cruel and indifferent words, Clarence had destroyed her world; but he had not destroyed her will to live. Not yet.

She glanced across the narrow space to the uncompleted building. The workmen who filled the daylight hours with a cacophony of rivets and protesting winches were gone now, leaving behind, for safety, hundreds of small bare light bulbs. In the mild breeze, they swung on their wires like chained fireflies in the dusk.

Tessa smiled at the thought. How long had it been since she had seen real fireflies drift through summer twilight? Surely not more than half a dozen times since marrying Clarence all those years ago—God! Was it really almost forty years now? She no longer hated the city, but she had never forgiven it for not having fireflies—nor for blocking out the Milky Way with its star-quenching skyscrapers.

When he first brought her away from the country, Clarence had probably loved her as much as he was capable of loving anyone; yet even then he hadn't understood her unease at living in a place so eternally and brilliantly lit. When his friends complimented them on the penthouse and marveled at the size of their terrace (enormous even by those booming postwar standards of the fifties), he would laugh and say, "I bought it for Tessa. Can't fence in a country girl. They need 'land, lots of land 'neath the starry skies above!' "

It hadn't taken her long to realize he'd bought the penthouse to feed his own vanity, not to still her unspoken needs. Eventually, she stopped caring. If this terrace wasn't high enough above the neon glare to see her favorite stars, it at least provided as much quiet as one could expect in a city. She could always lie back on one of the cushioned chaises and remember how the Milky Way swirled in and out of the constellations; remember the dainty charm of the Pleiades tucked away in Taurus the Bull.

But not tonight. Instead of star-studded skies, memory forced her to relive the past hour in every humiliating and painful detail.

She was long since reconciled to the fact that Clarence did not love her; but after years of trying to mold herself to his standards, she had thought that he was comfortable with her and that she was necessary to him in all the other spheres that hold a marriage together after passion fades away.

Tonight, Clarence had made it brutally clear: not only was she *not* necessary, she was a boring encumbrance. Further, the woman she'd become, in her efforts to please him, was the antithesis of the woman he'd chosen as her replacement.

Tessa had followed him through their apartment in a daze as he packed his suitcases to leave. Mechanically, she had handed him clean shirts and underwear; then, seeing what a mess he was making of those perfectly tailored suits, she had taken over the actual packing as she always did when he went away on business trips. Only this time, he was going farther away than he ever had before, to a midtown hotel, out of her life.

"But why?" she asked, smoothing a crease in his gray slacks.

They had met Lynn Herrick at one of his sister-in-law's parties. Aggressive and uninhibited, her dress was blatantly sexual and her long black hair frizzed in a cloud around her bare shoulders. Tessa had thought the young woman brittle and obvious, hardly Clarence's type, and she had been amused by Ms. Herrick's brazenly flirtatious approach.

"Why this one?" she demanded again, knowing there had been other, more suitable women over the years.

A fatuous expression spread across Clarence's face, a blend of pride, sheepishness and defiance. "Because she's going to bear my child," he said pompously.

It was the ultimate blow. For years Tessa had pleaded for a child, only to have Clarence take every precaution to prevent one.

"You've always loathed children. You said they were whining, slobbering nuisances!"

"It wasn't my fault," Clarence protested. "Accidents happen."

"I'll bet!" Tessa muttered crudely, knowing that nothing accidental ever happens to the Lynn Herricks of the world.

Clarence chose to ignore her remark. "Now that it's happened, Lynn's made me see how much I owe it to myself. And to the company. Another Loughlin to carry our name into the next century since it doesn't look as if Richard and Alison will ever produce an heir."

Richard Loughlin was Clarence's much younger brother and only living relative. Together they had inherited control of a prosperous chain of department stores begun by their grandfather. Although Tessa had heard Richard remark wistfully that a child might be fun, his wife Alison shared Clarence's previous attitude toward offspring; and her distaste was strengthened by the fear of what a child might do to her size-eight figure.

With Clarence reveling in the newfound joys of prospective fatherhood, Tessa had snapped shut the final suitcase. Still in a daze, she stared at her reflection in the mirror over his dresser and was appalled.

In her conscious mind, she had known that she was past fifty, that her hair was gray, her figure no longer slim; and she had known that Clarence would never let her have children—but deep inside, down at the primal core of her being, a young, half-wild girl cried out in protest at the old and barren woman she had become.

The siren of a fire engine on the street far below drew Tessa to the edge of the terrace again. Night had fallen completely and traffic was thin now. The sidewalks were nearly deserted.

She still felt outraged at being cast aside so summarily—as if a pat on the shoulder, the promise of lavish alimony, and an "I told Lynn you'd be sensible about everything" were enough to compensate for thirty-six years of her life—but at least her brief urge toward self-destruction had dissipated.

She stared again at the bobbing safety lights of the uncompleted building and remembered that the last time she'd seen fireflies had been six years ago, after Richard and Alison returned from their honeymoon. She and Clarence had gone down to Pennsylvania to help warm the old farmhouse Richard had bought as a wedding surprise for Alison.

The hundred and thirty acres of overgrown fields and woodlands had indeed been a surprise to that urban young woman. Alison's idea of a suitable weekend retreat was a modern beach house on Martha's Vineyard.

Tessa had loved it and had tramped the woods with Richard, windblown and exhilarated, while Alison and Clarence complained about mosquitoes and dredged up pressing reasons to cut short their stay. Although Alison had been charming and had assured Richard that she was delighted with his gift, she found excellent excuses not to accompany him on his infrequent trips to the farm.

Remembering its isolation, Tessa wondered if Richard would mind if she buried herself there for a while. Perhaps in the country she could sort things out and grope her way back to the wild freedom she had known all those years ago, before Clarence took her to the city and "housebroke" her, as he'd expressed it in the early years of their marriage.

A cat's terrified yowl caught her attention. She looked up and saw it running along one of the steel girders that stuck out several feet from a higher level of the new building. The cat raced out as if pursued by the three-headed Hound of Hell, and its momentum was too great to stop when it realized the danger.

It soared off the end of the girder and landed with a sickening thump on the terrace awning. With an awkward twist of its furry body, the cat leaped to the terrace floor and cowered under one of the chaises, quivering with panic.

Tessa watched the end of the girder, expecting to see a battle-scarred tom spoiling for a fight. Although cats seldom made it up this high, it was not unusual to see one taking a shortcut across her terrace from one rooftop to another, up and down fire escapes.

When no other cat appeared, Tessa turned her attention to the frightened animal. The night air had roused that touch of arthritis that had begun to bother her this year, and it was an effort to bend down beside the lounge chair. She tried to coax the cat out, but it shrank away from her hand.

"Here, kitty, kitty," she murmured. "It's all right. There's no one chasing you now."

She had always liked cats and, for that reason, refused to own one. It was too easy to let a small animal become a proxy child.

She sympathized with Richard's mild disapproval whenever Alison called their dachshund "baby."

Patiently, she waited for the cat to stop trembling and to sniff her outstretched hand; but even though she kept her voice low and soothing, it would not abandon its shelter. Tessa's calcified joints protested against her crouch and creaked as she straightened up and stepped back a few feet.

The cat edged out then, suspiciously poised for flight. From the living-room lamps beyond the glass doors, light fell across it and revealed a young female with crisp black-and-gray markings and white paws. Judging from its leggy thinness, it hadn't eaten in some time.

"You poor thing," Tessa said, moved by its uneasy trust. "I'll bet you're starving."

As if it understood Tessa meant no harm, the cat did not skitter aside when she moved past it into the apartment.

Soon she was back with a saucer of milk and a generous chunk of rare beef which she'd recklessly cut from the heart of their untouched dinner roast. "Better you than a garbage bag, kitty. No one else wants it."

Stiff-legged and wary, the young cat approached the food and sniffed; then, clumsily, it tore at the meat and almost choked in its haste.

"Slow down!" Tessa warned, and bent over heavily to pull the meat into smaller pieces. "You're an odd one. Didn't you ever eat meat before?" She tried to stroke the cat's thin back, but it quivered and slipped away from her plump hand. "Sorry, cat. I was just being friendly."

She sank down onto one of the chaises and watched the animal finish its meal. When the meat was gone, it turned to the saucer of milk and drank messily with much sneezing and shaking of its small head as it inadvertently got milk in its nose.

Tessa was amused but a bit puzzled. She'd never seen a cat so graceless and awkward. It acted almost like a young, untutored kitten; and when it finished eating and sat staring at her, Tessa couldn't help laughing aloud. "Didn't your mother teach you *any*thing, silly? You're supposed to wash your paws and whiskers now."

The cat moved from the patch of light where it had sat silhouetted, its face in darkness. With purposeful caution, it circled the chaise until Tessa was between it and the terrace doors. Light from the living room fell full in its eyes there and was caught and reflected with an eerie intensity.

Tessa shivered uneasily as the animal's luminous eyes met her own with unblinking steadiness. "Now I see why cats are always linked with the supernatu—"

Suddenly it was as if she were a rabbit frozen in the middle of a back-country road by the headlights of a speeding car. Those feral eyes bored into her brain with a spiraling vortex of blinding light. A roaring numbness gripped her. Her mind was assaulted —mauled and dragged down and under and through—existence without shape, time without boundaries.

It lasted forever; it was over in an instant; and somewhere amid the splintered, whirling clamor came an awareness of another's existence, a being formless and desperate and terrified beyond sanity.

There was mingling.

Tessa felt the other's panic.

There was passing.

Then fierce exultation.

There was a brief, weird sensation of being unbearably compacted and compressed; the universe seemed to tilt and swirl; then it was over. The light faded to normal city darkness, the roaring stopped, and she knew she was sprawled upon the cool flagstones of the terrace.

She tried to push herself up, but her body responded queerly. Dazed, she looked around and screamed at the madness of a world suddenly magnified in size—a scream which choked off as she caught sight of someone enormous sitting on the now-huge chaise.

A plump, middle-aged, gray-haired woman held her face between trembling hands and moaned, "Thank God! Thank God!"

Shocked, Tessa realized that she was seeing her own face for the first time without the reversing effect of a mirror. Her shock intensified as she looked down through slitted eyes and saw neat white paws instead of her own hands. With alien instinct, she felt the ridge of her spine quiver as fur stood on end. She tried to speak and was horrified to hear a feline yowl emerge.

The woman on the chaise—Tessa could no longer think of that body as herself—stopped moaning then and watched her warily. "You're not mad, if that's what you're wondering. Not yet, anyhow. Though you'll maybe go mad if you don't get out of that skin in time."

She snatched up a cushion and flung it at Tessa.

"Shoo! G'wan, scat!" she gibbered. "You can't make me look in your eyes. I'll never get caught again. Scat, damn you!"

Startled, Tessa sprang to the railing of the terrace and teetered there awkwardly. The body had begun to respond, but she wasn't sure how well she could control it, and twenty-six stories above street level was too high to allow for much error.

The woman who had stolen her body seemed afraid to come closer. "You might as well go!" she snarled at Tessa. She threw a calculating glance at the luxurious interior beyond the glass doors.

"It's a lousy body—too old and too fat—but it looks like a rich one and it's human and I'm keeping it, so *scat!*"

Tessa's new reflexes were quicker than those of her old body. Before the shoe even left the other's hand, she had dropped to the narrow ledge that circled the exterior of the penthouse. Residual instinct made her footing firm as she followed the ledge around the corner of the building to the fire escape for an easy climb to the roof. There, in comparative safety from flying shoes and incipient plunges to the street, Tessa drew up to consider the situation.

Cat's body or not, came the wry thought, *it's still my mind.*

Absently licking away the dried milk that stuck to her whiskers, she plumbed the sensations of her new body and discovered that vestigial traces of former identities clung to this brain. Mere wisps they were, like perfume hanging in a closed room, yet enough to piece together a picture of what had happened to her on the terrace below.

The one who had just stolen her body had been young and sly, but not overly bright. Judging from the terror and panic so freshly imprinted, she had fled through the city and taken the first body she could.

Behind those raw emotions lay a cooler, more calculating undertone and Tessa knew *that* one had been more mature; had chosen the girl's body deliberately and after much thought. Not for her the hasty grabbing of the first opportunity. Instead, she had stalked her prey with care, taking a body that was pretty, healthy and, above all, young.

Beyond those two, Tessa could not sort out the other personalities whose lingering traces she felt. Nor could she know who had been the first or how it had all started. Probing too deeply, she recoiled from the touch of a totally alien animal essence struggling for consciousness—the underlying basic *catness* of this creature whose body she now inhabited.

Tessa clamped down ruthlessly on these primeval stirrings, forcing them back under. This must be what the girl meant about going mad. How long could a person stay in control?

The answer, of course, was to get back into a human body. Tessa pattered softly to the edge of the roof and peered down at the terrace. Below, the girl in her body still cowered on the chaise as if unable to walk into the apartment and assume possession. Her shoulders slumped and she looked old and defeated.

She's right, thought Tessa. *It is a lousy body. Let her keep it.*

At that moment, she could almost pity the young thief who had stolen her most personal possession; but the moment was short-lived. With spirits soaring, Tessa danced across the black-tarred roof on nimble paws. Joyfully she experimented with her new body and essayed small leaps into the night air. No more arthritis, no excess flab to make her gasp for breath. What bliss to *think* a motion and have lithe muscles respond!

Drunk with new physical prowess, she raced to the fire escape, leaped to the railing and recklessly threw herself out into space. There was one sickening moment when she felt she must have

The Beast Within

misjudged, then she caught herself on a jutting scaffold and scrambled onto it.

Adrenalin coursed in her veins and her confidence grew with each step that carried her farther and farther away from familiar haunts. She prowled the night streets boldly, recapturing memories and emotions almost forgotten in those air-conditioned, temperature-controlled, insulated years with Clarence. Never again, she vowed, would she settle for less than this.

Freed of her old woman's body, she felt a oneness again with —what? The world? Nature? God?

The name didn't matter, only the feeling. Even here in the city, in the heart of man's farthest retreat into artifice, she felt it, and a nameless longing welled within her.

What it must be to have a cat's body in the country! Yet even as the thought formed in her mind, Tessa shivered in sudden fear. It would be too much. To be in this body with grass and dirt underneath, surrounded by trees and bushes alive with small rustlings, with uncluttered sky overhead—a human mind might well go mad with so much sensory stimulation.

No, better the city with its concrete and cars and crush of people to remind her that she was human and that this body was only temporary.

Still, she thought, descending gracefully from the top of a shuttered newsstand, *how dangerous could a small taste be?*

She ran west along half-deserted streets, heading for the park. On the crosstown streets, traffic was light; but crossing the avenues scared her. The rumble and throb of all those motors, the many lights and impatient horns kept her fur on end. She had to force herself to step off the curb at Fifth Avenue; and as she darted across its wide expanse, she half expected to be crushed beneath a cab.

The park was a haven now. Gratefully she dived between its fence railings and melted into the safety of its dark bushes.

In the next few hours, Tessa shed the rest of the shackles of her life with Clarence, her years of thinking "What will Clarence say?" when she gave way to an impulsive act; the fear of being considered quaint by his friends if she spoke her inmost thoughts.

If Pan were a god, she truly worshiped him that night! Abandoning herself to instinctual joys, she raced headlong down grassy hills, rolled paws over tail-tip in the moonlight, chased a sleepy, crotchety squirrel through the treetops, then skimmed down to the duck pond to lap daintily at the water and dabble at goldfish turned silver in the moonbeams.

As the moon slid below the tall buildings west of the park, she ate flesh of her own killing. Later—behind the Mad Hatter's bronze toadstool—she crooned a voluptuous invitation and allowed the huge ginger male who had stalked her for an hour to approach her, to circle ever nearer . . .

As he grasped her by the scruff and began to mount, the alien animal consciousness below exploded into dominance, surging across her will in wave after roiling wave of raw sexuality with every pelvic thrust. Thrice more they coupled in excruciating ecstasy, and only when the ginger tom had spent himself into exhaustion was she able to reassert her will and force that embryonic consciousness back to submission.

Just before dawn, a neat feline head poked through the railing at Fifth and East Sixty-fourth Street and hesitated as it surveyed the deserted avenue, empty now of all traffic save an occasional bus.

Reassured, Tessa stepped out onto the sidewalk and sat on narrow haunches to smooth and groom her ruffled striped fur. She was shaken by the night's experiences, but complacently unrepentant. No matter what lay ahead, these last few hours were now part of her soul and worth any price she might yet have to pay.

Nevertheless, the strength of this body's true owner was growing and Tessa knew that another night would be a dangerous risk. She had to find another body, and soon.

Whose?

Lynn Herrick flashed to mind. How wickedly poetic it would be to take her rival's sexy young body, bear Clarence's child, and stick Lynn with a body which, after last night, would soon be producing offspring of its own. But she knew too little about that man-eating tramp to feel confident taking over that particular life.

No, she was limited to someone familiar, someone young, someone unpleasantly deserving and, above all, someone *close*. She must be within transferring distance before the city's morning rush hour forced her back into the park until dark—an unthinkable risk.

The logical candidate sprang to mind.

Of course! she thought. *Keep it in the family.*

Angling across Fifth Avenue, she pattered north toward the luxurious building that housed the younger Loughlins. Her tail twitched jauntily as she scampered along the sidewalk and considered the potentials of Alison's body. For starters, it was almost thirty years younger.

The deception might be tricky at first, but she had met all of Alison's few near relatives. As for surface friends who filled the aimless rounds of her sister-in-law's social life, Tessa knew they could be dropped without causing a ripple of curiosity—especially if her life became filled with babies. That should please Richard. *Dear Richard!*

Dear Richard? Tessa was intrigued. When had her brother-in-law become so dear? Richard was a small boy when she and Clarence married, and she had always considered the tenderness he roused in her a sort of frustrated maternalism, especially since he was so comfortable to be with. Somewhere along the line, tender maternalism had apparently transmuted into something earthier; and all at once, wistful might-have-beens were suddenly exciting possibilities.

Behind the heavy bronze and glass doors of Richard's building, a sleepy doorman nodded on his feet. The sun was not yet high enough to lighten the doorway under its pink-and-gray striped awning, and deep shadows camouflaged her own stripes.

Keeping a low silhouette, she crouched outside and waited. When the doorman opened the door for an early-rising tenant, she darted inside and streaked across the lobby to hide behind a large marble ashstand beside the elevator.

The rest would be simple as the elevator was large, dimly lit, and paneled in dark mahogany. She would conceal herself under the pink velvet bench at the rear of the car and wait until it eventually stopped at Alison and Richard's floor.

Her tail twitched with impatience. When the elevator finally descended, she poised herself to spring.

The door slid back and bedlam broke loose in a welter of shrill barks, tangled leash and startled, angry exclamations. The dog was upon her, front and back, yipping and snapping before she knew what was happening.

Automatically, she spat and raked the dog's nose with her sharp claws, which set off a frenzy of jumping and straining against the leash and sent his master sprawling.

Tessa only had time to recognize that it was Richard, taking Liebchen out for a prebreakfast walk, before she felt herself being whacked by the elevator man's newspaper.

All avenues of escape were closed to her and she was given no time to think or gather her wits before the street doors were flung open and she was harried out onto the sidewalk.

Angry and disgusted with herself and the dog, Tessa checked her headlong flight some yards down the sidewalk and glared back at the entrance of the building where the dachshund smugly waddled down the shallow steps and pulled Richard off in the opposite direction.

So the front is out, thought Tessa. *I wonder if their flank is so well-guarded?*

It pleased her to discover that those years of easy compliance with Clarence's wishes had not blunted her initiative. She was not about to be thwarted now by any little canine frankfurter.

Halfway around the block, she found an alley that led to a

small service court. From the top of a dumpster, she managed to spring to the first rung of a fire escape and scramble up.

As she climbed, the night's exertions began to pull at her physical reserves. Emotional exhaustion added its weight, too. Paw over paw, up and up, while every muscle begged for rest and her mind became a foggy treadmill able to hold but a single thought: paw in front of paw.

It seemed to take hours. Up thirteen steps to the landing, right turn; up thirteen steps to the landing, left turn, with such regular monotony that her mind became stupid with the endless repetition of black iron steps.

At the top landing, a ten-rung ladder rose straight to the roof. Her body responded sluggishly to this final effort and she sank down upon the tarred rooftop in utter exhaustion. The sun was high in the sky now; and with the last dregs of energy, Tessa crept into the shade of an overhanging ledge and was instantly asleep.

When she awoke in the late afternoon, the last rays of sunlight were slanting across the city. Hunger and thirst she could ignore for the time, but what of the quickening excitement that twilight was bringing?

She crept to the roof's edge and peered down at the empty terrace overlooking the park. An ivied trellis offered easy descent and she crouched behind a potted shrub to look through the doors. On such a mild day, the glass doors had been left open behind their fine-meshed screens.

Inside, beyond an elegant living room, Alison's housekeeper set the table in the connecting dining room. There was no sign of Alison or Richard—or of Liebchen. Cautiously, Tessa pattered along the terrace to the screened doors of their bedroom, but it too was empty.

As she waited, darkness fell completely. From deep within she felt the impatient tail-flick of awareness. She felt it respond to a cat's guttural cry two rooftops away, felt it surfacing against her will, pulled by the promise of another night of dark paths and wild ecstasy.

Desperately, she struggled with that other ego, fought it blindly and knew that soon her strength would not be enough.

Suddenly the terrace was flooded with light as all the lamps inside the apartment were switched on. Startled, the other self retreated; and Tessa heard Alison's light voice tell the housekeeper, "Just leave dinner on the stove, Mitchum. You can clear away in the morning."

"Yes, Mrs. Loughlin, and I want you and Mr. Loughlin to know how sorry I am that—"

"Thank you, Mitchum," came Richard's voice, cutting her off.

Tessa sat motionless in the shadows outside and watched Liebchen trot across the room and scramble onto a low chair, unmindful of her nearness.

As Richard mixed drinks, Alison said, "It's so horrible. Poor Tessa. Those delusions that she's really a young girl—that she's never met Clarence or either of us. Do you suppose she's trying to fake a mental breakdown?"

"How can you say that? You saw her wretchedness. It wasn't an act."

"But—"

"What a shock it must have been to have him ask for a divorce after all these years. Did you know about it?" His voice was harsh with emotion. "You introduced Lynn to Clarence. Did you encourage them?"

"Honestly, darling," Alison said scornfully. "You act as if *Tessa's* been victimized."

"Maybe she has." Richard sounded tired now and infinitely sad. "In more ways than either of us can possibly know. You should have seen her when they were first married—so fresh and open and full of laughter. I was only a kid, but I remember. I'd never met an adult like her. All our stodgy relatives were snide to her. They thought she was a gold-digging country hick. *I* thought she was like an April breeze blowing through this family and I was proud of Clarence for breaking out of the mold."

He gazed bleakly into his glass. "After Father died, they sent me away to school and it was years before I really saw her again. I couldn't believe the change: all the laughter gone, her guarded words. Clarence did a thorough job of cramming both of them back into the Loughlin mold. First he kills her spirit and then he has the nerve to call her dull! No wonder she's retreated into her youth, to a time before she knew him. You heard the psychiatrist. He doesn't think she's faking."

"Perhaps not," Alison said coolly, "but you seem to keep forgetting: Clarence may have killed her spirit, but Tessa's killed *him*."

In the shadows outside the screen, Tessa quivered. So they had found Clarence's body! That poor thieving child! At the sight of Clarence lying on the bedroom floor with his head crushed in, she must have panicked again.

"I haven't forgotten," Richard said. "And I haven't forgotten Lynn Herrick either. If what Clarence told me yesterday is true, I'll have to make some sort of arrangement for the child out of Clarence's estate."

"Don't be naive," said Alison. "I'm sure she merely let Clarence believe what he wanted. Trust me, darling. Lynn's far too clever to take on motherhood without a wedding ring and community property laws."

"You mean the divorce—his death—Tessa's insanity—all this was based on lies? And you knew it? You *did*! I can see it in your face!"

"Oh, please!" Alison snapped. She stood abruptly and stalked across the room. "Yes, I introduced them, but you can't blame me for your brother's stupidity. Clarence was sixty-three years old and Lynn made him feel like a young stud again. If Tessa couldn't hang on to him, why shouldn't Lynn have tried to land him?"

Richard stood, too, and freshened his drink. "Is that what marriage is to you? A hanging-on?"

But Alison had gone into the kitchen and appeared not to have heard when she returned with a large tray. As she began to arrange dishes and food on a low table in front of the couch, Liebchen put interested paws on the edge of the table, but Richard shoved him aside.

"There's no need to take it out on Liebchen," she said angrily.

"Come along, baby. Mummy has something nice for you in the kitchen."

On little short legs, the dachshund trotted after Alison and disappeared into the kitchen. Relieved, Tessa moved nearer to the screen.

When Alison reentered the room, she left the kitchen door closed and her flash of anger had been replaced by a mask of solicitude. She brought silverware, poured hot tea and spoke in soothing tones.

Richard ate mechanically, then stood up and reached for his jacket.

"Must you really go out again tonight, darling? Can't things wait till morning?"

"You know lawyers," he sighed. "Everything's going to be doubly complicated by the way he died."

"That's right," Alison said thoughtfully. "Murderers can't inherit from their victims, can they? No, don't pull away from me like that, darling. I feel just as badly for Tessa as you do, but we have to face up to it. Insane or not, she did kill him."

"Sorry." Richard straightened his tie. "I guess I just can't take it all in yet."

He went down the hall to his study and came back with his briefcase. Alison remained on the couch with her back to him. As Richard sorted through some papers, she said with careful casualness, "If they decide poor Tessa did kill him while of unsound mind and she later snaps out of it, would she then be able to inherit?"

"Probably not legally," Richard answered absently, his mind on the papers. "Wouldn't matter though, since we'd feel morally obliged to see she's fairly provided for."

"Oh, of course," Alison agreed, but her eyes narrowed.

Richard leaned over the couch and kissed her cheek. "I don't know how long this will take. If you're tired, don't wait up."

Alison smiled up at him, but once he was gone and the outer door had latched shut, her smile faded and was replaced by a look of greedy calculation.

Lost in thought, she gazed blindly at the dark square of the screened doorway, unaware of someone watching. Slowly, slowly, Tessa eased up on narrow haunches until lamplight hit her eyes—eyes that were slitted and glowed with abnormal intensity . . .

It was after midnight before Richard came home again. Lying awake on that wide bed, she heard him drop his briefcase on the floor inside his study, then continue on down the hall to the dimly lit bedroom. She held her breath as he opened the door and whispered, "Alison?"

"I'm awake." She turned between the linen sheets. "Oh, Richard, you look absolutely drained. Come to bed."

When at last he lay beside her in the darkness, she touched him shyly and said, "All evening I've been thinking about Tessa and Clarence—about their life together. I've been as rotten to you as he was to Tessa."

Richard made a sound of protest, but she placed slim young fingers against his lips. "No, dearest, let me say it. I've been thinking how empty their marriage was and how ours would be the same if I didn't change. I want to become a whole new person. Will you let me? Let me pretend we just met and that I barely know you? Start new? Please?"

"Alison—"

"No, let me finish. As soon as the funeral's over—as soon as we've arranged for the best legal and medical care that we can give Tessa—could we go away to the farm for a few weeks? Just the two of us?"

Incredulous, Richard propped himself on one elbow and peered into her face. "Do you really mean that?"

She nodded solemnly and he gathered her into his arms, but before he could kiss her properly, the night was broken by an angry, hissing cry.

He sat up abruptly. "What the devil's that?"

"Just a stray cat. It's been out on the terrace all evening."

With slender, eager arms, she pulled Richard back down to her, then pitched her voice just loud enough to carry through the screen to the terrace. "If it's still there in the morning, I'll call the animal shelter and have them take it away."

KITTY LITTER

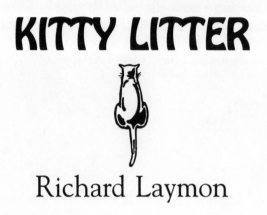

Richard Laymon

"SHE'S HERE FOR A KITTY!"

My flinch came to an end before the second word was out of her mouth, but my heart still thudded fast and hard. I'd thought I was alone, you see. I was stretched out on my lounge beside my backyard pool, surrounded by a redwood fence, enjoying a new 87th Precinct paperback, savoring the feel of the sunlight and the warm breeze.

The invasion took me by complete surprise.

After the jolt by the imperious voice, I jerked my head sideways and saw the girl.

Already, she was inside the gate and marching boldly toward me.

I knew right away who she was.

Monica from down the block.

Though we'd never actually met, I'd seen Monica around. And *heard* her. She had a loud, nasal voice which she operated primarily to snap back at her poor mother and berate her little friends.

I knew her name because she was often the subject of shouted warnings and threats. I also knew it because she used it herself. She belonged to the odd tribe that refers to itself in the third person.

She was about ten years old, I suppose.

If I had not been so unfortunate as to observe her behavior on previous occasions, I certainly would've been struck by the beauty of the girl striding toward me. She had rich brown hair, gleaming eyes, excellent facial features, a flawless complexion, and a slender body. She didn't look beautiful to me, however.

Nor did she look cute, though she wore a delightful outfit comprised of a pink cap with a jauntily upturned bill, a denim jumper, a white blouse, white knee socks and athletic shoes of pink to match her cap.

She was neither beautiful nor cute because she was Monica.

To my way of thinking, there is no such thing as a beautiful or cute snot.

She halted beyond the foot of my lounge and scowled at me. Her eyes flicked up and down my body.

My swimsuit had never been meant for public inspection. I quickly sheltered myself with the open book. It lay like a pitched roof atop my lap.

"You *are* Mr. Bishop?" she demanded.

"That's right."

"The man with the kitties?"

I nodded.

She nodded back at me. She bobbed on her toes. "And you're giving them away for free?"

"I'm hoping to find good homes for them, yes."

"Monica will have one, then."

"And who is Monica?" I asked, though obviously I knew the answer.

She pumped a small thumb against her chest, dead center between the denim straps of her jumper.

"You're Monica?" I asked.

"Of course."

"You want one of my kittens?"

"Where are they?"

In spite of my dislike for this particular child, I was eager to find homes for the kittens. My ad in the newspaper and the fliers I'd tacked to several neighborhood trees had not been a great success. Of the four kittens born to the litter, I still had three.

They were not getting any younger. Or any smaller.

Soon, they would pass out of the cute, romping, frisky kitten stage altogether. Who would want to adopt any of them, then?

In other words, I had no wish to be choosy. If Monica wanted a kitten, a kitten she would have.

"They're in my house," I said. "I'll bring them out for you to . . . inspect."

As I leaned forward on the lounge and wondered what to do about my immodest swimsuit, Monica scowled across the pool at the sliding glass door of my house.

"It isn't locked, is it?" she asked.

"No, but you stay . . ."

Ignoring me, she skipped off along the edge of the pool.

I took the opportunity to stand, set down my paperback, and snatch my beach towel off the lounge pad. Quickly, I wrapped the towel around my waist.

Corner tucked under to hold the towel, I hurried after Monica. She was already striding briskly past the far end of the pool.

"*I'll* get the kittens," I called to her. "You wait outside."

I did not want her in my house.

I did not want her to ogle my possessions. I did not want her to touch them, or break them or steal them. I did not want her to leave the taint of her pushy, pestilent *self* inside the sanctuary of my home.

She reached for the handle of the sliding door. Clutched it.

"Monica! No!"

"Don't have a cow, man," she said. And then she rumbled open the door and entered.

"Come out of there!" I yelled.

She hadn't gone far. Stepping over the runner, I spotted her standing near the center of my den. Her fists were planted on her hips as she swiveled her head from side to side.

"I asked you to stay outside."

"Where are they?"

I shrugged and sighed. She was in. There was no way to undo it. "This way," I said.

She followed me toward the kitchen.

"Why are you wearing that towel?" she asked.

"Because it suits me."

"Where'd your suit go?"

"It didn't go anywhere."

"Did you take it off?"

"No!"

"You'd better not've."

"I didn't. I assure you. I also assure you, young lady, that I'm on the very verge of asking you to leave."

A small wooden gate was stretched across the kitchen doorway to keep the kittens corralled. I hiked up my towel as if it were a skirt, and stepped over the gate.

I turned around to watch Monica. "Careful," I warned.

It would serve her right to fall and mash her impish little nose flat, I thought. But she swung one leg, then the other, over the top of the gate and made it to the other side without misadventure.

She sniffed. Her upper lip reached for the bottom of her nose. "What's that stink?"

"I don't detect a stink."

"Monica may barf."

"You might be smelling the litter box."

"Yug."

"There it is, now." I pointed at the plastic tub. Its desert landscape appeared a trifle bumpy. "You'll have to get used to some rather unpleasant aromas if you wish to keep a cat in . . ."

"Oh! Kitty!"

She rushed past me, dodged the table, and pranced to the far corner of the kitchen where the cats were at play on their blanket.

By the time I caught up to her, she had already made her pick.

She was on her knees, clutching Lazzy to her chest, stroking the little tabby's striped head.

Lazzy had a rather frantic look in her eyes, but she wasn't struggling much.

The kittens rubbed against Monica's knees, purring and meowing.

"She'll take this one," the girl said.

"I'm afraid she won't."

Monica slowly twisted herself around. Her eyes said, *How dare you!* Her mouth said, "Oh, yes she will."

"No. I offered you one of the kittens. That isn't one of the kittens."

"Of course she is! She's the tiniest, cutest little kitty of the bunch, and she'll go home with Monica."

"You may have one of the others."

"Who *wants* them? They're big! They aren't cute little kitties. *This* is the cute little kitty."

She nuzzled her cheek against Lazzy's face.

"You don't want that one," I said.

She started to get up. I grabbed her shoulder and pushed her down until she was on her knees again.

"Now you're in trouble," she said.

"No doubt."

"You touched Monica."

"You're a trespasser in my house. You came in uninvited even after I told you to stay out. You were preparing to leave with property that belongs to me. So I had every right to touch you."

"Oh, yeah?"

"Yeah."

"You'd better just let Monica take this cat home, right now, or else."

In spite of what I'd said about trespassing, etc., her threats could not be ignored. Here I was, a thirty-eight-year-old bachelor wearing next to nothing, alone in my house with a ten-year-old girl.

It wouldn't look good.

The notion of facing accusations sickened me.

"All right. If you want that cat, she's yours. Go on, take her and get out of here."

With a victorious grin, Monica rose to her feet. "Thank you," she said.

"If you want to know the truth, Lazzy always did give me the creeps."

"The creeps?"

"Never mind."

Monica narrowed her eyes. "What's wrong with her?"

"Nothing."

"Tell. You'd better tell, or else."

"Well . . ." I dragged a chair away from the kitchen table, swung it around, and sat down on it.

"Is this going to take long?"

Ignoring her question, I said, "It all started with Lazzy falling in the toilet."

She gasped as if the cat had suddenly turned white-hot, and tossed her aside.

Lazzy let out a *reeeeooow!* as she twisted and rolled through the air. But she did a quiet, four-point landing. Heading for the blanket, she glanced over her shoulder and gave Monica a look that was clearly miffed.

"You didn't have to throw her like that," I said.

"She fell in a *toilet!*"

"The toilet had nothing in it except for clean water. Besides, this was some time ago."

"You mean she isn't dirty any more?"

"She's perfectly clean."

"Then what's the big deal?"

"She drowned."

Monica tucked her chin down and gazed at me as if peering over the top of invisible eyeglasses. She folded her arms across her chest. I wondered if she had picked up the stance from an elderly relative. "Drowned?" she said. "Puh-leese."

"I'm serious," I said.

Monica tilted her head to one side. "If she drowned, she would be dead."

I chose not to argue. Instead, I proceeded with the story. "It began when Mrs. Brown gave birth. She was a tabby who belonged to my friend, James, in Long Beach. When he told me about the litter, I expressed an interest in taking one of the kittens off his hands. Of course, I couldn't take one immediately. I needed to wait until they'd been weaned."

Monica narrowed an eye. "What does that mean?"

"A kitty can't be taken away from its mother right away. It needs the mother's milk."

"Oh, that."

"Yes. At any rate, we set a date for me to visit James and select a kitten. Do you know where Long Beach is?"

She rolled her eyes toward the ceiling. "Monica has been to the Spruce Goose and the Queen Mary . . . oh, so many times that she is totally *bored* by them both."

"Then she knows that the drive takes about an hour from here."

She nodded. She sighed. She looked over her shoulder, apparently checking up on Lazzy.

I went on with my story.

"I drank quite a lot of coffee before setting out in the morning for Long Beach. By the time I reached James's house, I was very uncomfortable."

This won her attention away from the cat. "What?"

"I had to pee. Badly."

"Oh, for heaven's sake."

"I hurried to the front door and rang the doorbell. I rang it again and again, but James didn't answer. As it turns out, he had forgotten about our date, and gone shopping. I didn't know that at the time, however. I knew only that the door was not being opened, and that my teeth were afloat."

"You should not be talking to a child about such things."

"I'm afraid the condition of my bladder is integral to the story. Anyway, I was becoming frantic. I pounded on the door and called out James's name, but to no avail. I considered rushing over to a neighbor's house, but the idea appalled me. How could I ask a stranger for the use of a toilet? Besides, who would allow me inside for such a purpose? There were no gas stations, restaurants, or shopping malls near enough . . ." Monica interrupted me with a sigh. "Anyway, I had no choice but to let *myself* into James's house. It was either that or . . ."

"You are a very crude person."

"Not so crude that I wanted to pee outside. And fortunately, matters didn't reach that stage. At the back of the house, I found an open window. The screen was in my way, of course. But I was too desperate to care about niceties. I fairly tore the screen from its moorings, boosted myself through the window, tumbled onto the floor of James's bedroom, and raced for the bathroom.

"As it turned out, the bathroom was where James had been keeping the new litter—with the door shut, you know, so they wouldn't scamper all over the house. And to confine the aroma of the litter box, I'm sure."

"This is a *very* long story," Monica complained. "Long *and* gross."

"All right. I'll make it quick, then. I burst into the bathroom, pranced about to avoid mashing several kitties underfoot, and prepared to relieve myself. But when I looked down into the toilet bowl . . ."

"Lazzy," Monica said.

"Lazzy. Yes. Though, of course, that wasn't her name at the time. At any rate, she must've climbed onto the rim of the toilet for a drink, and tumbled in. She was floating on her side, her little face down in the water. I had no idea how long she might've been that way. But she wasn't moving at all. Not of her own accord. She was turning slightly as if being spun by a very slow, lazy whirlpool.

"Well, I fished her right out and laid her out on the floor. She looked horrid. Have you ever seen a dead cat?"

"She was *not* dead. She's right there." Monica pointed, her arm so straight and stiff that it seemed to be bent just a trifle bit the wrong way at the elbow.

Lazzy lay on her side, head up, licking one of her forelegs.

"She doesn't look dead now," I agreed, "but you should've

seen her shortly after I pulled her out of the toilet. She had that *awful* look—fur all matted down, ears flattened back. Her eyes were shut, so all you could see were dark slits. And she looked as if she'd died snarling." I bared my teeth at Monica to give her the idea.

Monica was doing her best to appear bored and annoyed and superior to all this. In spite of her efforts, however, she had a rather slack look to her face.

"The kitten was cold," I said. "Sopping. The feel of it sent chills through me. But that didn't stop me from examining the poor thing. It had no heartbeat."

"I'm sure," Monica said. But she was definitely looking a trifle distressed.

"The little kitten was dead."

"No, it wasn't."

"It had drowned in the toilet. It was as dead as dead can be."

"Was not!"

"Dead dead dead!"

Monica pounded her fists against her thighs. Red-faced, she snapped, "You're an *awful* person!"

"No, I'm not. I'm a very nice person, because I brought the dead kitten back to life. I rolled her onto her back and covered her little mouth with my mouth and breathed into her. At the same time, I used my thumb to push at her heart. Have you ever heard of CPR?"

Monica nodded. "CPR was a robot in *Star Wars*."

I was glad to find that she was not quite as smart as she thought she was.

"CPR stands for cardiopulmonary resuscitation. It's a technique used to revive people who . . ."

"Oh, *that!*" She suddenly looked very pleased with herself. And very prim and very superior. Her head dipped from one side to the other while her shoulders oscillated. "*So, the kitty wasn't* dead. Monica *told* you she wasn't dead."

"Oh, but she was very dead."

Monica shook her head. "Was not."

"She was dead, and I brought her back to life with the CPR.

Right there in the bathroom. Pretty soon, James came home. I told him what had happened, and he let me have the kitten I'd saved. So I named her Lazzy, short for Lazarus. Do you know who Lazarus was?"

"Of course."

"Who?"

"None of your business."

"Whatever you say. Anyway, I brought Lazzy home with me. And do you know what?"

Monica sneered at me.

"Lazzy never grew any larger after the day I brought her back from the dead. That was six years ago. She has been the size of a little kitty ever since. So you see, she's my pet. She's not part of the litter I want to give away. She's the *mother* of the litter."

"But she's *tinier* than they are!"

"*And* she's been dead."

Monica stared at Lazzy for a long while. Then she turned to me, no longer looking the least bit shaken. "She isn't *either* the mother. You made the whole thing up just so you could keep the cute one."

She rushed over to the blanket, snatched up Lazzy and hugged her and kissed the dark brown **M** on her honey-colored brow.

"Put her down," I said.

"No."

"Don't make me take her from you."

"You'd better not." She glanced at the kitchen doorway behind me. "You'd better get out of the way, or you'll be in very very bad trouble."

"Put down Lazzy. You may still take one of the other kittens, but . . ."

"Get out of the way," she said, and walked straight toward me.

"As soon as you've . . ."

"Mr. Bishop said, 'Come into my house. I have a little kitty for you.'" She halted and leered at me. "But when Monica went into his house, he told her a urine story and he took off the towel he was wearing and he said, 'This is the little kitty I have for you. His name is Peter.' "

I could only gasp, "You!"

"And he told me to pet Peter and kiss Peter. I didn't *want* to do it, but he grabbed me and . . ."

"Stop it!" I blurted, and stumbled sideways out of her way. "Take the cat! Take her and get out of here!"

As she strutted by, taking away my Lazzy, she winked at me. "Thank you so much for the kitten, Mr. Bishop."

I watched her leave.

Just stood and stared as she sashayed through the den and stepped over the threshold of the open sliding door. Immediately after setting foot on the concrete, she burst into a run.

Apparently afraid I might find a smidgen of nerve and attempt to retrieve my cat.

But I didn't move a muscle.

An accusation such as she had threatened to make . . . How does one disprove such a thing? One doesn't. Such an accusation, once made, would cling to me like leprous skin for all the days of my life.

I would forever be known as a pervert, a child molester.

So I let her *steal* my dear Lazzy.

I stood frozen with terror and *let* her.

And from outside came a familiar *reeooow!* followed by a quick harsh yelp—the sort of yelp a girl might make if the cat in her arms decided to claw its way to freedom—followed by a thudding splash.

I still stood motionless.

No longer terrified.

Amused, actually.

The poor dear. Fell and got herself all wet.

Lazzy leaped over the threshold and came scampering through the den, fur abristle over the ridge of her spine, her tiny ears swept back, tail curled up in a small, bushy question mark.

She slowed down, then rubbed her side against my bare ankle.

I picked up my tiny little cat. I held her in front of my face with both hands.

From outside came more splashing sounds.

Cries of "Help!" and "Help!"

Was it possible that Monica's bag of tricks did not include swimming?

I dared not get my hopes up.

There were no more cries for help. I did hear some choky gasps and quite a good deal of splashing, however, before silence replaced the disturbance.

I carried Lazzy out to poolside.

Monica was at the deep end. Face down, arms and legs spread out, hair drifting above her head, blouse and jumper shimmering slightly.

She rather looked like a skydiver enjoying a freefall, waiting for the very last moment to pull her ripcord.

"I suppose I ought to pull her out," I told Lazzy. "Give her some CPR."

Then I shook my head.

"No. Not a good idea—a man my age putting his hands on a ten-year-old girl? What would people say?"

I headed for the sliding glass door.

"Why don't we go pay a visit to James? Who knows, maybe someone will be lucky enough to find Monica while we're away."

Lazzy purred, her little body vibrating like a warm engine.

A LONG TIME SITTING

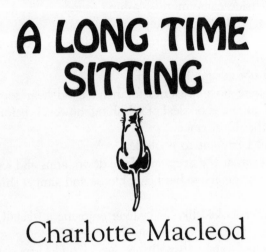

Charlotte Macleod

SHE HAD BEEN SITTING there a very long time. She had no notion
of how long, it didn't matter. Nothing mattered. Nothing had
mattered for many years. There seemed to be no life left in her,
she sat quite immobile in her rush-seated chair, the folds of her
long black gown lying just as they had fallen when she'd last sat
down, her eyes fixed on the one red coal that still glowed in the
fireplace. Only her mind still worked, carrying her to far-off
worlds.

Lost in her thought, she did not hear the taxi drive up the
overgrown lane or the key turn in the lock that had not been
turned all the while she had been sitting. Yet she was not surprised when the door was pushed open and a woman came into
the kitchen, a pale, thin woman who smiled and spoke.

"Oh! How do you do? I didn't expect—that is, Mr. Mowl at
the real estate office seemed to think—but what a nice surprise
to find you here. Are you Mrs. Hittle?"

Was she? She supposed she must have been, once. For a long

time she'd been invisible, apparently that was no longer so. Mowl must have told this woman that the owner of the cottage was dead, perhaps he was right. She moved not a muscle, spoke not a word, the woman seemed not at all disconcerted. She was young, she looked oddly dressed, but perhaps fashions had changed. She was putting a bagful of groceries and another filled with cleaning supplies on the bare wooden table, going back outside to bring in two large blue suitcases. Then she was planning to stay.

The old woman was not surprised to have acquired a tenant, nothing surprised her, but she did feel a small, long-forgotten sense of obligation to her house. The front bedroom must be cleaned, a bed made ready with lavender-scented sheets, a bright patchwork quilt, plump down-filled pillows. It was a tight squeeze, but she managed. The young woman called down, "Mrs. Hittle, it's beautiful!"

Feeling some slight nudge of satisfaction, the old woman willed the groceries into the pantry and the cleaning stuff into the broom closet, wafted a yellow tablecloth over the dingy table top, and directed the kettle to fill the teapot. What next? Food, that was it, there should be something to go with the tea. Scones were all she could think of, a plate of warm scones. It was not until she heard the young woman coming downstairs that she remembered the raisins, she tucked the last one in without a moment to spare and set the fire to dancing.

"How dear of you to make the tea. And fresh scones, too! You really mustn't spoil me like this, Mrs. Hittle, I'd expected to fend for myself. I'm Jenny Wrenne, in case Mr. Mowl didn't tell you. I'm an artist. Sort of one anyway, I paint little vignettes for greeting cards. It doesn't pay much, but it's fun."

While she was chatting, Jenny Wrenne had been fetching the cups, pouring the tea, carrying a cupful and a scone on a little plate over to the old woman before she fixed her own, bringing her chair over by the fire. Not too close, she wasn't pushy like the animal who was shoving his way in through the leather-hinged cat hole.

"What a gorgeous cat!"

Beauty was clearly in the eye of the beholder. Asphodemus, for that was his name, although nobody but he and the old woman knew it, was overlarge and bony of frame, gangly in the legs, frayed about the ears, lumpy in the tail, ragged and unkempt of pelt. Perhaps Jenny Wrenne's artist's eye was able to penetrate through the disreputable outer integument to the noble heart within, or maybe she was just sick and tired of painting cute kitties with bows around their necks. Anyway, she and Asphodemus took to each other right away although there could be no doubt in the cat's agile mind as to where his true allegiance lay. He rubbed against Jenny's legs, permitted her to serve him a saucer of milk and a corner of buttered scone with the raisins considerately picked out (Jenny ate them herself), then went to curl up in the old woman's lap.

The tea that the new tenant had poured for her silent hostess sat untouched until Jenny went back upstairs to get her painting materials, then Asphodemus made quick work of it and went back to sleep. Jenny would have liked to sketch Mrs. Hittle but didn't think she should go ahead without asking permission; it seemed too early in their acquaintance for that. She did move Asphodemus in her mind's eye to the hearth rug and paint a charming idealization of him with the firelight bringing out red gold glints in his ruddy coat, his ears nicely evened off around the edges, and an expression of content on his face.

The cat would look ever so distinguished, if not precisely handsome, if he'd wash more often and take better care of his whiskers, Jenny thought. As though he had read her mind, Asphodemus woke up and began to tidy himself. Despite his contortions, the old woman did not stir, but sat as she had been, gazing straight into the dancing flames. How long had it been since her fire had last burned clear?

She began willing away the cobwebs that had gathered inside the fireplace, and along the ceiling beams, running her mind like a vacuum cleaner into all the corners where dust had collected. She had been a good housekeeper back then; no dried bats or fillets of fenny snakes cluttering up her kitchen, she had been above such petty chicaneries. Not that she had been a good woman. She had been a particularly wicked woman and a first-class sorceress, until she had committed the arrogant folly of laying an extra-powerful curse without first erecting herself a safety net of protective charms. The curse had backfired, locking her here in limbo bereft of speech, of movement, of all physical functions, with no living soul except Asphodemus to look after her. He was an old cat now, each of his nine lives had been a long one but the last of them was by now nearly spent. She would, and this surprised her, miss him when he crossed over.

Was it possible that she retained some tiny grain of human feeling despite the backfired curse? Was the mild pleasure she'd been getting from utilizing what little power she still possessed to sweep away the cobwebs and conjure up a clean bed for an unexpected guest based on something other than the retained vanity of a once houseproud woman? This was something new to think about, she had not thought about anything new for a great span of time. She willed the woodbox full and sent another log to the fire. Intent on getting Asphodemus's whiskers just right, Jenny Wrenne didn't notice.

The afternoon was wearing on, Jenny began wondering about lamps and candles. There was no electricity in the cottage, Mr. Mowl had told her that much anyway. No telephone either, and no running water. But that pump in the sink must work because Mrs. Hittle's kettle had been full. Mr. Mowl had cautioned Jenny to boil the water before she drank, the house had not been occupied for a long time and he could not guarantee the well.

The taxi driver had laughed when she'd told him she was going to live in the old Hittle house, he wouldn't tell her why. Perhaps he'd known, as Mr. Mowl seemed not to, that the owner was still in residence and that, despite its lack of modern amenities, the house was beautifully kept and very comfortable. Jenny felt rather embarrassed about all those cleaning supplies Mr. Mowl had seemed to think she would need, she hoped they had not offended her landlady. Maybe that was why Mrs. Hittle still wasn't speaking to her.

No, Jenny could feel no atmosphere of disapproval, and she

was good at atmospheres. More likely, Mrs. Hittle had suffered a stroke that left her bereft of speech and perhaps awkward in her movements. That would explain why she preferred not to leave her chair in her new tenant's presence. She must manage well enough when she was alone, to have prepared that lovely tea so quickly.

Well, Jenny could talk enough for two, she'd just as soon be doing the chores herself but she wasn't about to quarrel if Mrs. Hittle chose to run the house her own way. She was in no position to quarrel, she'd come here for the sole reason that she couldn't find another place cheaper to rent. Her greeting card designs were nothing special, even so she couldn't turn them out fast enough to earn more money than would barely keep her head above water. Mr. Mowl had been almost contemptuous when she'd told him how little she could afford, he hadn't troubled himself even to show her where the cottage stood.

Perhaps that was just as well. If he'd seen how nice the place was inside, he'd surely have asked a higher rent. It was too late now, she'd signed the lease and paid her deposit, he couldn't back out if he wanted to. Jenny added one last triumphant whisker to the cat's noble face. There, her sketch was done. She did feel a trifle odd about not having tied a red bow around the cat's neck as greeting card convention required, but her artistic soul had rebelled against it. He was not the type for ribbons and frills.

This painting had turned out to be quite different from Jenny's usual style, it was the best thing she'd done in ages, maybe her best ever. She would, she decided, try a whole series of paintings with so splendid a model. But not tonight, it was getting dark, time to clear away her paints and think about supper. She'd planned to have sardines on toast as a special treat for her first night in her new lodging. It would be only decent to share with Mrs. Hittle and the cat, but would one small canful stretch to feed three? Jenny was an optimist and besides, they'd had that lovely tea not so long ago. Too bad the scones were all gone, but she'd brought a loaf of bread.

Making toast over an open fire sounded romantic. However, it might be safer to try the black iron stove where the kettle was singing again, though she hadn't been aware of its gentle purr before now. Nor had she noticed the funny little hatlike contraption that could only be an old-fashioned tin toaster. The cat probably wouldn't care for toast, he could have the sardine oil instead, it would be good for his coat.

The toaster worked well enough. Jenny laid browned slices on two flowered china plates she'd found in the cupboard and arranged an even third of the sardines for each of them, adding a garnish of lettuce and tomato from her grocery bag to provide extra vitamins and make the servings appear less meager. She set what remained in the can down on the hearth for the cat to eat, and carried a filled plate, a cup of tea, a fork and a napkin to Mrs. Hittle, all prettily set out on a tray with more flowers painted on it. This house was full of charming surprises, why had she been led to suppose it was little more than a shack?

The old woman was making no sign that she knew the food was there, but that was all right, Jenny was getting used to Mrs. Hittle's odd ways. She went back to the table and sat down to her supper with an appetite too hearty for the small amount of food before her. At least she'd thought it was; somehow these sardines turned out to be more filling than sardines usually were. She ate them slowly, in tiny bites, thinking how much better they tasted than all the other sardines she'd ever eaten. Perhaps it was the stove-browned toast that made the difference.

The tomato and lettuce seemed almost too much of a good thing, by the time she'd finished the last bite she felt altogether replete and ready to fall asleep. She rinsed her plate and cup under the pump, which worked beautifully, refilled the kettle, set it back on the stove, and excused herself to her landlady and cat. Mrs. Hittle wouldn't mind the new tenant's going, she still hadn't touched her supper, it would be only courteous of Jenny to let her eat in peace.

While Jenny was struggling into the lavender-smelling bed and pulling the bright patchwork quilt up around her ears, Asphodemus was finishing Mrs. Hittle's sardines, toast and all. He didn't even much mind having to eat the lettuce and tomato, meals had been few and far between here over the years. The old woman had been too far off in that other place to give more than an occasional thought to feeding her familiar, he'd had to catch most of his breakfasts and suppers before he could eat them. He was sick and tired of spitting out fur and feathers, not to mention bones and beaks. A cat his age was used to a little pampering and some variety in his diet, though Asphodemus did hope this new member of the household would lay off the tomato next time it was her turn to cook.

Come morning, Jenny woke to the smell of coffee brewing and bacon frying. Mrs. Hittle and her pet must already have breakfasted, an empty plate and cup were draining on the sinkboard and the cat was looking smug. Jenny's plateful of fried eggs, bacon, hashed brown potatoes, and two perfectly browned pieces of toast was keeping warm on the back of the stove. She ate every bite and was glad to get it, when it was all gone she went over and kissed Mrs. Hittle on the cheek. Then she got out her paints and sketching pad, coaxed the big cat outdoors, and spent a happy day on a perfectly splendid painting of him sitting on the doorstep like a king on a throne.

And so it went, Mrs. Hittle never moving, never speaking, but always having Jenny's breakfast warming on the stove no matter what time she got up, Jenny and the cat going off to some picturesque spot where he could pose and she could paint. If it rained, they stayed indoors and found some equally beguiling spot, often one that Mrs. Hittle had arranged for them only moments before they got there, though of course Jenny didn't know that. The cat could not have been a more obliging model, the artist's brush had never before been plied so deftly or so productively.

Somehow the housework got done while Jenny was painting, somehow the limited supply of groceries she'd brought with her had not yet run out. Mrs. Hittle must have both a root cellar and a preserve closet somewhere, though Jenny had not yet seen either. Potatoes, carrots, green stuff, jars of fruit, pickles, even jams and honey would be lying on the table when Jenny and the cat got back from their day's work. Jenny would contribute whatever she could and prepare a meal, always different, always good. The cat's fur was beginning to shine, his gaunt frame to fill out, he was washing regularly and thoroughly now, he was even beginning to purr a little now and then, when he happened to think of it.

As the days passed, Jenny's paintings accumulated, each of them better than the one before. Counting them up, she was astonished to find that she had almost two weeks' worth. How could the time have gone by so fast? She must quit having such a good time and become more businesslike. Much as she loved gloating over her finished works, she could not afford to keep them here, they must be mailed off to the greeting card company before another month's rent came due and she found herself with no money to pay.

It was only a two-mile walk to the village, the taxi driver had told her so. She could ask him to bring her back if she felt too tired to carry the groceries she must buy, she must not continue to batten on Mrs. Hittle's bounty as she'd been doing. Jenny explained all this to Mrs. Hittle and the cat, made up her stack of sketches into a neat package for mailing, and set off down the road. Mrs. Hittle felt a distinct twinge of disappointment when the door closed behind Jenny. Why should this be so? Now she had yet another new thing to think about.

Mrs. Hittle was not the only one to be given food for thought that day. A jowly man with a rather mean-looking mouth was just leaving the post office with his mail when a smiling young woman carrying a large brown envelope said to him, "Why, hello, Mr. Mowl."

At first he didn't recognize her, she looked about ten years younger and a good deal rosier than the pale, thin woman who'd shown up in his real estate office a couple of weeks ago, looking for a cheap place to live. He'd rented her the old Hittle place, sight unseen, there was no other way it would ever get rented. In fact, however, Mr. Mowl had done pretty well out of the old Hittle place over the years, always insisting on a six-month lease, always collecting a deposit in advance, almost invariably having the would-be tenants storming into his office the next morning claiming the place was unlivable and demanding their money back; always letting them know, gently but firmly, that they couldn't have it. This young woman had actually spoken pleasantly to him, what could have gone wrong?

Mowl put out a cautious feeler. "Things going along all right out there, Miz Wrenne?"

"Oh yes, everything's wonderful!" Too late Jenny realized she'd sounded far too enthusiastic, she tried to back off. "That is, it's adequate for my purposes. I'm outside sketching most of the time. Of course without electricity or running water . . ." she couldn't think of anything really negative to say about the Hittle house, she was simply no good at lying.

"Awful nuisance having nothing to cook on but an open fire, though, isn't it? And sitting in the dark by yourself every night must get kind of lonesome."

Then Mr. Mowl hadn't the faintest idea what the house was like, or that Mrs. Hittle was still living there! How could he be taking on tenants and issuing leases without knowing where to send the owner her share of money from the rents? Maybe he thought his client was still in the hospital on account of her stroke. Should Jenny explain that she'd come back? No! It was his to find out, not hers to tell. She was quite put out with Mr. Mowl.

"Oh, I manage well enough," she said shortly. "I'm a working woman, you know, I must get this package in the mail to my publishers. So nice to see you, Mr. Mowl."

It hadn't been nice at all, but polite lies didn't count. Jenny mailed her sketches and went on to the market. As people always do, she bought more than she had intended and was standing on the sidewalk, debating whether she could afford to take the taxi now that she'd overspent her budget buying little dainties to tempt Mrs. Hittle, and how she'd get her purchases home if she didn't get a ride, when who should drive by but Mr. Mowl.

"Hop in, Miz Wrenne, I'll run you back."

Burdened as she was, Jenny still didn't want to accept. "Oh no, I mustn't put you to the trouble."

"No trouble at all. I've got business out your way."

He was out of the car, snatching away her bundles before she could resist. She'd just have to tell him to let her off at the roadside because the lane wasn't drivable, Jenny decided. Actually the lane wasn't too bad, though not very good, but the car was new and elegant, surely he wouldn't want it all scratched up. Anyway, a lift was a lift and she really could not have afforded the taxi. She got in and spent the short ride trying to evade Mr. Mowl's searching questions, which seemed to add up to why she wasn't furious with him for sticking her out at the old Hittle place. She thought of a few things she'd have liked to ask him in return, but knew better than to start a conversation she might not be able to control.

She might have known she couldn't control Mr. Mowl either. Despite her protests, he swung into the lane and drove right up to the house. Jenny herself had been doing a little weeding and pruning, little could she reck that Mrs. Hittle had beguiled the morning tidying up the house itself: causing shingles to be replaced, straightening the roof line where the ridgepole had sagged, rehanging shutters that had dangled by one hinge or fallen off entirely, even giving them a fresh lick of green paint. Jenny herself didn't notice particularly as this was how her mind's eye had envisioned the cottage all the time, but Mowl almost threw a conniption.

"What the Sam Hill's been going on here?"

"I don't know what you mean, Mr. Mowl," said Jenny with a new dignity that she'd learned from Asphodemus. "May I have my bundles please?"

"B-buh—phm'f—ar—num. I'll carry them in for you."

"No, please don't. Mrs. Hittle may be sleeping, I don't want her disturbed."

"Mrs. Hittle?" Mowl gave Jenny a very odd look. Then he bulldozed his way past her, caught one horrified glimpse of the silent old woman sitting in front of the fireplace, dropped the bags of groceries on the floor, and fled. As Jenny went to pick up the scattered foodstuffs, she was relieved to hear him driving away, a good deal faster than he ought to be driving on that narrow, rutted lane. She hoped he'd stay away.

But he didn't. Mowl's cupidity was great enough to overcome his cowardice. Once back in his own house he sacrificed a couple of perfectly good silver spoons and melted them down to make silver bullets, he told himself that he could always reclaim the bullets afterward and try his hand at turning them back into spoons. He loaded an old horse pistol of his great-grandfather's, it was high time he got some use out of the weapon, and drove back up the lane the following night under cover of darkness.

That young woman who called herself Wrenne, she had to be a witch, or a wizard in disguise he told himself. She, or he, or maybe it must surely be in league with the powers of darkness. How else could she have brought back that evil hag from wherever the old besom had been for the past hundred years or so?

Mowl could remember his own grandparents talking about the old woman in hushed voices. He'd been startled to learn that his great-grandfather had died in some strange and horrible way on account of a woman named Hittle, a woman dressed all in black from head to toe, who'd sat in front of her fireplace still as a statue and worked her devilish spells.

After the earlier Mr. Mowl's terrible death, a few bold souls had gone to Mrs. Hittle's house. Too awed to wreak the vengeance they'd had in mind, they'd found her sitting there in her old rush-seated chair, silent, unmoving. They'd watched her in relays night and day for a whole week long, she'd never batted an eyelid. On the seventh day Mrs. Hittle had gradually faded away and never been seen since. But there was always a coldness in front of the fireplace, no matter how high the fire was built up. And every time anybody tried to move that old rush-seated chair out of the way, it would scoot right back to the spot where she'd been sitting.

That stubborn chair was the main thing that had always so far put tenants off staying, that and the feeling that somebody was in the house, not doing anything, just being there. Nobody wanted an invisible presence butting in on their privacy, Mr. Mowl could hardly blame them for that. What he planned to do with those silver bullets was no more than any decent, respectable resident with a sense of civic responsibility ought to be proud and honored to do for the good of the community.

Fixed up the way it was now, that cottage could be bringing in a pretty penny in local real estate tax dollars, not to mention a hefty commission for a smart real estate agent. Mowl would have to fiddle the paperwork, that would be no great problem except for the lease he'd got Miz Wrenne to sign. Well, that was just too bad for Miz Wrenne, there was a sinkhole down back over the hill plenty big enough to hold both the young witch and the old one. Who'd ever know? He tossed off a heartening jolt of whiskey to prove he wasn't a bit scared and set off on his civic betterment project.

The moon had been shining brightly when he'd left the village. Now a cloud must have come over it or something, it was pitch black out here on the back road. He'd have missed his turnoff if it hadn't been for a damn great big tomcat's green eyes catching his headlights as he rounded a curve. Mowl had always hated cats, he swerved deliberately to run this critter over, missed it, but found himself just where he wanted to be, heading straight for the old Hittle place.

Fortune favored the brave, or the slightly drunk. Grasping his horse pistol, making sure his powder was dry, Mowl left the car and advanced on the cottage. Something scooted ahead of him and seemed to pass right through the closed door. He almost dropped the gun, then emitted a sigh of relief. Only that cussed cat going in through its cat hole. Might have known a witch could keep a cat around. Well, she wouldn't have it much longer, he'd see to that. The door wasn't locked. That figured, the old key was iron. Witches wouldn't touch iron. He turned the knob and strode inside.

Yes, there she sat, stiff as a waxwork, just the way he'd seen her the day before, only now the cat was up on her lap. Great big orange thing with eyes like a panther's, he'd teach it to glare at him like that. Mr. Mowl raised his pistol.

Consarned trigger was stuck, it wouldn't budge. Mowl worked at the gun frantically, in a panic now, all his cowardice to the fore. "Damn you, fire!" he roared.

His shout woke Jenny, she leaped out of bed and flew down the stairs in her nightgown and bare feet, spied the frenzied man waving the pistol and the spitting cat standing up on Mrs. Hittle's lap, back arched, eyes flashing green fire. She rushed to shield them with her own body.

"No! Don't hurt them!"

Then everything happened at once. Asphodemus sprang clear over Jenny's head, straight at Mr. Mowl. The gun went off, the first silver bullet passed straight through the cat and struck Jenny in the shoulder. Stunned by the impact, she dropped to the floor beside the murdered cat. Mowl reloaded, cocked the pistol again, sent his second bullet into Mrs. Hittle's back, turned and fled the house. Still too stunned to move, Jenny heard his car start and go pell mell down the lane. He would crash. He did. The car exploded, the blast brought Jenny to her feet. Her first coherent thought was for the old woman.

"Mrs. Hittle! Mrs. Hittle! Oh, please speak. Are you badly hurt?"

"Yes, my dear." The voice was gentle, almost musical. "Be happy for me, I am released. I'll be going now, you stay here. Asphodemus will take care of you, as he did of me."

"Asphodemus? The cat? But—but he's dead. Mr. Mowl shot him. And I never even knew his name!"

"It's all right, Jenny. Everything will work out. I promise." Rising with no sign of stiffness from the chair she had so long occupied, Mrs. Hittle put her hand for a moment on the wound in Jenny's shoulder. At once the bleeding stopped, the bullet hole healed, the bloodstains faded from Jenny's nightgown, and a small tear in the cloth was invisibly mended. Mrs. Hittle then stooped over the body of her late familiar, and whispered something Jenny couldn't hear. He vanished, Jenny could not repress a sniffle.

"I hate to see him go. I—I loved him so."

"Don't worry, Jenny, Asphodemus will be back. You may kiss me goodbye if you want to."

Perhaps it was the kiss that broke the spell. Mrs. Hittle was gone, Asphodemus was gone, Jenny was alone. Strangely, she didn't mind. She knew there was no sense in her going to see what had happened to Mr. Mowl, whatever it was, he'd asked for it. But now whom would she pay her rent to?

Time enough to think of that later. She went back to bed and slept soundly, waking up an hour later than usual because there was nobody left to fix her breakfast. She made toast and a pot of coffee, she was sitting at the table drinking her second cup when a man came to the door, a youngish man with hair the color of burnished brass with coppery highlights and a beard to match. It was a beautiful beard, short and silky, that matched his hair and all but covered his face. His eyes were a magical clear green. He was carrying a kitten, a tiny orange tiger, adorable as all kittens were but somehow not the type to have a ribbon around its neck.

"Good morning," said the man. "Is this your kitten? And are you Miss Hittle?"

"No, I'm only a tenant. My name is Jenny Wrenne. Mrs. Hittle has—passed away."

"Then there are no Hittles left around here at all?"

The taxi driver had told Jenny there weren't. "None," she said. "She was the last."

"But this is the old Hittle house?"

"Oh, yes."

"Then it looks as if I'm your new landlord." He showed Jenny his driver's license. Hittle, the name was. A. James Hittle.

"Is the A for Asphodemus?" she asked with her heart in her mouth.

"Almost. Actually, it's for Amadeus, my mother was a Mozart freak. What made you ask?"

"I had to know. Then this must be Asphodemus." She took the kitten from him. "Do come in. And make yourselves at home, both of you."

She didn't have to say that, they already were. As Mrs. Hittle had promised, it was going to be all right.

CAT LADY

Carolyn Wheat

THE KNOCK AT THE DOOR made her jump, nearly out of her skin. She dropped the cracked coffee mug, spilling the dregs of her strong, black coffee on the floor. The family scattered—kittens tumbling under tables, tomcats jumping onto shelves and knocking off knicknacks. Aunt Jemima, the big black longhair, scrunched herself down and crept toward the coffee. When she reached the scalding puddle, the cat lowered a dainty pink tongue and began to lap up the spill. "Don't, baby," the old lady pleaded, hoisting herself out of her overstuffed armchair with a thrust of powerful arms. "Caffeine'll keep you awake all night."

Reluctantly, she plodded toward the door. *Oh, God, who would come here? Nobody with half a brain, that's for sure. Nobody who had a better place to go.*

She stopped, looking around at the mess. "Can't let anyone in," she muttered. "Not till I redd up a bit." She bustled about, emptying ashtrays, hiding her unfinished breakfast under the bed, plopping dirty clothes in the sink. *Oh, God, they couldn't know, could they? I was so careful.*

She took a deep breath of cat-odor-laden air and shuffled

toward the door. As she went, she mumbled, "I'm comin', I'm comin'. Keep your paws on."

Her sweaty palm reached for the doorknob. She hoped its coolness would calm her somehow, but instead the knob got as damp and sooty as her unwashed hand.

She opened the door a crack, peering out suspiciously. "Who's there?" she asked. *They won't answer. They're too smart for that.*

She was right; there was no answer. *I suppose I've got to; they'll just come back.*

As she pulled the heavy door toward her, it brushed against a gray tabby, big with unborn kittens. The cat stared up at her with unforgiving eyes, then stalked away, tail held high. "Sorry, Cleo," she murmured.

It was a man. A man in a suit! *Oh, God, it can't be the Health!* Her heart thumped wildly, and she clutched at her bosom. *Not the Health!*

"Miz Jasperson," the man said in a rusty voice that evidently hadn't been used in some time, "I'd like to come in, if I may."

"Well, I don't know," she said doubtfully. She looked past him toward the front yard. Maybe there was someplace there they could sit and conduct their business. She looked at the tree, dead from the blight seven years ago. In the lowest branch, crouched expectantly, perched Primrose, her calico cat. The once-painted bench beneath it was rotted and sawdusty, being eaten by termites before her very eyes. The deaf white kitten she called Beethoven lay sleeping in the shade behind it. In the tall, unmown grass next to the rusty lawnmower that seemed to have tired out one day and just stopped stood the back seat of a 1967 Ford. *Maybe we could sit there and talk*—no, she wasn't *that* crazy. People didn't sit in back seats of cars when there wasn't any car there anymore. Even when that back seat didn't house a whole family of Siamese.

They're closing in. My God, they're closing in. Busybody neighbors—I hope they fry in hell.

"Why can't you just go away?" she whispered, talking less to her visitor than to herself.

"Official business, ma'am," the man replied. "I could come back with the sheriff, but I wouldn't want—"

"Oh, all right," she grumbled, turning. "You better come inside. Just don't step on the moggies."

The moggies jumped and scattered, circled and skittered, meowing and hissing and purring like a feline tornado. The man from the Health stepped back, alarm on his face. "How—how many *are* there?" he asked, his fingers plucking at his pants leg.

As if he didn't know. As if those Nosy Parkers didn't tell him everything. Well, I'll go along with it. I'll pretend I'm the fool they think I am.

"Forty-seven," she said in a tone that wavered between defiance and pride. "Andromeda had a new litter last night. One poor darling died, but five lived, so now there's forty-seven all told."

Just then Big Tom came in, making an entrance as always, his huge orange body a pleasure to watch as he strode like a sultan past his harem, his bushy tail brushing her leg. He faced the stranger, challenge in his laid-back ears and swishing tail.

The Health raised a shaking hand. "Nice kitty," he croaked.

"He's a monster," she informed him with relish. "Ate a whole boot once."

The Health, sidling backward, said he could believe it. He bumped into a chair and began to lower himself into it, then jumped up when an indignant squeak told him he'd just sat on a pair of Siamese kittens.

"Frankie and Johnny, you move now," she said in a brisk tone, "and let the man from the Health sit down."

"Ah, Miz Jasperson?" He made it a question, like he'd suddenly forgotten whom he'd come to visit. "I'm not from the Health, I'm from the Internal Revenue Service."

As if I'd believe that! Those people at the Health must really take me for a porcupine! What business would I have with Revenuers, and me a teetotaller?

"It seems, ma'am," the Health went on, still playing his little game, "you haven't paid your taxes in, oh, seventeen years."

"Well, I make it eighteen," she said affably, "but then maybe

I've got it wrong." She reached down without looking and deftly picked up a tiny black kitten. She held it in one strong hand, stroking its tiny neck with huge fingers.

"Uh, ma'am, seventeen or eighteen, it's still a long time, and Uncle Sam—"

"Uncle Sam wants *you*," she said with a deep, throaty chuckle, pointing her catless hand at the man from the Health. He shrank back, then laughed unconvincingly. Worry lines sprang up on his pale forehead, and just stayed there.

"Don't you remember the war? My brother Faron went. He said if Uncle Sam wanted him, then he was going to give the man what he asked for. Got to go to Paris, France and everything. A regular doughboy."

"Oh, *that* war," the man replied, running his hand over his wrinkled forehead and rubbing hard.

They didn't even send me a smart one this time. Never heard of the Great War.

The man reached into his pocket. "I have a paper here," he began.

"Never read 'em," she said firmly. "Ever since they was wrong about Tom Dewey. Newspapers got nothing to say to *me*."

"It's not a newspaper." The man was raising his voice. *Like he was talking to a foreigner or something.* "It's a lien on this property, for back taxes. The government's going to take your house."

He was looking at the cats, at Big Tom especially. She could almost hear him thinking: what if one of them jumps on me, or claws at me? What if they sink those fangs into my legs? She knew what they said about her in town, called her a witch and her sweet darlings demon familiars. She chuckled inside, thinking of this city slicker falling for that old story. He shrank back in his chair as Asmodeus, the three-legged patriarch of her clan, sidled past in his ungainly way. Then he rubbed his forehead so hard he made red marks on the pale skin.

"Got a headache?" she asked, leaning over and setting the kitten on the floor with a gentle pat on its tiny rear end. The kitten mewed and scampered under the chair in which the man sat. All around him swirled a storm of cats. He watched them uneasily, with the air of a man who had never really *trusted* cats. "Yes," he admitted in a weak voice, "a *bad* headache."

"Let me rub your temples," she purred, walking over to the chair. Just as she moved toward him, the three-legged feline leapt into his lap. The man squeaked, brushing at the animal with ineffectual hands. Stepping behind his chair, she placed her giant fingers on his throbbing head and began, slowly, lazily, to make circles.

"No, really," he protested. "It's all right. I don't need any . . ." His voice trailed off. The lines on his forehead smoothed themselves out.

The man leaned back in the chair, which was covered with a thick layer of soft cat hair. He drowsed, letting his head fall back, as her massaging hands made gentle movements. She felt his muscles relax; he was limp.

I've got him now! Just like the other one. The Health isn't going to tell me how many children I can have!

She snapped his neck with one powerful twist of her thick wrist. Killing chickens on the farm when she was a girl had turned out to be the best training she'd ever had. Asmodeus jumped off the stranger's lap and hobbled toward the kitchen.

She reached into his wallet and pulled out a card. "Oh, my God," she said to Big Tom, "he *was* from the Revenue, after all!" *I can't figure what they'd want with me; Lord knows, there's no still up here.*

"Unless that's just another trick," she continued, addressing her favorite pet. "After all, that last one said he was from the County, but *we* knew better, didn't we, Tomkins?"

I thought sure this one was the Health. I know they're coming; I just don't know when.

Then she shrugged her powerful shoulders and walked into the kitchen. Pausing to take the clothes out of the sink, she reached into the cabinet and pulled out an enormous meat grinder.

She hefted the meat grinder onto the zinc table and took a saw down from the wall.

Cleo came into the room, her swollen body with its pink tits dragging down her spindly legs. Big Tom walked over and sniffed her, biting her ear for old times' sake. Frankie and Johnny tumbled on the floor in an all-out wrestling match. "That's right, babies," she said. "Anything I love to see, it's my sweet ones having a good time."

She lifted the old washtub and set it under the table, directly underneath the meat grinder. She unearthed a meat cleaver and laid it on the counter, ready to hand.

"The Lord," she explained to her family, "helps those who help themselves." *And, the Lord knows, it takes a lot of meat to feed forty-seven cats.*

She was just about finished when there came another knock at the door. *Finally! The Health!*

THE NEW BLACK CAT

Bill Crider

IT WAS THE CAT'S FAULT.

There are those who will say, of course, that what I write is not possible, that it is merely the raving of a lunatic—either they will say that I am mad or that I am merely trying to shift the blame for what I have done, but all of those things are quite untrue. It was the cat, there can be no doubt of that; it was the loathsome, hideous cat, as black as sin, with its unearthly yellow eyes that watched my every move while its frighteningly elongated tail twitched slowly, slowly, and its unclipped claws sheathed and unsheathed themselves and glistened with the ghostly, ghastly whiteness of a spectre's breath in winter—it was the cat, I say, that brought me to this place, with its cold stone walls and its cold iron bars and its stony hearts as cold as any iron.

My wife bought the cat.

She knew that I did not like cats. I do not like dogs, either, for that matter (as well she knew), nor do I like hamsters, goldfish, serpents, white mice, ferrets, or any form of bird, whether parakeet, parrot, cockatoo, or canary. Animals, in general, have quite low standards of cleanliness, are well known to be carriers of disease, and they of course play host to innumerable parasites such as ringworm, fleas, mites, and other disgusting, albeit microscopic, creatures.

And yet *she bought the cat.*

I explained my feelings to her again, as I had done with some vehemence after the first cat she bought, once more making plain my aversion not just to this particular cat but to any cat at all, to any *animal* at all, and especially to any animal that was brought into my own home. A man's home may no longer be his castle, but it is, at least, a refuge from the wearying world of corporate commerce, with its constant browbeating, harassment, and petty persecutions; a refuge that, along with a soothing libation of alcoholic potency, I seek with exceeding eagerness each day after putting in hours of unpaid overtime in the pursuit of money and promotions.

There can be no refuge, no sense of sanctuary, if your habitation is shared with an animal, but at least the first cat, which was brought into the house over my strenuous protestations, had the decency to rush into the street one early morning as I went to fetch the newspaper, where it was flattened by a passing automobile, a not unusual type of accident, but one for which I was blamed in one tearful tirade after another for weeks on end, though the tears eventually stopped, at which time I believed the cat to be forgotten.

I was wrong, as I discovered to my considerable chagrin late one afternoon after I came home from work and drank the first of what I hoped would be a series of very dry martinis, stirred, not shaken, and just the thing I needed after a day which I must confess had not gone particularly well at the office, thanks to a mistake in the Donner account, an account for which I am solely responsible, although I am convinced that the error was not mine. There was, however, no one else to whom the blame could be conveniently shifted; therefore I was forced to bear the brunt of Mr. Tyson's considerable wrath, a wrath which had caused my hands to tremble whenever I thought about it, which was often throughout the day. But I had arrived at home, at my refuge, and the trembling had at last begun to subside, when I heard the cat.

To say his *voice*, if such a sound as a cat makes may be called by that name, was guttural and unpleasant would be to understate the case. It sounded worse than fingernails on a blackboard; it grated on the nerves like tinfoil on a tooth.

His appearance was even worse. He was black: totally, completely, and hideously black. There was not the merest trace of any other color (except for the glaring yellow of his frightful eyes, his watchful, frightful eyes) to offer a mark of contrast to the grotesque blackness of his fur, his claws, or his rubbery lips, for even *they* were of the inky blackness that might be seen in a glimpse between the stars of deepest space on a clear night when there is no moon to lend the faintest hint of the reflected glory of the sun.

And he was huge. My wife is not a small woman, yet she had difficulty holding him in her arms, for it was indeed Clara who had brought him into the room where I sat meditatively drinking; she who had brought him into my refuge to show him to me in all his offensive felinity. He must have weighed twenty-five pounds, perhaps more, and as he made his rasping purring sound and rubbed his head against my wife's pillowy breasts, I saw that his reproductive equipment was in proportion to the rest of him —his testes were immense, almost like the eggs of two bantam hens encased in skin and fur.

But it was his tail that fascinated me. It was long, far longer than it had any right to be, and black, yes, black; and it writhed and twisted as if it had a will of its own, sliding across Clara's breasts, down her bare white arm, over her hips, almost as if it were caressing a lover. It was serpentine and sinuous, and it seemed to wander where it would with insulting familiarity and ease.

I set my glass down carefully on the small wooden table beside my chair and stood up. I was quite calm. I remember that distinctly. I was quite sober, and quite calm. Quite.

"There will be no more cats," I said. "Not in this house. I believe that we have spoken of this before. Clara. No. More. Cats."

Clara smiled. She was wearing a dress of scarlet red, against which the blackness of the cat shone with an almost satanic luster, and her lipstick was equally red, giving her teeth a startling whiteness. They were fine teeth, intensely white, small, and perfectly formed. She ran her tongue over them before she spoke, and she rubbed the top of the cat's head, causing it to increase its odious purring.

"Don't you wike 'ims?—'e is my new itsy-beesums." She crushed him tightly to her breasts, and the purring sound became even louder, if that was possible, and the beast looked at me and smiled.

I know that some might say that a cat cannot smile, that for an animal a smile is a physical impossibility, yet that is exactly what this one did. It parted its repugnant black lips, and it smiled. At me.

Its teeth, for a wonder, its teeth were not black. They were small and white, like Clara's teeth, but they were pointed like needles, and its tongue was red as it slid over the white teeth in an obscene parody of what Clara's tongue had done.

I felt an acute desire for another taste of the drink that was sitting on the table, and while I was sipping it, Clara mercifully took the cat from the room.

I finished the first martini, and then I had another. No one could deny that I needed it. First the Donner account, and now the cat. Yes, indeed, I needed the drink very much. There was another drink after that, and there might have been another later on. Perhaps two more. Or even three. I was not counting, and I do not remember.

I do remember, however, that I ate very little dinner that night. It was chicken, prepared with some kind of sauce from a jar and simmered in a pan. While I tried to eat it, the cat, the new black cat, sat just inside the doorway to the back hall, watching me with its brutish yellow eyes, its tail twitching, its larynx vibrating with the throaty noise of its hateful purr.

And every time that Clara would glance at it, she would say, "Is my itsy-beesums hun-gee? I will give itsy-beesums some of the chicken for its wittle supper. My itsy-beesums is sooooo *sweeeet!*"

I believe I may have had another drink after dinner. Perhaps two, but surely no more than that. The memory of the fiasco over the Donner account was fast fading, but the presence of the cat made the drinks more than necessary.

What happened next requires some explanation. Upon calm reflection, it seems quite unlikely to me that it ever actually occurred, yet I am certain that it did, as certain as I am of anything in this wretched concatenation of events. I was not drunk, however; on that point I must insist, though my lawyer, an oily, court-appointed time-server, seems to think that alcoholism might somehow mitigate the circumstances. Need I say that I neither agree with nor trust him?

It happened when I was going up the stairs to my bedroom. Yes, I say *my* bedroom, for Clara and I had, within the last few years, developed the habit of sleeping separately, the result of a combination of things, not the least of which was her annoying habit of sleeping on her back, mouth agape, as she gasped and puffed like a beached whale.

Not that I spoke to her of this. I had not mentioned it since the time that she rebutted me by making reference to certain faults which I attributed to perhaps a touch too much alcohol and which she insisted were instead the result of a seriously declining masculinity, an aspersion that of course had absolutely no basis in fact—none whatsoever—though that did not stop Clara from making her noxious slurs.

"Soft as a boiled noodle," was one of her favorites, as I recall, not that I paid her the least attention.

"Droopy as wilted lettuce," was another.

You will note that most of her slights allude to food, another of her weaknesses, and while not as bad as her undue fondness for cats, it is the one which causes her to be such a large woman and to have such cushiony breasts.

"Floppy as—"

But I have drifted far from my point, which was to relate the incident that occurred as I made my way up the stairs that night. My hand was quite steady on the rail; that much I remember distinctly. The light was dim. I had left a desk lamp on in my study, and the door was open, but the bulb was a small one; it did not illuminate the stairway as well as it might have done, and the yellow glow seemed to dance and waver as I climbed upward.

I had nearly reached the top of the stairs when I saw the cat. Or at least I *believed* that what I saw was the cat. There is actually nothing else that I could have seen, though what appeared there was not precisely like a cat.

I am a well-educated man, quite proud of being sensible, prudent, and logical—all the things that a good accountant should be. A wild imagination has no place in the world of precise reality that numbers provide, a world in which mistakes are of course made, as I had explained to Mr. Tyson earlier that day—who among us is perfect, after all?—but a world in which the errors can be detected and corrected with no harm done to anyone, no matter what Tyson, that pompous ass, might say.

At any rate, I am sure that I saw what I am about to describe, no matter how much my lawyer, a self-involved twit in a shiny blue suit, says that it could not have happened and that it will be laughed out of court if he presents it as a part of his defense.

Defense! As if he knew the meaning of the word! He wants to say that I am insane—delusional, if you will!—a concept that is absurd on the face of it. On the contrary, I am only *too sane*. I *know* what I have seen.

And what I saw was this: The new black cat sat atop the stair, but he did not appear to be a cat any longer. Or he did, but he did not. It is impossible to say exactly what I mean. Even as I watched him, he was changing, growing, his back enlarging, his yellow eyes glowing, his mouth smiling, his black lips stretching around the pristinely white teeth that sparkled in the indistinct light as he prepared to spring on me and devour me.

I screamed.

The cat pounced. Its claws tore at my face, shredding my flesh as its disgusting red tongue snaked out to lap the blood that welled up in the freshly rent furrows. I could taste its musky fur filling my mouth, sticking to my teeth, choking me, as my blood dribbled down my cheeks.

I put my hands around the thing's neck, though they could hardly encompass it, and I squeezed with all my fast-fading strength as I tried to tear it from my face. It would not move, and I forced my thumbs into its terrifying eyes, trying to punch the gelid orbs from their sockets. I did not succeed, but the thing opened its hideous mouth and yowled.

Or perhaps it did not. It may have been my own screams that I heard, for I am sure that I was screaming. Nevertheless, no matter what the sound, I pried the cat from my face and threw it against the wall with all the force that I could muster. I am quite certain that I heard its back—or perhaps its neck—break as it struck against the wall, for let me assure you, I threw it very hard.

And then I fell. It was as if something had twined itself between my legs and tangled them together, and I fell backward, crashing down the stairs.

That was all I remembered for quite some time.

I awoke to blackness, blackness and a professional voice that had nothing of comfort in it, saying, "He'll be just fine. You don't have a thing to worry about. Nothing's broken, but he did hit his head pretty hard. Concussion, maybe, but nothing serious, no broken bones or anything like that. Give him a few days, he'll be okay."

I wanted to laugh. A concussion! *What about my face? What about the claw-torn flesh?* Didn't the fool know about the terrible dangers of infection?

I did not open my eyes. Somehow I could not bring myself to open my eyes. But I put my hand to my face, fearing what my exploring fingertips would discover. I had never been a strikingly handsome man, but I was sure that I would now be disfigured in such a way as to make passersby turn away in loathing and disgust.

To my great surprise, however, my fingers encountered only my undamaged skin, roughened by a day's growth of whiskers, but nothing more than that. No bandages, no sutures. No caked and drying blood.

I started up, my eyes wide, my mouth forming a scream.

The paramedic who had been speaking forced me back down, his hands on my shoulders. "Take it easy, fella. You're gonna be just fine. Bumped your head on the stairs a little, but that's all. You were lucky." With the last words, his nose wrinkled in disgust at the alcoholic fumes that issued from my mouth. "You oughta take it a little easier on the booze, you know?"

"The cat!" I said. "It was the cat!"

"Cat? What cat?"

I looked wildly around the room, my head thrashing on the pillow. I saw only Clara and the paramedic she had called, no one else. And no cat.

"You got a cat?" the paramedic said to Clara.

"Yes," she answered. "I just got him today at the pound."

"Hey, neat. I like cats. What kind is it?"

"Just a plain black cat."

I laughed bitterly. A plain black cat indeed. "He tried to kill me," I said. "He tripped me on the stairs."

"That right?" the paramedic asked Clara.

"Of course not. It's ridiculous. The cat was in the bed with me."

The paramedic gave her an appreciative up-and-down look. "Hey, lucky cat."

Clara smiled a very self-satisfied smile, and at that moment the cat entered the room. It stood in the doorway, looking at me and smiling, just like Clara.

"The cat!" I said, pointing. "The cat!"

They turned to see, but there was nothing in the doorway. The cat was much too fast for them, and by the time they had turned around it had disappeared.

"Sure," the paramedic said. "The cat. Right. But take a tip

from me, fella, and don't do so much drinking right before bed-time. You might not be so lucky if you fall down those stairs again."

With that, he and Clara left the room, and I eventually drifted into a fitful sleep in which I dreamed endlessly of cats, huge black cats with smiling mouths, white teeth, snatching claws, and lips of rubbery black.

The cat knew that I was wary of it—wary, let me repeat, but not afraid; never afraid—but my wariness seemed merely to increase its desire to be near me, as if by following me around, by turning up when least expected, it could fray my nerves, destroy my composure and, if it could not kill me, somehow drive me from the house.

For that was what it intended. There can be no doubt of it. Either I would be murdered or I would be removed from the premises. It was not enough for the cat to have all of Clara's attention, to be her itsy-beesums. No. That was not sufficient. It could triumph completely only if I were no longer a part of the household.

And Clara seemed not to care. Habits that in any other animal would never have been tolerated were in the cat looked upon as merely endearing foibles.

During the day, it slept upon the dining room table, and when it was awake, it destroyed the house plants. It shredded the upholstery on the couch and chairs. It leapt onto the china cabinet and broke expensive pieces of R. S. Prussia that Clara had collected.

She merely laughed, gathered the beast into her arms, and crushed it to her breasts, cooing to it in baby talk. " 'E is 'is mama's itsy-beesums, an' 'e is a baaaaaaad boooooooy."

The cat would smirk—at me—and rub its black head against the outthrust breasts and undulate its reptilian tail over her bare white arms and purr outlandishly, closing its eyes in sheer ec-stasy.

It was not long after my fall that I decided to kill the cat.

A simple matter, really. Our house was at the edge of the town's last subdivision, and behind our seven-foot board fence there was a field of deep grass that stretched for several blocks. Then the trees began. No one would think it strange to find a dead cat there, if indeed anyone cared to look.

I had a pistol. There is nothing so very strange in that; everyone has a pistol these days. We live at the edge of a city where drugs are sold openly on the streets, where panhandlers are gunned down in convenience store parking lots for asking the wrong person for spare change, where going to an ATM machine after dark is as risky as Russian roulette, where—but never mind. Suffice it to say that I had a pistol, a little .32 automatic, made in Germany and quite expensive. A .32 is considered underpowered by many people, but I had taken a firearms safety course and learned to shoot with a high degree of accuracy at close range. A .32 would serve me very well, especially if the target was only a cat, albeit quite a large one.

First I made an insincere effort to befriend the creature, but that availed me nothing. It seemed to realize that I had some hidden purpose, and whenever it apprehended that I was in the vicinity, it would somehow dematerialize, only to turn up later in another location. I began to recall stories I had heard as a child about cats and their relationship to witches. Foolish tales, of course, but somehow I could not get them out of my mind.

The cat was Clara's beloved companion, of course; they were virtually inseparable. It sat curled in her lap, snuggling its flat, repulsive head deep between her thighs, purring loudly for hours on end; and every night it pranced into her bedroom, its abhorrent tail erect, to sleep in her bed. But it would have nothing to do with me by way of companionship. It had other plans for me.

Not that it tried anything so blatant as the murder attempt on the stairway again. It now preferred to lurk in dark hallways and leap out at me, trying to startle me and give me heart failure; or to jump on my head when I was sitting on the couch to watch a movie on TV, hoping by surprise to induce a stroke or seizure of some sort; or to crouch beside a doorway and sink its claws into my leg as I entered a room.

So we would never be friends. But it *would* take food from me. It responded very well to the sound of the can opener and to the clink of a spoon against the side of its bowl. And that was its undoing.

One evening I was drinking a martini. I may have had more than one, though that is irrelevant now. There had been another of those days at the office, and Mr. Tyson had *not* been pleased with my work. I admit that he had reason; I was distracted by the cat and its plots against my life, and my work had suffered therefore. I had turned more and more to libations of gin to alleviate my troubles or at least to make them bearable for a time.

I was sitting quietly in my study, drinking. The pitcher of martinis was on a side table, and I was thinking of nothing in particular. I was deliberately trying to think of nothing, to forget the day, to forget Tyson's wrath, to forget the fact that my wife seemed to prefer the company of her new black cat to that of her husband.

Not that one could entirely blame her. I freely acknowledge that I had not been all that a husband should be to her; I had ceased to be so from the moment the cat entered the house, no matter the implications of her frequent references to "drooping" and "flopping," references which I note had ended upon the day of the cat's arrival. I suppose that I had at least one thing for which to be grateful to the brute.

But I was not feeling grateful at the time. I was sitting, I say, in my study, when the cat charged in, leapt over the top of my chair, landed briefly on my head and sank its claws into my scalp, causing me to scream and throw my drink into the air, glass and all, and then jumped to the side table, dashing the martini pitcher to the floor, breaking both the pitcher and the glasses that sat on the silver tray beside it.

When Clara rushed into the room to see what had happened, the cat was of course nowhere in sight. It was as if it had never been there, though it certainly had. I would never have been so clumsy as to cause such damage myself. Clara listened halfheartedly to my complaints and went looking for the cat, calling for her itsy-beesums, while I was left alone to clean up the mess, which I did, but not before I looked in the locked drawer of my desk where the pistol was kept. It was there, in a sheepskin-lined leather case, oiled and loaded. Seeing it brought a sense of peace and comfort to my heart that it would be impossible to describe. I closed the drawer and smiled.

I do not remember having smiled for quite a long time.

Late that night I crept down the hall to Clara's room. In my hands I held a spoon and a bowl of cat food that smelled of oily, rotting fish and decaying chicken. In my pocket was the pistol and a very sharp knife. I put my ear to the door and heard no snoring; there was only the sound of contented purring, which I could hear clearly through the heavy wood of the door.

I turned the knob—very slowly—and opened the door—equally slowly—as wide as need be for a gigantic cat to squeeze through.

Then I clinked the spoon against the side of the bowl. Not loudly. I made hardly any sound at all, but it was enough, for the cat was always ravenous, as if it had been engaging in some strenuous physical activity rather than spending its life in vacuous sleep.

The sound I made was sufficient, as I had known it must be. I heard a dull thud as the cat jumped from the bed, then the padding of its feet across the rug.

By the time it reached the doorway, I was at the bottom of the stairway—I would be taking no chances of being tripped up that night of all nights—and again I clinked the bowl with the spoon.

The cat came down the stairs, eager for food, and it followed me faithfully across the back yard, through the gate in the fence, into the field and to the edge of the trees. When I set down the bowl, it plunged its face eagerly into the disgusting mess of ground animal parts.

I stuck the pistol in its ear and blew out its brains.
And after it stopped twitching, I cut off its tail.

The next day was a Saturday, and I slept late. I had not had such a good night's sleep since the arrival of the new black cat, nor had I felt so refreshed on awakening. The sun was shining through my window, and the birds were singing joyfully outside as if they, too, were glad to be rid of the offensive feline.

I was reading the morning paper and reclining comfortably on the couch, the couch that would no longer be torn to tatters by the claws of the black cat, when the police came to the door, badges in hand.

To say that I was shocked to see them there would be a gross understatement, though perhaps there should have been no surprise in it. If Clara had noted by now that the cat was missing, as she surely must have, she would have called out the National Guard and the FBI as well as the police.

But it was not the cat they sought. They were looking for a missing man whom they said had been seen often in the neighborhood, though not by me.

I ushered them in and listened to their questions. I glanced politely but without recognition at the picture they showed me. They were about to leave when Clara came crying into the room.

"He did it!" she sobbed, pointing directly at me. "He did it! Ask him if he can deny it!"

"Did what, lady?" one of the policeman said. He was stocky and dark, and he looked with interest at the loose robe Clara was wearing.

"Killed him!" Clara said. "Killed him!"

The policemen both turned to face me with looks like stone. "Maybe you'd better explain," the stocky one said.

I laughed. "I suppose she means the cat. Her cat is missing, and she is probably possessed of some wild idea that I killed it."

"Well, did you?"

I glanced at Clara, who had now retreated to the far side of the room and sunk into a chair, her face buried in her hands. She was too far away to hear anything that I might say, providing I did not raise my voice.

"Well, yes, I did. But it was only a cat."

"Maybe you'd better let us take a look."

I laughed again. It was a cheerful laugh, a merry laugh, a carefree laugh. Let them look. What difference could that possibly make to me?

I led them from the house, across the yard, through the gate and to the edge of the trees. I looked for the food bowl, but it was no longer there, not that it mattered. I recalled the spot well enough.

"Here," I said. "This is where I killed the cat."

"I don't see no cat," the stocky policeman said.

"I buried him," I said, and indeed I had. I did not want innocent neighborhood children, who often played among the trees, to stumble across the body of the cat and perhaps bring it to Clara's attention.

"Where?"

"Right over there." I indicated the spot, a place where the dirt was obviously displaced. I had made no attempt to hide the shallow grave.

"I guess we better take a look," the stocky man's partner said. He was fair and tall, with cold blue eyes.

"Let me help you," I said, my chipper voice accompanied by a manic burst of activity as I began kicking away clods of earth. I saw a rotten tree branch nearby and grabbed it up, digging into the still-soft dirt and sending it flying.

It was not long before the body was exposed.

"I cut off its tail, as you can see," I explained happily, "and I shoved it in its mouth."

"Jesus Christ," the stocky cop said, just before he stepped behind a tree and threw up.

I did not understand his reaction. You might think he had never seen a dead cat before.

"It's only a cat," I said. "A black cat."

"That's not a cat," the tall policeman said. "And that sure as hell ain't no tail in its mouth."

I looked into the grave again, and then I began to scream.

And so that is how I came to this place. I suppose in some ways it is not so bad. At least there are no cats here, for which I am thankful. I remain convinced that at my trial I will be found not guilty of any crime. How can I be guilty? I killed only a cat. What jury could see any harm in that?

Yes, soon I will be free, and I will go home to Clara, who, for some reason, has not been a frequent visitor here, and who, I understand from my barely-competent lawyer, has already found a new cat.

The cat, he says, has yellow eyes, is very large, very black, and has a long, thick tail.

I can almost see its smile.

TO KILL A CAT

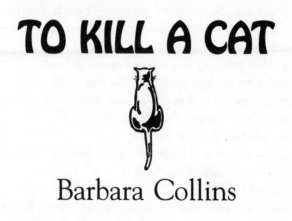

Barbara Collins

IT HAD BEEN A YEAR since Maggie's husband died.

Tom's cruel death of pancreatic cancer came quickly; and yet was kind enough to allow him time to fully appreciate life, and say goodbye to friends.

In his final days he seemed at peace, in his drugged semicoma, surrounded by loving family members.

He had the easy part—dying—while Maggie was left living with sadness and guilt that drove her to the brink of suicide.

Unable to teach, she took a leave of absence from the college, and sought professional help to cope with her grief.

Now, buoyed by time, she had the strength to visit the park where Tom proposed to her fifteen years ago. Beneath this stone bridge, on the grassy bank of the pond, surrounded by weeping willows, he had kissed her and promised never to leave.

She stood there, in the dusk of a cool summer evening, and stared out at the water. The branches of the willows, blown by the wind, reached out, as if to comfort her.

But she did not weep.

She'd come up from the depths of depression, to break its hold and gasp for air. She wanted to live—though she knew she would never forget the helplessness of standing by, watching someone die.

Perhaps that was why she reacted as she did, when something sailed off the bridge and splashed into the pond.

For an instant, she thought it was a sack of garbage, and looked up sharply toward the bridge in disgust.

In the darkness, she saw no one.

The sack—which was beginning to sink—was squirming; an unearthly screech came from within.

Something *live* was in it!

The water was cold, the pond, surprisingly deep. Weeds grabbing at her legs threatened to hold her back. Her jeans and sweater, heavy and cumbersome, slowed her down.

The sack had gone under.

Reaching out in the water, Maggie searched with her hands, but found nothing. Then she kicked with her feet, and felt it!

Quickly, she yanked the sack to the surface, and putting it on the back of her head and shoulders, held it there with one hand as she swam back to shore with the other.

On the bank, on her knees, she tore off the twine that sealed the burlap bag, and emptied it.

A large black cat lay lifeless.

Rhythmically, she pushed on its swollen stomach.

The cat didn't move.

Instinctively, she grabbed its hind legs, held the animal upside down like a newborn baby, and shook it!

Water streamed from its mouth, and the cat sputtered and spasmed as it fought its way back from the dead.

Maggie cried out with joy and relief as the terrified animal clung to her.

"Meow! Meow!" it shrieked. "Meow! Meow!"

"There, there," she soothed, holding it tightly, rocking slightly. "There, there."

For a moment she stayed on her knees, caressing the trembling cat. Then she stood up with it. Outraged.

"Who would *do* such a thing?" she said loudly, angrily, for the benefit of a person who had long since fled.

She gazed down into the cat's golden eyes. "Who would do such a thing?" she repeated softly, sadly.

The cat said nothing, clinging to her, its claws buried in Maggie's soaked sweater.

Maggie shivered, as much from the thought some bastard could be so sadistic, as from her damp, cold clothes.

"I'm taking you home!" she said to the cat, firmly, indignantly. She bent down and picked up the sack and twine, then walked toward her car, her tennis shoes sloshing as she went.

She opened the trunk and threw in the burlap bag and twine —perhaps later they might be useful in locating the owner and bringing that vile person to justice! Then Maggie pulled out a stadium blanket and wrapped herself up with the cat and got behind the wheel of her car and drove home, the animal quivering against her.

In the spacious kitchen of her Victorian house, Maggie stood at the stove in a terry-cloth robe, stirring a pan of hot chicken soup.

The cat was on the floor, next to the round oak table, in a large box Maggie found in the basement. She thought the arrangement best, as she'd never had a pet, and wasn't sure *what* to expect.

She gave the cat a bowl of the soup—cooled down with tap water—and it greedily ate.

After cleaning up the dishes, Maggie went off to bed, leaving a small light on in the kitchen for her guest.

Soon she fell into a deep, deep sleep . . . at first restful, then suddenly filled with delirious dreams of witches and goblins and demons from hell . . .

If she could only wake up! In the distant corner of her subconscious she recognized the barking of her neighbor's dog—the yapping was a nightly annoyance she tried to ignore, but now she fought her way toward it. In the limboland of half-asleep, her eyes lidded, she sensed the presence of something.

Large glowing eyes stared into hers.

She sat up in bed. She looked around. Had she imagined it? A movement caught her eye. But it was just the curtains being tossed about from the brisk night air coming in the open window.

In the kitchen, the cat lay sleeping, curled in a ball, its back rising and falling peacefully. Maggie returned to her bedroom.

With a sigh, she crawled under the quilts and closed her eyes. She needed a good night's sleep! Tomorrow she had to find the nice cat a new home.

Maggie had driven by the sign a hundred times, but had never given it much thought; now she followed the directions and turned off the highway onto a blacktop that led out of town.

The brilliant morning sun streaked in the car window across the cat that lay on the front seat, making its black coat shine. Maggie looked at the cat and smiled, happy about the good deed she was about to perform.

After several miles the blacktop ended and Maggie slowed as the road turned to gravel. Though her tires kicked up dust, she kept the windows down, reveling in the smell of ripening corn fields that had just begun to turn brown.

Another sign appeared, and she turned off the gravel and into the grassy lane of the County Animal Shelter. To her right, enclosed by a low, rustic wooden fence, was a pet cemetery. Each of the tiny graves had its own little marker, and many were decorated with plastic flowers. Butterflies danced among them.

To her left loomed a white metal building, and Maggie pulled her car up to it and shut off the engine.

The cat, alert, began to stiffen, its ears rotating forward. Maggie picked it up and its claws dug into the soft fabric of her shirt.

The cat made a pitiful noise.

"It's all right," Maggie answered cheerfully, getting out of the car. "They're going to help us."

Inside the building, the sounds and smells of the caged animals assaulted her. The cat dug in further, and Maggie had to hold it tightly to keep it from clawing all the way up to the top of her head.

A young woman with puffy blond hair and ratted-up bangs sat behind a metal desk just inside the door. She was reading a book, and looked up from it. Her features were so perfect, so completely void of anything unique or interesting, that Maggie felt if she ever saw the woman again she would never recognize her.

"I have a cat," Maggie said, raising her voice above the din of the yapping, yowling animals.

"Uh-huh," the woman said, putting the book down.

"I hope you can find it a home."

The woman eyed her slowly. "You don't want to keep it?" she asked.

"Well . . . no," Maggie said, taken slightly aback. "I don't *want* a pet. That's why I'm here."

The woman sighed, seemingly annoyed, and opened a drawer. She pulled out a form and picked up a pencil. "Where did you find it?" she asked flatly.

"In the pond," Maggie answered. "At the park." Then she added, somewhat sanctimoniously, *"Someone* tried to *drown* it."

The young woman stopped writing, and said almost smugly, "Maybe you didn't do it a favor."

"What do you mean?" Maggie demanded, bristling a little.

The woman sat back in her chair and crossed her legs, showing large holes in the knees of her jeans. "We got room for just eighteen cats here," she explained. "About forty come in every week." The young woman paused. "If we're *lucky* we give away two."

Maggie stared at her and clutched the cat tighter. "What happens to the rest?" she asked.

The woman didn't answer, but looked past Maggie and hollered, "Rusty!"

Maggie turned to see a thin young man in shorts and a t-shirt. On his shirt was a picture of a heavy metal rock group, with the word MEGADEATH above it. The kid had a face full of freckles and small eyes with no eyebrows at all. Strands of unruly red hair stuck out from under a baseball cap he wore backward on his head.

"Rusty," the young woman said, "put the cat somewhere—*anywhere*—until we can find it a cage."

"Okay," he answered dully. He reached for the cat, and pulled it off Maggie, and the animal's claws caught in her blouse, undoing one button, revealing her lacy white bra.

Rusty grinned, showing sharp little teeth.

Maggie glared back, clutching her shirt closed, and watched as he left with the cat, down the cement corridor, disappearing through a door beyond which she glimpsed caged animals. Then she turned to the woman.

"You will *try* to find the cat a home?" Maggie asked. It was more a statement than a question.

The young woman nodded indifferently, her lips a tight sullen line.

"It's a *nice* cat," Maggie defended.

"It's a male Bombay," the young woman said coldly. "They're not all that friendly."

Now this upset Maggie, and the woman, seeing she'd gone too far, and perhaps sensing she might get into trouble, tried her best to look sincere. "But we'll do what we can," the young woman promised.

Maggie was hesitant.

"You check back with us at the end of the week, if you like," the woman suggested.

"Yes," Maggie said, brightening. "Yes, I'll do that." Then she dug into her purse and found a twenty-dollar bill. "I want to make a donation," she said, holding out the money.

"Thank you," the young woman said, taking it, smiling at last. "We do rely on donations."

Maggie nodded, and left.

Getting into her car, she wondered if the twenty would buy pet food or hair spray. But it just didn't matter. It bought Maggie relief from the guilt she felt as she drove out of the lane, leaving the cat behind, not looking at the pet cemetery as she went by.

* * *

At home, Maggie vacuumed the oriental rug in the living room —something she'd have to do constantly if she had a cat. Then she dusted the Queen Anne furniture she inherited from her grandmother; its delicate needlepoint would never survive destructive sharp claws.

But in the hallway, while polishing the mirror, she stopped, rag suspended in midair as she stared at the reflection of the cat's box, behind her, still in the kitchen.

"What's the matter?" she sneered at herself. "Are you afraid to love even a *cat?*"

She threw down the rag, and ran out the door and got in her car.

In a race against time—it was late and the shelter soon would be closing—Maggie sped along the country road, dust encompassing the car, and, before long, wheeled into its grassy lane only to have to throw on her brakes.

In front of the building the red lights of a police car and ambulance were flashing.

Puzzled, Maggie rolled down her dirty car window to see better, and slowly pulled off to the side, next to the cemetery. She shut off the engine and got out.

Quietly she entered the building.

"I don't know *how* it happened!" the young woman was wailing; so cool and collected earlier, she was now quite hysterical.

"Just take it slow," said a policeman who stood near the woman. He made a calm-down gesture with both hands.

The young woman breathed deeply, composing herself, then looked at the cop with wet, mascara-blackened eyes.

"He was getting ready to do some dogs," she said in a quavering voice. "We use gas pellets and . . ." She halted and swallowed thickly.

"Go on," the cop said.

"When I hadn't seen him for a while, I went looking . . ." Now she stared down at her feet, her face contorting. "Somehow the door must have *closed*, locking him in!"

The young woman buried her face in her hands and sobbed, "Christ! It shouldn't happen to a dog."

"Excuse me," Maggie said from the doorway.

The young woman looked over at her with the eyes of a startled animal.

The cop took a step toward Maggie. "Ma'am, you're going to have to leave," he ordered.

"I came back for my cat," Maggie said, speaking to the woman who continued to stare.

"I'm sorry if I've come at a bad time," Maggie continued, undeterred, "but I want that cat before you do anything to it."

"Lady," the young woman said, her eyes now half-crazed, "there's nobody *to* do anything to it!"

"I'm going to ask you just once more to *leave*," the policeman barked.

Intimidated, Maggie backed out of the building, and for a moment stood off to one side in the grass, indecisive about what to do next, when the front door of the shelter flew open.

Two men came out carrying a stretcher. Maggie watched them, rather detached—the cat, after all, was her main concern —as they made their way to the ambulance. The men didn't seem to be in much of a hurry.

But suddenly Maggie realized that the stretcher was *covered*; underneath she could make out a form. With mounting horror she stared, unable to look away. As the gurney was lifted into the back of the van it got jostled.

The blanket slipped. Red hair sprang out from under.

Rusty.

Maggie stumbled back a few steps, then turned and fled to her car. She opened the door and quickly got in.

On the front seat, sleeping serenely, was the cat.

"Kitty!" she cried, her horror turning to joy. "Oh, Kitty!"

She reached for the cat. "But how . . . ?" she began, then burst into tears. "Forgive me," she whispered, her face lost in its fur.

Then she started the car, turned it around, and tore out of the lane, burying the pet cemetery in a cloud of dust.

* * *

Maggie stood anxiously in the reception area of the Animal Care Clinic, a rambling wooden affair that looked more like a lodge than a pet hospital. It was located just a few miles outside of town, on an old winding road that ran along the river. The clinic was owned by Dr. Goodman and his wife Edna.

"I hope I didn't do the wrong thing," Maggie sighed.

Dr. Goodman smiled reassuringly. "I don't think so," he said. He was a stout man in his sixties, with white hair and kind eyes that were made even kinder by the magnification of his glasses. Maggie knew him from church where he sang in the choir with a vibrant yet compassionate voice, traits she had heard he brought to his work with animals.

"Although," the doctor admitted, nodding his head slightly, "there are those who think differently—cat experts who say this kind of thing should never be done."

Maggie frowned.

"However," Dr. Goodman continued, "if it means that a cat might be adopted instead of put to sleep . . ."

A door in the back of the reception area opened and a portly, attractive woman entered. She had short gray hair and round, rosy cheeks that dimpled as she smiled.

She was carrying Maggie's cat.

"Ah, here's Edna now," the doctor said.

Maggie smiled as Mrs. Goodman came toward her; but the smile vanished when she got a closer look at her pet.

"Oh, dear," Maggie said, concerned, "what's wrong with him?"

"It's just the effects of the anesthesia," Dr. Goodman said. "He'll be fine in a couple of hours."

"But his paws . . ." Maggie said, gesturing to the cat's bandaged feet. ". . . I didn't think they had to be . . ."

"We like to wrap them for protection and to keep the incisions clean," the doctor explained. "You may untape them in a few days."

Maggie gingerly took the cat from Mrs. Goodman; the animal felt limp in her arms.

"Just let him sleep," the doctor advised.

Maggie nodded slowly.

"You can call us if you have any questions," his wife added helpfully. "We're here until nine o'clock tonight."

Maggie thanked them and left.

She put the cat in the car on the front seat, right next to her, but it crawled away in slow motion, toward the opposite door, and turned itself around until its back was to her.

Maggie drove home, feeling rejected, thinking that she shouldn't have had the cat declawed.

In the kitchen, she put the cat on the floor, on a special pillow she had bought for its homecoming; but after a minute, it stood unsteadily, and moved away, and staggered like a drunk into the bedroom to be alone.

Maggie felt heartsick.

Later, around supper time, when Maggie was cooking some fish, the cat emerged from seclusion, and, walking quite well on its bandaged paws, joined her by the stove. Relieved, Maggie bent down to pet it.

"Feeling better?" Maggie smiled, feeling better.

She put some of the fish on a plate, and set it down on the floor and watched as the cat ravenously ate. When it was done, it went to the back door, and meowed. Maggie complied, and the cat went out.

After Maggie had finished washing the dishes, she stepped outside and called for the cat.

But it didn't come.

She looked around the yard, but saw no sign of it.

Now Maggie began to worry—twilight had arrived—and she frantically searched up and down the street. When that failed to produce her pet, she alerted her neighbors, who promised to call her if they should see the cat.

In her kitchen, Maggie paced back and forth, looking out the back door every fifteen minutes or so. Darkness closed in. Sometime after nine, a siren pierced the peaceful night like a knife, then grew distant as the vehicle headed out of town. Except for that, all was quiet—even the Doberman pinscher next door.

Maggie set the cat's pillow out on the stoop, and—leaving the porch light on—locked the back door. Then she went off to bed.

Her rest was fitful at best, however, and during the night she got up and peered out the window; she could see the little pillow from there . . .

But it lay empty.

In the morning, she awoke with a start, and jumped out of bed as if guilty for having slept, and ran to the window.

The cat was curled up on the pillow!

Her heart pounding, robe flapping, bare feet slapping the floor, Maggie ran to the kitchen and flung open the door.

"Where have you been?" she practically shouted.

The cat looked up. Unperturbed.

"Never mind," Maggie sighed, bending down to get it. "I'm just glad you're home."

Then she held the cat out. "But just look at you!" she scolded. "You're full of cockleburs and . . . oh! Your paws!"

The bandages on its front feet were ragged and filthy.

Maggie took the cat into the hallway and picked up the phone. "I'm going to call the vet!" she said, and dialed the number with her free hand.

A woman's voice answered; it wasn't Mrs. Goodman.

"Dr. Goodman, please," said Maggie urgently.

"I'm afraid all calls to our Animal Care Clinic are being referred to another veterinarian service."

"But I want to talk to Dr. Goodman," Maggie insisted.

There was a pause. "I'm afraid that's not possible."

"Why?" Maggie asked.

The voice, now softer, said, "The doctor and his wife were in an automobile accident last night."

"Oh, no!" Maggie moaned. She set the cat down. "Please . . . tell me . . ."

"On their way home from the clinic they lost control of their car and ran into a guardrail, broke through and went into the river."

"Dear God," Maggie gasped. "What could have happened?"

"According to Mrs. Goodman, an animal ran onto the road in front of them and the doctor swerved so they wouldn't hit it."

Maggie looked down at the cat, licking one half-bandaged front paw, its pink tongue darting. "A deer, perhaps?" she asked weakly.

"Something much smaller," the woman said, then sighed. "I'm afraid the doctor was more concerned about saving the animal's life than saving his own. So typical of him . . ."

"What do you mean?" said Maggie, alarmed. "Dr. Goodman's all right, isn't he?" Out of the corner of her eye she saw the cat, trotting off to the bedroom, head high, tail erect, bandages trailing behind.

"Dr. Goodman drowned."

Maggie hummed a little tune as she set the dining room table with her best crystal and china. When she had finished, she stepped back and surveyed her work.

She smiled, then frowned.

"What should I use for a centerpiece?" she asked the cat.

The cat, lying on a window seat nearby, basking in the rays of the fading, late afternoon sun, stretched out its body and flexed its paws, which had healed nicely in the past week.

Maggie went to the cat and wagged a finger in its face. "Now I want you to be on your *best* behavior," she warned. "This is a colleague of mine. A *professor!*"

The cat yawned, unimpressed.

Maggie leaned over the animal and opened the window.

"It would be *so* nice to have some fresh air," she said, looking out.

But the woman next door and her two little girls were having a picnic in their back yard, which was adjacent to Maggie's. The children yelled and screamed as they chased each other around with sticks. Their mother, a single parent in her thirties with short curly brown hair and a tired-looking face, was in the process of lighting a small candle on the table; she stopped and hollered at them. The family dog, chained nearby, determined not to be left out of the excitement, barked frantically, running in and out of his doghouse, kicking up straw.

Maggie shut the window. "So much for *that* idea," she sighed.

The front doorbell chimed.

Maggie answered it, and greeted Professor Fudder, who stood uncomfortably in a three-piece suit. A bachelor in his early fifties with a close-cropped gray beard, he was holding a bouquet of roses.

"What beautiful flowers!" Maggie said, then added, "But you shouldn't have."

"Nonsense," the professor scoffed. "Merely a token of my gratitude for being invited to partake in your culinary delights."

"Thank you," Maggie smiled, amused. "I think." She gestured inside. "Please, come in, Professor."

"Throckmorton," he corrected, stepping past her.

"Just make yourself at home . . . Throckmorton . . . while I put the roses in water."

She went into the kitchen, then returned with the flowers in a crystal vase and set them on the table.

Maggie was surprised at how well the dinner went, considering her nervousness in preparing something she'd never served before, and to someone who had such gourmet tastes; but the professor really seemed to enjoy her appetizer of fried banana chips and entree of curried lamb with rice . . . and Maggie knew *nothing* could beat her mother's recipe for German chocolate pie.

The time passed quickly with shoptalk about their upcoming classes; Maggie told the professor she was anxious to return to teaching. When the conversation drifted to their pets—Maggie knew the professor had four cats—she suggested they leave the dishes in the dining room and move to the kitchen for coffee.

The professor took a seat at the oak table and Maggie went to get some cups from the cupboard. Out the window above the sink, she could see that the family next door had gone inside. The lone candle left flickering on the picnic table softly illuminated the doghouse in the night; the chain led inside, indicating the animal had also retired. Maggie opened the window and let in the cool breeze.

"Professor . . . Throckmorton," she said, now pouring him a cup of coffee, "I wanted to find some way of repaying you for taking over my classes last year when . . ." She couldn't finish the sentence.

"No payment necessary," said the professor, jumping in graciously.

Maggie sat down and poured herself a cup. "I thought inviting you to dinner might be a nice way of saying thanks."

"You've provided the most delicious thank-you note I ever ate, my dear."

Maggie smiled, then stared down at her coffee. "I'm afraid I had another reason for inviting you here tonight."

"A hidden agenda? How delightful."

She nodded, running one finger around the rim of her cup. "I need to tap into your expertise . . ."

The professor leaned forward, just slightly.

"Can cats kill the way people can kill?"

The professor blinked, and it seemed to Maggie that his face registered disappointment before taking on a look of puzzlement. "Come again?" he said.

"I know this may sound silly . . . but do you think it's possible for a cat to kill—maliciously, cunningly—like a human can kill?"

The professor sat back in his chair. "Well, cats *are* extraordinary hunters . . ."

"I don't mean kill for food," Maggie interrupted. "I mean kill for *revenge*—or just the hell of it!"

The professor stared. "You can't be serious," he said, after a moment. "Have you been reading horror novels on your sabbatical?"

"What I've been reading," Maggie said, feeling her face begin to flush, "is that . . ."

She shut her mouth. The cat, curled up by the stove, was watching them intently, as if it could understand their conversation. Maggie got up from the table and picked up the cat and put it out the back door, then returned to her chair.

"What I've been reading," she began again, almost in a whisper, "is that a kitten's mother will first bring back food to her babies and kill it in front of them, to teach them how. Then, she brings back prey for *them* to kill."

"Continue."

"Cats learn everything from their mothers—or *mother-substitutes*: humans that raise them from kittens."

"Point being?"

"Point being that a cat raised by Mother Teresa is going to be a very different animal than the one that learned the lifestyle of, say, mass-murderer John Wayne Gacey."

The professor laughed. "My dear," he said, "your conjecture is pure nonsense. Cats are not that intelligent. Furthermore, today's feline has remained close to its ancestral form; its behavior is still remarkably like the African wild cat from which it was gradually developed thousands of years ago."

"I don't agree," Maggie argued. "I think years of manhandling and coddling have caused the modern cat to forget most of its instincts, much less its purpose. And prolonged exposure to sophisticated human beings has perhaps spawned a new breed of cat—a much more intelligent and crafty animal than you can imagine."

"Hogwash, my dear."

"Then *how*, for example, do you explain the cat that learned to run a toy train on 'Stupid Pet Tricks'?" Maggie asked.

The professor opened his mouth to speak, but instead of words came a terrible screech, and it took Maggie a second or two before she realized that the shriek had not emanated from the professor at all, but from something outside. As the horrible screeching continued—she couldn't tell if it was man or beast— Maggie jumped out of her chair and ran to the back door and flung it open.

The night was blacker than India ink, but Maggie had no trouble seeing, because the doghouse in the yard next door lit up the sky.

It was aflame.

The Doberman pinscher—the source of the screeching—raced back and forth, as far as the chain would take him, his body a torch. Perhaps in his doggy-mind he thought that action might help, but it only made things worse.

Maggie stood in frozen horror, one hand to her mouth, the other holding the door open, when suddenly her attention was diverted from the tragedy before her, as her cat shot out of the darkness, and moved swiftly up the steps, and past her, into the kitchen, on its way to the bedroom, no doubt.

She could not help the thought that popped into her head: *Now what have you done?*

The two little girls, hearing the commotion, came running out of their house and stopped a few feet away from the blazing fire. They held onto each other, jumping up and down like demented cheerleaders, their high-pitched screams blending together to make one continuous one, as they watched their beloved pet shudder and drop, its legs finally getting the message that the rest of it was dead.

Something touched Maggie and *she* jumped.

"I've called the fire department," the professor said solemnly, one hand on her arm. "Come in and sit down. Nothing can help that poor beast now."

But Maggie moved away from him, toward the fire which had begun to die down, her eyes searching.

The candle on the picnic table was missing; knocked into the dog house by a cat's paw . . . ?

Mercifully, the siren of the approaching fire truck drowned out the sobbing of the girls, and their mother, who had joined them, her arms around them both, head lowered in grief.

Maggie shrank back into the shadows, then moved on wobbly legs up the back steps and into the kitchen. She sat down numbly at the table.

"Maggie?" the professor asked, concerned. He was standing beside her, a hand lifted to, but not quite touching, her shoulder.

"I'm all right," she responded, not looking at him but through him. "I must ask you to go," she said softly.

"I'll telephone you later," he said.

She nodded.

He thanked her again for the dinner, but she hardly heard him; he found his way out, forgotten by his hostess.

She continued to sit until the cat came back, rubbing itself against her leg. She picked it up and kissed its face. "I love you," she whispered. "I really do."

Then she put it down and got up from the table and went outside.

A storm was coming; big drops of rain fell from the sky, hitting her face, running down it, mingling with her tears.

In the garage, she opened the trunk of her car and pulled out the blanket that she had used to warm herself, and the cat, what seemed like eons ago. For a moment, she held it to her cheek, tenderly, caressingly, like a baby's blanket. Then she let it fall back into the trunk, and reached in further, for the burlap bag and twine . . .

It had been six months since Jim's wife left him—for a woman for God's sake! During that time he thought he would die from the pain and embarrassment she caused him. Only one thing kept him going: his nine-year-old son, Nate.

Sitting in the rowboat across from his dad, Nate was a small mirror image of his father. They'd been out fishing, cramming as much fun as they could into the last few days before school started, when the storm suddenly came up.

They'd taken refuge under the old stone bridge.

Now the rain had stopped, and the clouds parted, showing a brilliant moon, and they drifted out tentatively in the old rowboat.

Something hit the water, off the stern, splashing them both. Jim had only to reach out to haul it in, whatever it was. But by then, he knew. He untied the twine from around the burlap bag, and pulled out the cat. He watched his son's eyes express surprise, then confusion, then sadness.

"Dad," the boy said; "who would do such a thing?"

"Son," replied his father, gently holding the shivering cat, "I'm afraid there are some pretty bad people in this world."

Nate reached out for the animal that seemed eager to go to him. "Can we keep it?" he asked excitedly.

"Now . . . Nate," Jim said slowly, "you seem to forget we already *have* a pet."

"Oh, *please?*" Nate pleaded, stroking the cat that was now nuzzling his neck.

"Well . . ." Jim said, waffling. He could deny his son nothing. "Okay. But I don't think Rover will like it."

"Yes!" Nate exclaimed, raising one small fist in the air. "You won't be sorry, you'll see!"

Then the boy smiled at the cat and petted its head. "Anyhow," he added, "ol' Rover won't live forever!"

NINE LIVES TO LIVE

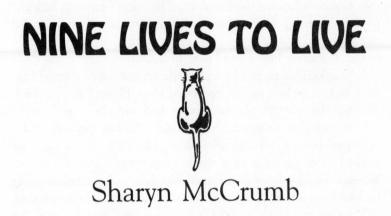

Sharyn McCrumb

IT HAD SEEMED like a good idea at the time. Of course, Philip
Danby had only been joking, but he had said it in a serious tone
in order to humor those idiot New Age clients who actually
seemed to believe in the stuff. "I want to come back as a cat,"
he'd said, smiling facetiously into the candlelight at the Eskeridge dinner table. He had to hold his breath to keep from laughing as the others babbled about reincarnation. The women
wanted to come back blonder and thinner, and the men wanted
to be everything from Dallas Cowboys to oak trees. *Oak trees?*
And he had to keep a straight face through it all, hoping these
dodos would give the firm some business.

The things he had to put up with to humor clients. His partner, Giles Eskeridge, seemed to have no difficulties in that quarter, however. Giles often said that rich and crazy went together;
therefore, architects who wanted a lucrative business had to be
prepared to put up with eccentrics. They also had to put up with
long hours, obstinate building contractors, and capricious zoning
boards. Perhaps that was why Danby had plumped for life as a
cat next time. As he had explained to his dinner companions

that night, "Cats are independent. They don't have to kowtow to anybody; they sleep sixteen hours a day; and yet they get fed and sheltered and even loved—just for being their contrary little selves. It sounds like a good deal to me."

Julie Eskeridge tapped him playfully on the cheek. "You'd better take care to be a pretty, pedigreed kitty, Philip," she laughed. "Because life isn't so pleasant for an ugly old alley cat!"

"I'll keep that in mind," he told her. "In fifty years or so."

It had been more like fifty days. The fact that Giles had wanted to come back as a shark should have tipped him off. When they found out that they'd just built a three-million-dollar building on top of a toxic landfill, the contractor was happy to keep his mouth shut about it for a mere ten grand, and Giles was perfectly prepared to bury the evidence to protect the firm from lawsuits and EPA fines. Looking back on it, Danby realized that he should not have insisted that they report the landfill to the authorities. In particular, he should not have insisted on it at 6:00 P.M. at the building site with no one present but himself and Giles. That was literally a fatal error. Before you could say "philosophical differences," Giles had picked up a shovel lying near the offending trench, and with one brisk swing, he had sent the matter to a higher court. As he pitched headlong into the reeking evidence, Danby's last thought was a flicker of cold anger at the injustice of it all.

His next thought was that he was watching a black-and-white movie, while his brain seemed intent upon sorting out a flood of olfactory sensations. *Furniture polish . . . stale coffee . . . sweaty socks . . . Prell Shampoo . . . potting soil . . .* He shook his head, trying to clear his thoughts. Where was he? The apparent answer to that was: lying on a gray sofa inside the black-and-white movie, because everywhere he looked he saw the same colorless vista. A concussion, maybe? The memory of Giles Eskeridge swinging a shovel came back in a flash. Danby decided to call the police before Giles turned up to try again. He stood up, and promptly fell off the sofa.

Of course, he landed on his feet.

All four of them.

Idly, to keep from thinking anything more ominous for the moment, Danby wondered what *else* the New Age clients had been right about. Was Stonehenge a flying saucer landing pad? Did crystals lower cholesterol? He was in no position to doubt anything just now. He sat twitching his plume of a tail and wishing he hadn't been so flippant about the afterlife at the Eskeridge dinner party. He didn't even particularly like cats. He also wished that he could get his paws on Giles in retribution for the shovel incident. First he would bite Giles's neck, snapping his spine, and then he would let him escape for a few seconds. Then he'd sneak up behind him and pounce. Then bat him into a corner. Danby began to purr in happy contemplation.

The sight of a coffee table looming a foot above his head brought the problem into perspective. At present Danby weighed approximately fifteen furry pounds, and he was unsure of his exact whereabouts. Under those circumstances avenging his murder would be difficult. On the other hand, he didn't have any other pressing business, apart from an eight-hour nap which he felt in need of. First things first, though. Danby wanted to know what he looked like, and then he needed to find out where the kitchen was, and whether Sweaty Socks and Prell Shampoo had left anything edible on the counter tops. There would be time enough for philosophical thoughts and revenge plans when he was cleaning his whiskers.

The living room was enough to make an architect shudder. Clunky early American sofas and clutter. He was glad he couldn't see the color scheme. There was a mirror above the sofa, though, and he hopped up on the cheap upholstery to take a look at his new self. The face that looked back at him was definitely feline, and so malevolent that Danby wondered how anyone could mistake cats for pets. The yellow (or possibly green) almond eyes glowered at him from a massive triangular face, tiger-striped, and surrounded by a ruff of gray-brown fur. Just visible beneath the ruff was a dark leather collar equipped with a little brass bell. That would explain the ringing in his ears. The rest of his body seemed massive, even allowing for the fur, and the great plumed tail swayed rhythmically as he watched. He resisted a silly urge to swat at the reflected movement. So he was a tortoiseshell, or tabby, or whatever they called those brown striped cats, and his hair was long. And he was still male. He didn't need to check beneath his tail to confirm that. Besides, the reek of ammonia in the vicinity of the sofa suggested that he was not shy about proclaiming his masculinity in various corners of his domain.

No doubt it would have interested those New Age clowns to learn that he was not a kitten, but a fully-grown cat. Apparently the arrival had been instantaneous as well. He had always been given to understand that the afterlife would provide some kind of preliminary orientation before assigning him a new identity. A deity resembling John Denver, in rimless glasses and a Sierra Club tee shirt, should have been on hand with some paperwork regarding his case, and in a nonthreatening conference, they would decide what his karma entitled him to become. At least, that's what the New Agers had led him to believe. But it hadn't been like that at all. One minute he had been tumbling into a sewage pit, and the next: he had a craving for Meow Mix. Just like that. He wondered what sort of consciousness had been flickering inside that narrow skull prior to his arrival. Probably not much. A brain with the wattage of a lightning bug could control most of the items on the feline agenda: eat, sleep, snack, doze, dine, nap, and so on. Speaking of eating . . .

He made it to the floor in two moderate bounds, and jingled toward the kitchen, conveniently signposted by the smell of lemon-scented dishwashing soap and stale coffee. The floor could do with a good sweeping, too, he thought, noting with distaste the gritty feel of tracked-in dirt on his velvet paws.

The cat dish, tucked in a corner beside the sink cabinet, confirmed his worst fears about the inhabitants' instinct for tackiness. Two plastic bowls were inserted into a plywood cat model, painted white, and decorated with a cartoonish cat-face. If his food hadn't been at stake, Danby would have sprayed *that* as an indication of his professional judgment. As it was, he summoned a regal sneer, and bent down to inspect the offering. The water wasn't fresh; there were bits of dry cat food floating in it. Did they expect him to drink *that?* Perhaps he ought to dump it out so that they'd take the hint. And the dry cat food hadn't been stored in an airtight container, either. He sniffed contemptuously: the cheap brand, mostly cereal. He supposed he'd have to go out and kill something just to keep his ribs from crashing together. Better check out the counters for other options. It took considerable force to launch his bulk from floor to counter top, and for a moment he teetered on the edge of the sink, fighting to regain his balance, while his bell tolled ominously, but once he righted himself, he strolled onto the counter with an expression of nonchalance suggesting that his dignity had never been imperiled. He found two breakfast plates stacked in the sink. The top one was a trove of congealing egg yolk and bits of buttered toast. He finished it off, licking off every scrap of egg with his rough tongue, and thinking what a favor he was doing the people by cleaning the plate for them.

While he was on the sink, he peeked out the kitchen window to see if he could figure out where he was. The lawn outside was thick and luxurious, and a spreading oak tree grew beside a low stone wall. Well, it wasn't Albuquerque. Probably not California, either, considering the healthy appearance of the grass. Maybe he was still in Maryland. It certainly looked like home. Perhaps the transmigration of souls has a limited geographic range, like AM radio stations. After a few moments consideration, while he washed an offending forepaw, it occurred to Danby to look at the wall phone above the counter. The numbers made sense to him, so apparently he hadn't lost the ability to read. Sure enough, the telephone area code was 301. He wasn't far from where he started. Theoretically, at least, Giles was within reach. He must mull that over, from the vantage point of the window sill, where the afternoon sun was marvelously warm, and soothing . . . zzzzz.

*   *   *

Danby awakened several hours later to a braying female voice calling out, "Tigger! Get down from there this minute! Are you glad Mommy's home, sweetie?"

Danby opened one eye, and regarded the woman with an insolent stare. *Tigger?* Was there no limit to the indignities he must bear? A fresh wave of Prell Shampoo told him that the self-proclaimed "Mommy" was chatelaine of this bourgeois bungalow. And didn't she look the part, too, with her polyester pants suit and her cascading chins! She set a grocery bag and a stack of letters on the counter top, and held out her arms to him. "And is my snook-ums ready for din-din?" she cooed.

He favored her with an extravagant yawn, followed by his most forbidding Mongol glare, but his hostility was wasted on the besotted Mrs. . . . (he glanced down at the pile of letters) . . . Sherrod. She continued to beam at him as if he had fawned at her feet. As it was, he was so busy studying the address on the Sherrod junk mail that he barely glanced at her. He hadn't left town! His tail twitched triumphantly. Morning Glory Lane was not familiar to him, but he'd be willing to bet that it was a street in Sussex Garden Estates, just off the by-pass. That was a couple of miles from Giles Eskeridge's mock-Tudor monstrosity, but with a little luck and some common sense about traffic he could walk there in a couple of hours. If he cut through the fields, he might be able to score a mouse or two on the way.

Spurred on by the thought of a fresh, tasty dinner that would beg for its life, Danby/Tigger trotted to the back door and began to meow piteously, putting his forepaws as far up the screen door as he could reach.

"Now, Tigger!" said Mrs. Sherrod in her most arch tone. "You know perfectly well that there's a litter box in the bathroom. You just want to get outdoors so that you can tomcat around, don't you?" With that she began to put away groceries, humming tunelessly to herself.

Danby fixed a venomous stare at her retreating figure, and then turned his attention back to the problem at hand. Or rather, at paw. That was just the trouble: Look, Ma, no hands! Still, he thought, there ought to be a way. Because it was warm outside, the outer door was open, leaving only the metal storm door between himself and freedom. Its latch was the straight-handled kind that you pushed down to open the door. Danby considered the factors: door handle three feet above floor; latch opens on downward pressure; one fifteen-pound cat intent upon going out. With a vertical bound that Michael Jordan would have envied, Danby catapulted himself upward and caught onto the handle, which obligingly twisted downward, as the door swung open at the weight of the feline cannonball. By the time gravity took over and returned him to the ground, he was claw-deep in scratchy, sweet-smelling grass.

As he loped off toward the street, he could hear a plaintive voice wailing, "Ti-iii-ggerr!" It almost drowned out the jingling of that damned little bell around his neck.

Twenty minutes later Danby was sunning himself on a rock in an abandoned field, recovering from the exertion of moving faster than a stroll. In the distance he could hear the drone of cars from the interstate, as the smell of gasoline wafted in on a gentle breeze. As he had trotted through the neighborhood, he'd read street signs, so he had a better idea of his whereabouts now. Windsor Forest, that pretentious little suburb that Giles called home, was only a few miles away, and once he crossed the inter-state, he could take a short cut through the woods. He hoped that La Sherrod wouldn't put out an all-points bulletin for her missing kitty. He didn't want any SPCA interruptions once he reached his destination. He ought to ditch the collar as well, he thought. He couldn't very well pose as a stray with a little bell under his chin.

Fortunately, the collar was loose, probably because the ruff around his head made his neck look twice as large. Once he determined that, it took only a few minutes of concentrated effort to work the collar forward with his paws until it slipped over his ears. After that, a shake of the head—jingle! jingle!—rid him of Tigger's identity. He wondered how many pets who "just disappeared one day" had acquired new identities and went off on more pressing business.

He managed to reach the by-pass before five o'clock, thus avoiding the commuter traffic of rush hour. Since he understood automobiles, it was a relatively simple matter for Danby to cross the highway during a lull between cars. He didn't see what the possums found so difficult about road crossing. Sure enough, there was a ripe gray corpse on the white line, a mute testimony to the dangers of indecision on highways. He took a perfunctory sniff, but the roadkill was too far gone to interest anything except the buzzards.

Once across the road, Danby stuck to the fields, making sure that he paralleled the road that led to Windsor Forest. His attention was occasionally diverted by a flock of birds overhead, or an enticing rustle in the grass that might have been a field mouse, but he kept going. If he didn't reach the Eskeridge house by nightfall, he would have to wait until morning to get himself noticed.

In order to get at Giles, Danby reasoned that he would first have to charm Julie Eskeridge. He wondered if she were susceptible to needy animals. He couldn't remember whether they had a cat or not. An unspayed female would be nice, he thought; a Siamese, perhaps, with big blue eyes and a sexy voice.

Danby reasoned that he wouldn't have too much trouble finding Giles's house. He had been there often enough as a guest. Besides, the firm had designed and built several of the overwrought mansions in the spacious subdivision. Danby had once suggested that they buy Palladian windows by the gross, since every nouveau riche homebuilder insisted on having a brace of them, no matter what style of house he had commissioned. Giles had not been amused by Danby's observation. He seldom was. What Giles lacked in humor, he also lacked in scruples and moral restraint, but he compensated for these deficiencies with a highly-developed instinct for making and holding onto money. While he'd lacked Danby's talent in design and execution, he had a genius for turning up wealthy clients, and for persuading these tasteless yobbos to spend a fortune on their showpiece homes. Danby did draw the line at carving up antique Sheraton sideboards to use as bathroom sink cabinets, though. When he also drew the line at environmental crime, Giles had apparently found his conscience an expensive luxury that the firm could not afford. Hence, the shallow grave at the new construction site, and Danby's new lease on life. It was really quite unfair of Giles, Danby reflected. They'd been friends since college, and after Danby's parents died, he had left a will leaving his share of the business to Giles. And how had Giles repaid this friendship? With the blunt end of a shovel. Danby stopped to sharpen his claws on the bark of a handy pine tree. Really, he thought, Giles deserved no mercy whatsoever. Which was just as well, because, catlike, Danby possessed none.

The sun was low behind the surrounding pines by the time Danby arrived at the Eskeridges' mock-Tudor home. He had been delayed en route by the scent of another cat, a neutered orange male. (Even to his color-blind eyes, an orange cat was recognizable. It might be the shade of gray, or the configuration of white at the throat and chest.) He had hunted up this fellow feline, and made considerable efforts to communicate, but as far as he could tell, there was no higher intelligence flickering behind its blank green eyes. There was no intelligence at all, as far as Danby was concerned; he'd as soon try talking to a shrub. Finally tiring of the eunuch's unblinking stare, he'd stalked off, forgoing more social experiments in favor of his mission.

He sat for a long time under the forsythia hedge in Giles's front yard, studying the house for signs of life. He refused to be distracted by a cluster of sparrows cavorting on the birdbath, but he realized that unless a meal was forthcoming soon, he would be reduced to foraging. The idea of hurling his bulk at a few ounces of twittering songbird made his scowl even more forbidding than usual. He licked a front paw and glowered at the silent house.

After twenty minutes or so, he heard the distant hum of a car engine, and smelled gasoline fumes. Danby peered out from the hedge in time to see Julie Eskeridge's Mercedes rounding the corner from Windsor Way. With a few hasty licks to smooth down his ruff, Danby sauntered toward the driveway, just as the car pulled in. Now for the hard part: how do you impress Julie Eskeridge without a checkbook?

He had never noticed before how much Giles's wife resembled a giraffe. He blinked at the sight of her huge feet swinging out of the car perilously close to his nose. They were followed by two replicas of the Alaska pipeline, both encased in nylon. Better not jump up on her; one claw on the stockings, and he'd have an enemy for life. Julie was one of those people who air-kissed because she couldn't bear to spoil her make-up. Instead of trying to attract her attention at the car (where she could have skewered him with one spike heel), Danby loped to the steps of the side porch, and began meowing piteously. As Julie approached the steps, he looked up at her with wide-eyed supplication, waiting to be admired.

"Shoo, cat!" said Julie, nudging him aside with her foot.

As the door slammed in his face, Danby realized that he had badly miscalculated. He had also neglected to devise a backup plan. A fine mess he was in now. It wasn't enough that he was murdered, and reassigned to cathood—now he was also homeless.

He was still hanging around the steps twenty minutes later when Giles came home, mainly because he couldn't think of an alternate plan just yet. When he saw Giles's black sports car pull up behind Julie's Mercedes, Danby's first impulse was to run, but then he realized that, while Giles might see him, he certainly wouldn't recognize him as his old business partner. Besides, he was curious to see how an uncaught murderer looked. Would

Giles be haggard with grief and remorse? Furtive, as he listened for police sirens in the distance?

Giles Eskeridge was whistling. He climbed out of his car, sun-tanned and smiling, with his lips pursed in a cheerfully tuneless whistle. Danby trotted forward to confront his murderer with his haughtiest scowl of indignation. The reaction was not quite what he expected.

Giles saw the huge, fluffy cat, and immediately knelt down, calling, "Here, kitty, kitty!"

Danby looked at him as if he had been propositioned.

"Aren't you a beauty!" said Giles, holding out his hand to the strange cat. "I'll bet you're a pedigreed animal, aren't you, fella? Are you lost, boy?"

Much as it pained him to associate with a remorseless killer, Danby sidled over to the outstretched hand, and allowed his ears to be scratched. He reasoned that Giles's interest in him was his one chance to gain entry to the house. It was obvious that Julie wasn't a cat fancier. Who would have taken heartless old Giles for an animal lover? Probably similarity of temperament, Danby decided.

He allowed himself to be picked up, and carried into the house, while Giles stroked his back and told him what a pretty fellow he was. This was an indignity, but still an improvement over Giles's behavior toward him during their last encounter. Once inside, Giles called out to Julie, "Look what I've got, honey!"

She came in from the kitchen, scowling. "That nasty cat!" she said. "Put him right back outside!"

At this point Danby concentrated all his energies toward making himself purr. It was something like snoring, he decided, but it had the desired effect on his intended victim, for at once Giles made for his den, and plumped down in an armchair, arranging Danby in his lap, with more petting and praise. "He's a wonderful cat, Julie," Giles told his wife. "I'll bet he's a pure-bred Maine Coon. Probably worth a couple of hundred bucks."

"So are my wool carpets," Mrs. Eskeridge replied. "So are my new sofas! And who's going to clean up his messes?"

That was Danby's cue. He had already thought out the piece de resistance in his campaign of endearment. With a trill that meant "This way, folks!", Danby hopped off his ex-partner's lap, and trotted to the downstairs bathroom. He had used it often enough at dinner parties, and he knew that the door was left ajar. He had been saving up for this moment. With Giles and his missus watching from the doorway, Danby hopped up on the toilet seat, twitched his elegant plumed tail, and proceeded to use the toilet in the correct manner.

He felt a strange tingling in his paws, and he longed to scratch at something and cover it up, but he ignored these urges, and basked instead in the effusive praise from his self-appointed champion. Why couldn't Giles have been that enthusiastic over his design for the Jenner building? Danby thought resentfully. Some people's sense of values were so warped. Meanwhile, though, he might as well savor the Eskeridges' transports of joy over his bowel control; there weren't too many ways for cats to demonstrate superior intelligence. He couldn't quote a little Shakespeare or identify the dinner wine. Fortunately, among felines toilet training passed for genius, and even Julie was impressed with his accomplishments. After that, there was no question of Giles turning him out into the cruel world. Instead, they carried him back to the kitchen, and opened a can of tuna fish for his dining pleasure. He had to eat it in a bowl on the floor, but the bowl was Royal Doulton, which was some consolation. And while he ate, he could still hear Giles in the background, raving about what a wonderful cat he was. He was in.

"No collar, Julie. Someone must have abandoned him on the highway. What shall we call him?"

"Varmint," his wife suggested. She was a hard sell.

Giles ignored her lack of enthusiasm for his newfound prodigy. "I think I'll call him Merlin. He's a wizard of a cat."

Merlin? Danby looked up with a mouthful of tuna. Oh well, he thought, Merlin and tuna were better than Tigger and cheap dry cat food. You couldn't have everything.

*   *   *

After that, he quickly became a full-fledged member of the household, with a newly-purchased plastic feeding bowl, a cat-nip mouse toy, and another little collar with another damned bell. Danby resisted the urge to bite Giles's thumb off while he was attaching this loathsome neckpiece over his ruff, but he restrained himself. By now he was accustomed to the accompaniment of a maniacal jingling with every step he took. What was it with human beings and bells?

Of course, that spoiled his plans for songbird hunting outdoors. He'd have to travel faster than the speed of sound to catch a sparrow now. Not that he got out much, anyhow. Giles seemed to think that he might wander off again, so he was generally careful to keep Danby housebound.

That was all right with Danby, though. It gave him an excellent opportunity to become familiar with the house, and with the routine of its inhabitants—all useful information for someone planning revenge. So far he (the old Danby, that is) had not been mentioned in the Eskeridge conversations. He wondered what story Giles was giving out about his disappearance. Apparently the body had not been found. It was up to him to punish the guilty, then.

Danby welcomed the days when both Giles and Julie left the house. Then he would forgo his morning, mid-morning, and early afternoon naps in order to investigate each room of his domain, looking for lethal opportunities: medicine bottles, perhaps, or perhaps a small electrical appliance that he could push into the bathtub.

So far, though, he had not attempted to stage any accidents, for fear that the wrong Eskeridge would fall victim to his snare. He didn't like Julie any more than she liked him, but he had no reason to kill her. The whole business needed careful study. He could afford to take his time analyzing the opportunities for revenge. The food was good, the job of house cat was undemanding, and he rather enjoyed the irony of being doted on by his intended victim. Giles was certainly better as an owner than he was as a partner.

An evening conversation between Giles and Julie convinced

him that he must accelerate his efforts. They were sitting in the den, after a meal of baked chicken. They wouldn't give him the bones, though. Giles kept insisting that they'd splinter in his stomach and kill him. Danby was lying on the hearth rug, pretending to be asleep until they forgot about him, at which time he would sneak back into the kitchen and raid the garbage. He'd given up smoking, hadn't he? And although he'd lapped up a bit of Giles's Scotch one night, he seemed to have lost the taste for it. How much prudence could he stand?

"If you're absolutely set on keeping this cat, Giles," said Julie Eskeridge, examining her newly-polished talons, "I suppose I'll have to be the one to take him to the vet."

"The vet. I hadn't thought about it. Of course, he'll have to have shots, won't he?" murmured Giles, still studying the newspaper. "Rabies, and so on."

"And while we're at it, we might as well have him neutered," said Julie. "Otherwise, he'll start spraying the drapes and all."

Danby rocketed to full alert. To keep them from suspecting his comprehension, he centered his attention on the cleaning of a perfectly tidy front paw. It was time to step up the pace on his plans for revenge, or he'd be meowing in soprano. And forget the scruples about innocent bystanders: now it was a matter of self-defense.

That night he waited until the house was dark and quiet. Giles and Julie usually went to bed about eleven-thirty, turning off all the lights, which didn't faze him in the least. He rather enjoyed skulking about the silent house using his infrared vision, although he rather missed late-night television. He had once considered turning the set on with his paw, but that seemed too precocious, even for a cat named Merlin. Danby didn't want to end up in somebody's behavior lab with wires coming out of his head.

He examined his collection of cat toys, stowed by Julie in his cat basket, because she hated clutter. He had a mouse-shaped catnip toy, a rubber fish, and a little red ball. Giles bought the ball under the ludicrous impression that Danby could be induced to play catch. When he'd rolled it across the floor, Danby lay down and gave him an insolent stare. He had enjoyed the next quarter of an hour, watching Giles on his hands and knees, batting the ball, and trying to teach Danby to fetch, but finally Giles gave up, and the ball had been tucked in the cat basket ever since. Danby picked it up with his teeth, and carried it upstairs. Giles and Julie came down the right side of the staircase, didn't they? That's where the banister was. He set the ball carefully on the third step, in the approximate place that a human foot would touch the stair. A tripwire would be more reliable, but Danby couldn't manage the technology involved.

What else could he devise for the Eskeridges' peril? He couldn't poison their food, and since they'd provided him with a flea collar, he couldn't even hope to get bubonic plague started in the household. Attacking them with tooth and claw seemed foolhardy, even if they were sleeping. The one he wasn't biting could always fight him off, and a fifteen-pound cat can be killed with relative ease by any human determined to do it. Even if they didn't kill him on the spot, they'd get rid of him immediately, and then he'd lose his chance forever. It was too risky.

It had to be stealth, then. Danby inspected the house, looking for lethal opportunities. There weren't any electrical appliances close to the bathtub, and besides, Giles took showers. In another life Danby might have been able to rewire the electric razor to shock its user, but such a feat was well beyond his present level of dexterity. No wonder human beings had taken over the earth; they were so damned hard to kill.

Even his efforts to enlist help in the task had proved fruitless. On one of his rare excursions out of the house (Giles went golfing, and he slipped out without Julie's noticing), Danby had roamed the neighborhood, looking for . . . well . . . pussy. Instead he'd found dimwitted tomcats, and a Doberman pinscher, who was definitely Somebody. Danby had kept conversation to a minimum, not quite liking the look of the beast's prominent fangs. Danby suspected that the Doberman had previously been an IRS agent. Of course, the dog had *said* that it had been a serial killer, but that was just to lull Danby into a false sense of security. Anyhow, much as the dog approved of

Danby's plan to kill his humans, he wasn't interested in forming a conspiracy. Why should he go to the gas chamber to solve someone else's problem?

Danby himself had similar qualms about doing anything too drastic—such as setting fire to the house. He didn't want to stage an accident that would include himself among the victims. After puttering about the darkened house for a wearying few hours, he stretched out on the sofa in the den to take a quick nap before resuming his plotting. He'd be able to think better after he rested.

The next thing Danby felt was a ruthless grip on his collar, dragging him forward. He opened his eyes to find that it was morning, and that the hand at his throat belonged to Julie Eskeridge, who was trying to stuff him into a metal cat carrier. He tried to dig his claws into the sofa, but it was too late. Before he could blink, he had been hoisted along by his tail, and shoved into the box. He barely got his tail out of the way before the door slammed shut behind him. Danby crouched in the plastic carrier, peeking out the side slits, and trying to figure out what to do next. Obviously the rubber ball on the steps had been a dismal failure as a murder weapon. Why couldn't he have come back as a mountain lion?

Danby fumed about the slings and arrows of outrageous fortune all the way out to the car. It didn't help to remember where he was going, and what was scheduled to be done with him shortly thereafter. Julie Eskeridge set the cat carrier on the back seat and slammed the door. When she started the car, Danby howled in protest.

"Be quiet back there!" Julie called out. "There's nothing you can do about it."

We'll see about that, thought Danby, turning to peer out the door of his cage. The steel bars of the door were about an inch apart, and there was no mesh or other obstruction between them. He found that he could easily slide one paw sideways out of the cage. Now, if he could just get a look at the workings of the latch, there was a slight chance that he could extricate himself. He lay down on his side and squinted up at the metal catch. It seemed to be a glorified bolt. To lock the carrier, a metal bar was slid into a socket and then rotated downward to latch. If he could push the bar back up and then slide it back . . .

It wasn't easy to maneuver with the car changing speed and turning corners. Danby felt himself getting quite dizzy with the effort of concentrating as the carrier gently rocked. But finally, when the car reached the interstate and sped along smoothly, he succeeded in positioning his paw at the right place on the bar, and easing it upward. Another three minutes of tense probing allowed him to slide the bar a fraction of an inch, and then another. The bolt was now clear of the latch. There was no getting out of the car, of course. Julie had rolled up the windows, and they were going sixty miles an hour. Danby spent a full minute pondering the implications of his dilemma. But no matter which way he looked at the problem, the alternative was always the same: do something desperate or go under the knife. It wasn't as if dying had been such a big deal, after all. There was always next time.

Quickly, before the fear could stop him, Danby hurled his furry bulk against the door of the cat carrier, landing in the floor of the backseat with a solid thump. He sprang back up on the seat, and launched himself into the air with a heartfelt snarl, landing precariously on Julie Eskeridge's right shoulder, and digging his claws in to keep from falling.

The last things he remembered were Julie's screams and the feel of the car swerving out of control.

When Danby opened his eyes, the world was still playing in black and white. He could hear muffled voices, and smell a jumble of scents: blood, gasoline, smoke. He struggled to get up, and found that he was still less than a foot off the ground. Still furry. Still the Eskeridges' cat. In the distance he could see the crumpled wreckage of Julie's car.

A familiar voice was droning on above him. "He must have been thrown free of the cat carrier during the wreck, Officer.

That's definitely Merlin, though. My poor wife was taking him to the vet."

A burly policeman was standing next to Giles, nodding sympathetically. "I guess it's true what they say about cats, sir. Having nine lives, I mean. I'm very sorry about your wife. She wasn't so lucky."

Giles hung his head. "No. It's been a great strain. First my business partner disappears, and now I lose my wife." He stooped and picked up Danby. "At least I have my beautiful kitty-cat for consolation. Come on, boy. Let's go home."

Danby's malevolent yellow stare did not waver. He allowed himself to be carried away to Giles's waiting car without protest. He could wait. Cats were good at waiting. And life with Giles wasn't so bad, now that Julie wouldn't be around to harass him. Danby would enjoy a spell of being doted on by an indulgent human; fed gourmet cat food; and given the run of the house. Meanwhile, he could continue to leave the occasional ball on the stairs, and think of other ways to toy with Giles, while he waited to see if the police ever turned up to ask Giles about his missing partner. If not, Danby could work on more ways to kill humans. Sooner or later he would succeed. Cats are endlessly patient at stalking their prey.

"It's just you and me, now, fella," said Giles, placing his cat on the seat beside him.

And after he killed Giles, perhaps he could go in search of the building contractor that Giles bribed to keep his dirty secret. He certainly deserved to die. And that nasty woman Danby used to live next door to, who used to complain about his stereo and his crabgrass. And perhaps the surly headwaiter at *Chantage*. Stray cats can turn up anywhere.

Danby began to purr.

FIVE STARVING CATS AND A DEAD DOG

Kristine Kathryn Rusch

WHENEVER A CAR RUMBLES UP THE DRIVE, he runs—four feet flying, orange and white tail a flag in the underbrush.

I wish I could run too.

Instead, I grab my husband's .22, and point it at the door, waiting. If I stand right next to the stairs, I can see through the glass panes without anyone seeing me. Usually, it's the man from the electric company out to read the meter. He doesn't seem to notice me. Once it was two Jehovah's Witnesses. I moved closer to the door; they saw the rifle and ran.

No one else comes up here.

I live on a knoll in a company-owned valley, my house hidden among twenty acres of trees that the company can't log. My husband and I bought the house a year ago, on a sun-dappled July afternoon. We had seen the ancient For Sale sign and followed its directions up a mile-long gravel driveway, catching glimpses of a brown building as we drove. We came up the ridge of the knoll and stopped, staring at the house.

Two stories, no basement, three balconies, and dozens of windows. The front door was unlocked, so we let ourselves in. We wandered through the first floor with its cavernous living room, formal dining room, and kitchen large enough to hold twenty comfortably. We didn't have to see the upstairs to know we had found home.

I wish it had stayed that simple. Lord knows, after all the work we did on our business and in our lives, we deserved simple. We had sold our computer company for twice its value and were looking forward to an early retirement in the hills. Neither of us over forty, enjoying our relative youth in relative quiet—or so we thought.

We should have noticed how odd things were from the start. The house's owners didn't want to sell. Their asking price was twice as high as the market would bear. They were waiting for the house to collapse, and the company to buy the land. But we insisted; we hardly negotiated. The house was what we were looking for, and we were determined to have it.

Then there were the cats. The skinny brown one who kept disappearing into the trees, and the starving pregnant Siamese who gave birth to a single orange kitten on the day we moved in. We put out food for them, not willing to let them inside with our four cats, and three more cats appeared, too-thin, starving, grateful for the attention but skittish. They liked me, but it took weeks before they went near Reg. They didn't like our male friends, either, something I'd never seen so uniform in a group of cats before. All five starving cats were purebreds, expensive purebreds: a Scottish Fold, a Tortoise-Shell Siamese, an Abyssinian, a Burmese, and a Manx. People didn't abandon cats like that. Even if they had no affinity for animals, the sheer expense of the cats made them worth keeping.

But the dog unnerved me the most. One afternoon in early September, with the sun setting along the hills, sending ridges of colored light through the trees, I decided to explore the property. I got to the edge of our knoll, where the grass tapered into trees, and found a skull.

Long and slender, canine, a bit too yellow to be sunbleached. It rested on top of a half-dug grave, with more bones littered inside. The skin was gone, but most of the gray matter remained in the cranium. Whatever had dug it up hadn't had time to finish its meal.

I called Reg over. He crouched, gave his inexpert opinion. "Been dead less than a year," he said. Then we stared at each other. People who would abandon purebred cats wouldn't bury a dog, would they? That showed more caring than we thought them capable of.

Reg promised to cover the grave, but dark was setting in, so we left it, forgotten, skull staring sightlessly at the clouds. Maybe if we had taken an extra fifteen minutes, I wouldn't be trapped here. Maybe things would have turned out differently.

We took the purebreds to the vet, got rid of their fleas and ear mites, had the Siamese fixed, renamed them, and brought them back into their old home. Our cats tolerated them with barely hidden displeasure, although few hissing fights occurred. I let them take over our lives, but the one that took over my heart was the orange kitten, whom we named Grubby.

He was a hardy little guy. Born to a starving mother, he barely moved during the first few weeks of his life. As she gained strength, so did he. But he never completely caught up. He remains, even now, two years later, a permanent kitten, stuck between eight and sixteen weeks of age.

But he can run faster than any other cat I have ever seen. And he can hunt. One evening, I sat in my study, reading, when I heard a thrashing on the front porch, followed by squawking, and several pounding noises. I hurried to the front door and stared through the panels at Grubby, who was not yet full-grown. He had trapped a crow three times his size on the porch and was trying to wring its neck. I was about to step out, to prevent my kitten from being pecked to death, when he pounced.

The crow squawked and jabbed at him. Grubby held its head

down with one paw while he used his back legs to break its spine. The bird twisted away from him, and Grubby pounced again, this time landing on the bird's neck with an audible snap. The bird stopped moving, and Grub stared at it as if he were a child who had just broken a favorite toy. He tried tossing it in the air a few times, and succeeded only in covering my porch with more feathers.

From that point on, we let him hunt anything he wanted. He brought me field mice, squirrels, shrews, and baby opossums. Once he fended off the raccoon that had been raiding our garbage. Not too bright, our Grubby, but courageous.

That courage fails him now. I don't know why he runs, because he won that last fight. Maybe because it startled him, or maybe because of Reg . . .

Yet I think it's something simpler than that. For Grubby is still a baby, and he reacts instinctively. I think he realized that human beings can be cruel, and the only one he trusts is me.

The day it happened started poorly. I woke with the acrid smell of smoke in my lungs. Reg was still asleep, his face twenty years younger in repose. Sometimes I stared at him while he slept, seeing the boy I had married in the man he had become. I nudged him awake, and he sat up bleary-eyed, black hair tousled.

"Smell that?" I asked.

"Jesus, smoke," he said.

Our smoke alarm hadn't gone off, but we walked through the house anyway, finding nothing. Then Reg called me from the back balcony. I hurried to him and peered out. On the other side of the ridge, fire licked at the hillside, orange against the October green.

"I'll call," he said, and disappeared. I watched it, eating away at the clearcut, trying to decide what possessions to take, which car would handle the cats.

Five minutes later, he was back. "They said to stay put. They think it's an unofficial slash-burn."

A slash-burn. Something the logging company does after it clearcuts to prime the soil for next year's planting. Oregonians seem to think that fire is the only way to add nutrients to the soil. Grass-growers in the nearby Willamette Valley do the same thing—and pitch-black smoke blowing across the interstate killed forty-three people the summer before.

We watched as the little green fire truck made its way up the logging road that branched off our driveway. It stopped, yellow lights flashing, near the source of the burn, and remained there for nearly fifteen minutes. Then the lights went out. It turned, followed the logging road until it met our driveway and drove up to the house.

Reg slid on a pair of jeans and was downstairs before they could knock. I took an extra minute to get dressed.

By the time I got downstairs, the fireman was already talking with Reg.

". . . slash-burn, like we thought. Don't know why they didn't report it. They been doing it too much lately." The fireman was stocky, in an oversized green plastic-looking uniform. He had clearly come to fight a fire.

"We're safe, then?"

"Oh, yeah," the fireman said. "They got it under control. Something you got to get used to out here. The company owns the valley, they do what they want."

"We were warned about that when we bought the place," Reg said.

We had been warned about a number of things, such as the fact that our twenty acres could be the only stand of trees for miles if the company decided to do some heavy logging in our area.

"Knew the guy who lived here before," the fireman said. "See him every day, and still don't know why he sold it."

My interest was piqued. "Do you work with him?"

"Naw. He works at the grocery down toward town. I stop every night for the wife. We talk some, although we been talking less."

"Did he ever say why he moved?"

The fireman shook his head. "All I know is that he wasn't sure if he wanted to sell the house. Don't know why since he hadn't lived in it for months. That's why he priced it so high. Didn't think nobody would buy it. Then you happened along. Wasn't sure if he was happy or not."

"Was that his dog buried out back?" Reg asked.

The fireman shrugged. "Don't rightly know. We just kinda talk every day, you know. We're not friends or nothing." He tipped his hat. "Best get back to the truck."

"Thank you for coming out here," I said.

"It's our job, ma'am," he said as he made his way through the trees.

Reg closed the door and coughed. "Something we'll have to get used to, huh?"

"Well, this is the first time in almost two months," I said. "Maybe it won't happen that often."

"Hope not," Reg said. "This isn't the way I like to wake up."

He went upstairs and took a shower. I followed soon after. We spent the rest of the day watching the fire slowly burn itself out. By twilight, it had become a glow of embers against the dark.

We were sitting down to a late dinner when we heard a car on the gravel road. It wasn't so unusual then; we just figured it was a friend stopping by for some conversation or wilderness star-gazing.

Reg was halfway to the door when footsteps sounded on the front porch. I had gotten up to put our meal on the counter, out of reach of the cats. The door burst open, and a shotgun stabbed Reg's sternum. The man behind it was short, squat, with brown hair tied in a ponytail. He was wearing a butcher's apron, dress slacks and a white shirt with the sleeves rolled up.

I had never seen him before.

"Didn't think I'd find out about the dog, did ya?"

"I d-d-don't know what you're talking about," Reg said.

I picked up the phone, set the receiver on its side and dialed 911. Not that it would do us any good right away. We were too far out.

"Get that bitch out here where I can see her," the man said. "Hon?"

I stepped into the foyer, wishing I had gone for the rifle we had in the pantry instead of dialing for help that wouldn't come.

Reg's face was ashen. I stood, hands at my sides, concentrating, trying to see out of the corner of my eye if there was something, anything I could use as a weapon. The hall table beside me was empty, and the coat rack near the door too light to do more than annoy the man, even if I could reach him.

"I didn't think I shoulda sold the house to you," the man said. "But the money, the goddamn money—"

"You sold the house?" Reg asked. *"You* owned it?"

Grubby jumped on the table. None too bright, my little cat. The others had run, smelling the fear and anger in the room.

"Why'd you have to snoop? Why didn't you leave it alone?"

"Can't we sit and talk about this like reasonable people?" Reg asked.

Reasonable people. The man holding the gun was not reasonable. He was red-faced and frightening.

"It's the dog," he said, raising his rifle some. I saw my chance. "If you hadn't said nothing about the dog—"

I picked up Grubby and hurled him at the man. The cat flew through the air, spitting and hissing. The rifle went off, Reg moaned and collapsed, and Grubby dug his claws into the man's face before bounding out the door.

The man turned to me, blood pouring down his cheeks from scratches that hadn't come close enough to his eyes. "You stupid bitch," he said, leveling the gun at me.

I wasn't about to stand still while he tried to shoot me. I turned, ran through the kitchen, grabbing the knife I had used for dinner off the counter as I passed. I let myself out the back door and into the yard as a gunshot smashed glass around me.

Down on the road, I could hear sirens.

I slid through the trees, gripping blackberry bushes and trying not to cry out as the thorns bit into my palms. I had left Reg in there with that madman. Reg.

I made it to the gravel road quicker than I thought. Sliding, sliding on the steep incline, I ran to the sound of the sirens. Two police cars hurried up, with more on the road behind. They had heard it and dispatched someone. Heard everything. Traced the call.

They stopped on the incline, near me.

"He's up there," I said, pointing toward the trees. The cops left their doors open and went up. I couldn't tell anyone that I needed an ambulance. I didn't know how to work the radio, and I was so scared I could barely breathe.

Other cars stopped. More police got out. "Up there," I said. Finally, a woman stayed back with me.

"We need an ambulance," I said. "My husband's still up there."

She called for help. And by the time the ambulance arrived, they had already stopped Reg's bleeding, and were waiting for backup. But they never found the man. He had run into the woods with his gun and disappeared.

The things they never tell you about the forests of the Pacific Northwest. Children disappear in them, only to be found, decades later, skeletal remains under a tree. Adults walk away from a car to take a leak and are never seen again. It's still wilderness here, even if it is wilderness owned by the company.

The search parties combed the woods for three days.

They never found him.

We should move, I know. Find a new place, with new people, get away from all the memories, the bloodstain too deep in the wood-grained floor to remove. But with Reg's medical bills, we can't afford to sell a house we paid too much for in the first place.

Besides, they assure us he's dead.

Reg believes them, even though I find him in his wheelchair staring out the window into the woods more times than not. As if he's looking for something. When we can afford it, I'm going to put in a lift to the second floor. He feels trapped down here, like I feel trapped in the house.

Reg believes the man is gone, forever. "He snapped, babe," Reg says. "He won't be back."

He snapped. As if that's unusual for him. He snapped in the spring and murdered a woman, whether she was a wife or girlfriend no one knew, and buried her in the backyard. Then he shot her dog (I believe all the animals were hers—they never liked men), and buried it on top of her, thinking no one would go past a dog's corpse to see what was buried beneath it. When his friend the fireman relayed his discussion with us, the man snapped—again. How many more times would he snap before he died?

Reg believes he's dead. But I don't. And Grubby doesn't. Sometimes I see that orange and white tail waving through the tall grass, and I realize Grubby's on the hunt. I like to imagine he's following footprints, looking for the man who haunts him in every car that pulls into our drive, in every stranger's glance, in my fear-filled eyes. I like to think that Grubby, our mighty hunter, will catch him someday, trap him on the porch, and use his powerful back legs to snap the man's spine as he once snapped a crow's spine, as a bullet snapped Reg's.

But that won't happen, because that would be justice. And if there were justice in this world, Reg would still be walking, that awful man would be dead, and I would be able to enjoy this house and the woods and the quiet, instead of seeing that gun go off every time I close my eyes. Instead of wondering what would have happened if I hadn't tossed Grubby, if I hadn't interfered. Maybe the police would have arrived in time. Maybe we would all be okay.

Maybe my little orange cat wouldn't scour the woods, searching for prey I hope he never, ever finds.

THE WINFIELD TRADE

Jeremiah Healy

ONE

VENETIA SCOTT SAID, "Slow down a bit and take this next right."

I looked over to her. "Much farther?"

She shook her head. "Not more than a mile now. I really *do* appreciate your driving me from work, Mr. Cuddy."

My new client said it like she was thanking a waiter for bringing her an extra cocktail napkin. About five-five and mid-thirties, Scott looked trim in a gray herringbone suit with a ruffled white blouse and two-inch heels. Her face was thin, but she had big green eyes and generous lips and auburn hair drawn back into a bun that hinted at shoulder length once loosened.

Scott had called me at my office. A lawyer who represented her bank in major loan deals had recommended me as a private investigator who could be trusted on a confidential matter. I told her I'd call her back, then dialed the lawyer. Venetia Scott had

256

checked out as a recently promoted vice-president in charge of computer lease agreements for one of the few Boston financial institutions still taking nourishment without government receivership. I'd picked her up just fifteen minutes ago outside one of the bank's branches, filling up the time more with small talk than business as she gave me directions to her home address.

"Ms. Scott, I take it whatever you want me to work on has to do with your house?"

"It does."

"Just what, exactly?"

My client took a deep breath. "Beginning about a month ago, someone has been staying there while I've been away on weekends."

It was Thursday as we were talking. "How do you know?"

"Little things. And feelings. I'm *very* sensitive that way."

Jesus. "Do you live alone?"

An icy tone. "What difference does that make?"

"What I mean is, could somebody else in the house be responsible?"

"No. Since my divorce, I live alone except for Winfield."

"Winfield?"

"My cat."

I smiled. "Named after Dave?"

"I beg your pardon?"

"Dave Winfield. Yankee outfielder who was unhappy in New York, moved to a couple of other teams since."

The icy tone again. "Winfield is not named after an *athlete*. He is named after Winfield Scott, a general in the Mexican-American War. I'm a traceable descendant."

"Oh."

The cat turned out to be a tubby orange tabby with yellow eyes and long whiskers. He was affectionate enough, brushing against my pant cuffs and purring like a snoring lumberjack when I scratched between his ears.

We were in the foyer of Scott's modest Cape Cod, the smallest house in a good neighborhood. A terrific investment in the mid-eighties, it was probably holding its value as well as could be expected now. I'd checked the front door on our way in. No sign of forced entry.

Scott walked me through a living room with colonial furniture, including an old-fashioned slider chair, to a kitchen extended via a deck into the backyard. The back door lock and jamb looked fine, too.

"You keep your windows locked?"

"Always."

"Security system?"

"No."

I stepped out onto the deck and looked left, then right. Each bordering house was nestled on about an acre, hers only a half-acre by the looks of the landscaping that acted as boundary lines.

"Neighbors?"

Scott pointed left. "That place has been empty for three months. Foreclosure, but not by my bank." She swung right. "The couple on the other side have been in Florida for six weeks. Which is my point, really."

"Your point?"

"Yes. If someone simply wanted to break into a house and occupy it like a *squatter*, there are better choices within easy reach. No, Mr. Cuddy, this is harassment."

"Harassment."

"Yes. Subtle, but clear."

"Could you share some of the subtleties with me?"

A labored sigh. "Toilet paper roll just *slightly* out of kilter."

I looked down at Winfield, who had followed us from room to room. "Maybe the cat, toying with it?"

The icy tone a third time. "Water glasses rinsed and dried, leaving no spots. Forks placed in drawer tines down rather than tines up."

"Forks."

"I beg your—"

"Forks plural, or just one each time?"

"Just one."

"Same for glasses?"

"Yes."

We moved back into the living room. "You think it's harassment, you must have somebody in mind."

"*Three* somebodies. Do you wish to take notes?"

I sat down in the slider chair. Comfortable and silent.

Scott used her left hand to tick off names on her right, as
though she were vigorously polishing her nails. "First, Chris
Murphy, my ex-husband. He's a police officer in the next town."

Uh-oh. "He still have a set of keys to this place?"

"No. The locks have been changed twice."

"Twice?"

"Yes. Once after the judge ordered him out during the divorce
three years ago, and again five weeks ago."

"Just before you noticed the 'subtle harassment.' "

"Exactly. That brings me to the second—what would you call
it, 'suspect'?"

"The second person will do fine."

"Second is Luther Dane, my assistant at the bank. I lost my
keys at work, which was the reason I had the locks changed
again. Luther would have access to my new key."

"This Dane have any motive?"

"Yes. He would love to see me foul up due to pressure here so
that he could get my job."

"Is that realistic?"

"It's how I got *my* promotion."

"By forcing out a boss?"

"Precisely. Which brings us to number three, Irene Presker."

"Your former boss."

A nod. "I'm sure she has it in for me after I nudged her out."

I found myself rooting for Presker but fought it. "She have
access to your keys?"

"Not that I know of."

"Who was the locksmith this last time?"

A wave of the hand. "A nice man, got on *famously* with

Winfield. Vietnamese, I think. He came by to change the locks on a Friday just as I was leaving."

"And the next week, the live-in stuff began happening."

"The next weekend."

"Why is it that you go away weekends, Ms. Scott?"

She glanced involuntarily toward a shelf on the wall. I could see a framed photo of Scott in casual clothes, hugging a handsome man of about fifty with gray hair that looked carefully styled even in the breeze that lifted it.

My client said, "I'm seeing a man who's allergic to cat dander, so I spend weekends at his home."

"Name?"

"I don't want you approaching him."

"I'd just like his name in case it comes up."

"Evan Speidel."

I looked at the photo again and took a guess. "Also in banking?"

"Yes. He'll be the next president of Ridgeview Savings and Loan, a *solid* institution."

Scott put more into "solid" than I could have with a hammer.

"Speidel have a key to your house?"

The icy tone got glacial. "I keep a spare at his home."

I glanced down at the cat. "Why not just give Winfield away?"

My client glared at me. "I bought him for Chris originally, but Winfield stayed with me as part of the divorce settlement."

I chewed on that awhile.

"If you're thinking that Evan has anything to do with this, forget it."

Actually, I was thinking that Venetia Scott might have been better off with the cop that liked cats than the banker who couldn't, but I kept it to myself.

TWO

On Friday morning I got up early and went over the addresses Venetia Scott had given me. Then I drove to the downtown area nearest her house.

The sign over the glass door said MAIN STREET LOCKSMITH in tintype. The walls of the six-by-seven shop were lined with brass knobs and sturdy plates and imposing deadbolts. A skinny man with Southeast Asian features sat behind a steel counter with an English-language newspaper open in front of him. His black hair hung over his forehead almost to his eyebrows, and he worked a bony index finger one word at a time through a column that had the phrase "Khmer Rouge" in its headline. Behind him, purple beads, strung vertically on wire, curtained entry to the back of the shop. The beads shimmered a little as I closed the front door.

The man looked up at me, smiled and said, "Can I help, sir?"

I said, "Mr. . . ."

"Hun is my name."

I showed him my ID. He looked at it a long time, reading "John Francis Cuddy" as carefully as he had the newspaper.

"What you want?"

I pocketed the leather holder and explained that I was asking questions for Venetia Scott.

Hun's eyes grew wary. "Ms. Scott?"

"Yes."

"What is problem?"

"No problem for you. I'd just like to ask you a few questions."

Hun looked resigned. "Ask."

I pointed at the article he'd been reading. "You're from Cambodia originally?"

"Why that matter?"

"No reason, except you're reading an article about the Khmer Rouge."

Hun's jaw clenched. "I no need to read about Khmer Rouge. I live through Khmer Rouge. In Phnom Penh, then in camp, then in jungle." He stabbed the paper with the tip of his finger. "Newspaper used to say two million people kill by Pol Pot. Now say only one million. How can this be?"

I didn't have an answer for him. "You changed the locks at Ms. Scott's house?"

"Yes, I do that for her."

"Anybody ever ask you for keys to the house?"

Hun's eyes widened. "Ask me?"

"Yes."

"Nobody."

I went through the names I had, including the new boyfriend, Evan Speidel. Hun shook his head no, the eyes stony at each one. I got the feeling that other interrogators hadn't treated him so well in the past.

"Anyone else here I could talk to?"

Hun's eyes went back down to the article. "Is nobody else. Only me."

Chris Murphy, about six-two and two hundred pounds, looked like a surfer who was losing his dishwater blond hair. And his temper at me.

"Cuddy, I don't get why you're asking me all these questions."

"I'm hired to ask questions. These are simple ones."

"Simple, huh? Like am I harassing my ex-wife and you won't even tell me what I'm supposed to be doing?"

I'd called Murphy at police headquarters in the neighboring town, then waited for him outside, as he'd asked me to. We were standing next to a dented, five-year-old Corvette that I took to be his car. Murphy had his arms crossed, beefy hands working on the outside of his sport coat.

"Murphy—"

"I mean, the hell position am I in with the department, I get accused of harassing my ex, this day and age?"

"So you haven't been in any kind of contact with Venetia Scott."

"No, I told you. Not her, not the bank, not the house. Not since the restraining order way back when."

I hadn't mentioned the house.

Murphy said, "You think I'm nuts or something, a cop violating a restraining order?"

I didn't think he was nuts. I did wonder how he and Venetia Scott ever got together, but I wasn't sure I wanted to find out.

"Seen your cat lately?"

"My—Winfield? Hell, that little bugger still around?"

"How do you mean?"

"Aw, Venny, she never cared much one way or the other for the cat. Just like another pawn in the chess game between her lawyer and me."

"Because you wanted him back?"

Murphy looked exasperated. "Cuddy, she held onto him because I made her *think* I wanted him back."

"Why would you do that?"

"So I could get what *I* wanted, like this car, some other stuff to set myself up in a new place."

"While she got the house."

"Right, right. Hell, it was like a negotiating tactic on my part. What do you think, I'm stupid?"

I let that one pass, too.

Irene Presker had answered her own telephone and now answered her own door. The condo complex was a nice one, low and by the sea about eight miles south of Boston. From the parking lot, I'd seen a little skyline through the smog in the distance and a couple of playful sailboats through the mist in the foreground.

Presker, however, did not look playful herself. About five feet tall, she was pushing a hundred fifty, mostly through the hips and thighs. Her hair was curly and too black to be natural, the make-up overdone considering she was apparently working at home that day.

Staring at my ID, Presker said, "Which would be easier for me, to talk with you or call the cops?"

"Calling the cops, definitely."

The hint of a grin. "You're really a private investigator?"

"Really and truly."

"All right, come in."

The living room was a little box without fireplace or harbor view, a small, open kitchen cloistered with it. A corridor ran off in one direction toward two closed doors, I assumed a bedroom and a bath. Presker took one barrel chair, me the other, there not being space enough for couch or even loveseat.

"So, what's this about?"

"A former associate of yours is being harassed. Your name came up."

"I'm supposed to know something about 'a former associate' being harassed?"

"That's what I'm here to find out."

"Hah. You wasted your gas. The only one I could . . ." Presker's eyes did grow playful. "Not Venetia Scott?"

"Yes."

"There is a God. I must thank Him."

"Ms. Presker—"

"So, is Venny going nuts?"

Venny. The nickname her ex-husband had used. "You're not even curious about what the harassment is?"

"Not unless it's really awful. I'd rather use my imagination."

"Why so down on Scott?"

"Down. Down, now there's a great word for Venny. Put down, shut down, shot down. Lots of possibilities there."

"Possibilities?"

"For who's harassing her. Let me tell you something about your client, Mr. Cuddy. Venny, basically speaking, is a witch.

An absolute witch. She begged me to take her on as my assistant at the bank, and her resumé wasn't in the personnel folder before she was laying the groundwork to replace me. Venny sucked up to people, slept with people, whatever it took. Oh, yeah, one other thing, too. She really did master the job."

"Which is?"

"Doing loan papers on complicated computer leases. You know the jargon?"

"None of it."

"Then I'll spare you. Just figure that she can understand complicated relationships, technical and financial, then protect the bank as to them."

"And you taught her?"

"That's right."

"And now she's in your office in a downtown skyscraper and you're working out of your house."

"Oh, but I'm con-*sult*-ing." A thick layer of sarcasm coated Presker's voice. "My own *home* office. It's really much *so* much more meaningful and satisfying than a *mere* salary and stock options."

It took me a minute to appreciate that Presker was lampooning Scott's speech patterns.

"Anything you can tell me about who might be after her?"

Presker laughed, not a pleasant sound. "Try the guy who replaced her. Maybe he's learning at the witch's knee."

Luther Dane was a young black man with horn-rimmed glasses. I met him sitting at a desk outside Venetia Scott's office in the skyscraper. He looked studious in a blue suit, white button-down shirt and quiet tie. At least until he started talking. Then he both looked and sounded studious.

"I don't have any idea what could be behind this, Mr. Cuddy."

Scott was at a meeting, so Dane and I had moved into her office, a nice view of the beige and gray airport and a verdant harbor island through a window that I was sure couldn't be opened. Dane had taken Scott's desk chair without seeming to think about it. I tried one of the captain's chairs, my shoulders covering the emblem of a local business school emblazoned on the backrest.

"No reason for anyone you know of to be harassing Ms. Scott?"

"Venetia Scott is a warm and wonderful human being."

Dane's words would have sounded fine to a bug planted in the office. His face and body language told a different story, like a Mideast hostage giving a canned television interview.

"You're not interested in scaring her out of her job?"

"Ms. V. Scott does not scare."

"Rattle her then. Enough so she starts to make mistakes here at work."

"Her mistakes would be looked upon as my mistakes, too."

"Not if you created the record correctly."

Dane smiled. "Law school, Mr. Cuddy?"

"A year, nights. You?"

"Four years, nights. Worked long and hard to get this far. I'm not about to pollute my own well."

"So, if you're not interested in scaring or rattling your boss, how do you plan to get ahead?"

"By outworking her. Her and anybody else I'm competing with."

"And you figure you can outwork Ms. Scott."

"The way she's spending her weekends? You bet."

I hadn't said anything about weekends. "How's that?"

"Her weekends, man. She's spending them somewhere else."

"How do you know?"

Dane spread his hands wide, encompassing Scott's office. "Because I come in every Saturday and half a day on Sunday, Mr. Cuddy. I'm here, and she isn't, and that means she's off somewhere."

"Like at her house?"

"Not when I try to reach her there."

"Why would you try to do that?"

Dane shrugged. "Even on weekends, questions come up that I'm not good enough to answer."

"Yet."

Just a smile.

THREE

After speaking with Luther Dane, I didn't wait for Venetia Scott to come back from her meeting. Instead I got my car out of hock at the parking garage next to the bank and drove to the suburban town where Ridgeview Savings and Loan had its offices.

I sat outside the red-bricked and gold-domed building for an hour before being rewarded by the appearance of Evan Speidel. He shook two sets of hands on his way from the main entrance to a black Lincoln Continental. Inside the Lincoln, Speidel drove sedately about three miles to a butcher block and ferns saloon just off a busy mall. I parked three slanting rows away from his car and followed him into the restaurant.

When he shook a few more hands and took a table, I slid onto a stool at the bar, the mirror above the top shelf bottles allowing me to watch Speidel in reflection. After a waiter presented him with a *Wall Street Journal* to skim, a cocktail waitress brought him what looked like a dry manhattan without his having to order it. He glanced up a couple of times, like a man watching for someone to join him.

Someone did.

Irene Presker swooshed through the place, still made up but now dressed like Venetia Scott had been in bankers' tweeds. Speidel took one of Presker's hands in both of his as greeting. Then they sat down across from each other and began talking. I couldn't see any way of getting out of there without her spotting me, so I sat still and nursed a beer.

They talked through a drink and lunch and were about to

order dessert when Presker caught me out of the corner of her eye. She barely paused, covering it with a palm-up gesture to support her chins. Waving off coffee, the consultant waited until Speidel covered the tab by signing for it, then shook hands goodbye with him as he moved toward the exit and she toward the rest rooms.

Presker made sure Speidel was gone before reversing direction and steaming up to the bar. "What's the idea of following me?"

"Maybe I didn't believe everything I heard at your condo."

"Does that mean you have to give me a heart attack in the middle of an interview?"

"Interview?"

"The man who just left is—"

Presker stopped, but I hadn't interrupted her.

I said, "Who is he?"

She tapped a stubby finger on my left arm. "He left before I did, but he was here before I was. I would have noticed you taking this stool if you came in after me. That means you were here before me." Presker looked playful again. "And that means that either you've tapped my phone, in which case you wouldn't have bothered covering this little meeting, or you're following my lunch date. But why?"

I got up before telling Presker anything else, feeling my client might be a little disappointed in me.

I sat in my car until Irene Presker came out. She noticed me, as I'd hoped she would, but just blew me a kiss, which meant I wasn't fooling her at all.

I started up and drove back toward the city, thinking as best I could. Chris Murphy might have intimidated Hun the locksmith into giving him the new key to Venetia Scott's house. Murphy also could have used a skeleton master from his department, but where was his motive three years after the divorce? Luther Dane could have lifted the new key sometime at work, had it copied, and returned it before Scott realized it was missing, but he really didn't seem to think he needed to reduce his boss to supplant her. Irene Presker might have gotten the spare key to the house from Evan Speidel, in which case her bluff at the bar was one for the record books. Speidel might be able to slip away from Scott on one of their weekends at his place, but why go to her place to do, essentially, nothing?

Shaking my head, I focused on the traffic. At least I knew where that was going.

Luther Dane's voice said, "Ms. Scott's office."

I said, "May I speak with her?"

"I'll see, Mr. Cuddy."

Good at recognizing voices, Mr. Dane.

"Venetia Scott."

"Can Dane hear us?"

"No."

"You're positive?"

"Yes. What is it?"

"Given that it's Friday, are you going to Speidel's place?"

"Yes. Why?"

"I have an idea."

It was something I'd hoped I could avoid. Solo, you can't really watch a house completely from the street or the back or the sides. Short of a high perch, there are just too many blind spots created by the building itself. But, owner willing, you can cover it pretty thoroughly from one place.

Inside it.

In the dark, I sat on the slider in the living room, Winfield curled up on my lap. I'd paced off the strides to both front and back doors. The slider was almost exactly equidistant from each.

It was barely eight o'clock when I heard something at the back door. Winfield jumped off my lap and did his rotund best to scamper out there. I moved to the wall by the kitchen, hoping I wasn't going to need a weapon. I heard the faint sound of the door opening, then closing, then nothing.

I waited five seconds. Then ten. At fifteen, I went into the kitchen.

Nobody. Not even Winfield.

I looked out the windows, but didn't see anything. I went back to the living room and sank into the slider. I thought about it, then thought some more. About what I'd told people, and what I hadn't told them.

And eventually I believed I saw it.

I knocked on the door to the mini-mansion a second time. Evan Speidel opened it. He was wearing a silk robe that probably cost more than my rent.

"Yes?" Nice baritone voice, too.

"I need to speak with Venetia Scott."

"At this hour?"

"Tell her it's John Cuddy."

The door closed in my face. Two minutes later, Scott reopened it.

Her robe matched Speidel's, her auburn hair indeed tumbling onto her shoulders. "This had better be important."

I stepped inside the house. "It won't take long. There's bad news and good news."

"What's the bad news?"

"I think we've lost Winfield."

I heard Speidel chuckle from the other room, but Scott's face stayed neutral. "That I can live with, I guess. What's the good news?"

"If you'll trust me to guarantee that it's over, I can end it tonight, nobody getting hurt or in trouble."

The executive in Scott stiffened. "Guaranteed?"

"Absolutely. But I keep everything I've learned to myself."

My client took ten seconds to weigh that. "Do it."

This time I kept knocking until a shadow loomed in the weak light behind the purple beads. Hun's head peered out, shook, then came forward slowly with the rest of his body as he let me into the shop.

I said, "Where's the cat?"

He thought about toughing it out, then said, "In the back. Where I live."

"Tied up?"

Hun gave me a derisive look and spat out a word I didn't understand. Winfield came running, slowed only a little by the bead curtain, most of which he could get under. He regarded me but cuddled up to Hun.

The locksmith said, "How you know it was me?"

"The other people I talked to, the other names I asked you about, I didn't tell any of them the problem had something to do with Ms. Scott's house."

Hun shook his head. "That is not enough."

"No, but Scott said you really liked the cat. And at her house only the smallest things were disturbed, like someone was visiting, not intimidating."

I stopped, but Hun nodded.

I said, "Only the things you would need to give him food and yourself water and relief."

"I like to give him food. I like to visit him."

"And based on what I told you, you might miss the chance to see him again."

"You tell me problem with house, maybe problem with locks. Maybe Ms. Scott not use me next time to change locks. Maybe I cannot see Winfield again without break in."

"Which you didn't want to do."

"I am locksmith! I do not break in houses!"

"But you'd risk your business to see the cat."

Hun reached down to stroke Winfield's head. "I lose my whole family, Khmer Rouge. This cat only creature all United States nice to me."

"So you were willing to trade your profession for being able to have him."

The stony look. "Yes."
"Ever hear of Dave Winfield?"
"Who?"
"Skip it."